Informality in Policymaking

Informality in Policymaking: Weaving the Threads of Everyday Policy Work

EDITED BY

LINDSEY GARNER-KNAPP
University of Edinburgh, UK

JOANNA MASON
University of Sydney, Australia

TAMARA MULHERIN
Northumbria University, UK

AND

E. LIANNE VISSER
Leiden University, The Netherlands

United Kingdom – North America – Japan – India – Malaysia – China

Emerald Publishing Limited
Emerald Publishing, Floor 5, Northspring, 21-23 Wellington Street, Leeds LS1 4DL.

First edition 2025

Editorial matter and selection © 2025 Lindsey Garner-Knapp, Joanna Mason, Tamara Mulherin, and E. Lianne Visser.

Individual chapters except chapter 6 © 2025 The authors.
Published under exclusive licence by Emerald Publishing Limited.

Chapter 6, Visualising Informal Repair: Exploring Photographic 'Routines' in Ethnographic Methodology copyright © 2025 Neha Mungekar, is Open Access with copyright assigned to respective chapter authors. Published by Emerald Publishing Limited. This work is published under the Creative Commons Attribution (CC BY 4.0) licence. Anyone may reproduce, distribute, translate and create derivative works of these works (for both commercial and non-commercial purposes), subject to full attribution to the original publication and authors. The full terms of this licence may be seen at http://creativecommons.org/licences/by/4.0/legalcode

Cover Art and section images: Emma Weale, 2023.

Reprints and permissions service
Contact: www.copyright.com

No part of this book may be reproduced, stored in a retrieval system, transmitted in any form or by any means electronic, mechanical, photocopying, recording or otherwise without either the prior written permission of the publisher or a licence permitting restricted copying issued in the UK by The Copyright Licensing Agency and in the USA by The Copyright Clearance Center. Any opinions expressed in the chapters are those of the authors. Whilst Emerald makes every effort to ensure the quality and accuracy of its content, Emerald makes no representation implied or otherwise, as to the chapters' suitability and application and disclaims any warranties, express or implied, to their use.

British Library Cataloguing in Publication Data
A catalogue record for this book is available from the British Library

ISBN: 978-1-83797-281-4 (Print)
ISBN: 978-1-83797-280-7 (Online)
ISBN: 978-1-83797-282-1 (Epub)

INVESTOR IN PEOPLE

Being able to think and act in the moment, as any administrator and politician knows, is the hallmark of being an effective practitioner. It is the only way to tame the intrinsic uncertainty and unpredictability of the organization and its environment. This insight, which is backed up by a sizeable literature - on practice, know how, tacit knowledge, improvisation, wisdom, administrative discretion, informal organization, playing the system – backs up this everyday observation. Yet, in policy analysis and political science this practical common sense is inexplicably ignored. Instead, the formal aspects of organizations – institutions, laws, rules, procedures, constitutions – are considered the standard of epistemic and social authority. One of the many achievements of this book is it brings the voice of practice back into the conversation. It invites us to think in a non-dualist way about the formal-informal distinction. Another strength is the all-female line-up of contributors, which in itself is a commentary on the hegemonic distribution of epistemic authority in policy research. Nine detailed, carefully researched case studies demonstrate that only a thorough immersion in the formal aspects of policy and organization allows the practitioner to improvise on the spot to get things done and successfully solve problems, and also what that means for the organization. I expect this book to be a lasting contribution to bridging the divide between the formal and informal aspects of public policy and administration.

Hendrik Wagenaar (Institute for Advanced Studies, Vienna; Centre for Deliberative Democracy and Global governance, University of Canberra)

Brilliant and insightful, this forceful intervention challenges the taken-for-granted assumptions and paradigms in public administration and governance. This book tells an alternative, less-told story of in/formality in policy studies, one that is grounded in feminist methodologies, contextualized practices and localized knowledges. Broad in its scope, the book details how informality is used to negotiate boundaries, transfer knowledge and maintain infrastructure using a fascinating array of visual, material, and ethnographic methods. It is a must-read for anyone wishing to develop a complete understanding of how governance actually works on the ground.

Ayesha Masood (Associate Professor, Suleman Dawood School of Business, Lahore University of Management Sciences)

This edited collection is an insightful reminder of the unseen interstitial spaces and occasions where the (hyphenated) work of doing policy gets done. Beautifully presented and full of rich ethnographic accounts from a range of contexts, a great read for practitioners, managers and academics alike.

Rob Wilson (Professor of Digital Social Innovation, Manchester Metropolitan University)

This book vividly presents how informality gains shape in the daily practice of professional policymakers. The refreshing approach goes beyond binary thinking and considers the complex intertwining of informality with formality. It will be a key resource for anyone interested in informality in policymaking, and recommended reading for those who want to understand how informality always seems to elude definition.

Martijn Koster (Sociology of Development and Change, Wageningen University)

Contents

List of Figures and Tables	*ix*
About the Editors	*xiii*
About the Contributors	*xv*
Foreword: By Richard Freeman	*xix*
Acknowledgements	*xxi*

Introduction

From Informality and Formality to In|formality: Troubling Absolutism in Policymaking
Joanna Mason, E. Lianne Visser, Lindsey Garner-Knapp and Tamara Mulherin — *3*

Setting the Stage of Informality

Chapter 1 'Knowing' the System: Public Administration and Informality during COVID-19
Claire Bynner — *23*

Chapter 2 The Informal Work of Policy Maintenance: Making Space for Local Knowledge in Indian Rural Electricity Governance
Meera Sudhakar — *39*

Informal Practices and Ethnomethodology

Chapter 3 Mastering Informality in Diplomacy
Kristin Anabel Eggeling and Larissa Versloot — *53*

Chapter 4 Bureaucratic Hustling and Knowledge Shuffling – Informality within Swiss Public Administration
Lisa Marie Borrelli — *67*

viii *Contents*

Chapter 5 Catching Up with Catching Up: Collaborative Policy Work, In|formality and Connective Talk
E. Lianne Visser   *81*

Methods to Study Informality

Chapter 6 Visualising Informal Repair: Exploring Photographic 'Routines' in Ethnographic Methodology
Neha Mungekar   *97*

Chapter 7 Traceless Transitions: Studying the Role of Drawings and Gestures in Construction Project Meetings
Evelijn Martinius   *113*

Chapter 8 Vehicles of In|formality – The Role of the Car as a Mobile Space of Policy and Relational Work
Tamara Mulherin   *127*

Concluding Thoughts

Chapter 9 Tracing Threads of In/Visibilities: The Knotty Mattering of Policymaking
Lindsey Garner-Knapp and Joanna Mason   *147*

Chapter 10 Dénouement: Why the How Comes to Matter
Tamara Mulherin and Lindsey Garner-Knapp   *163*

Afterword

Afterword: Reflecting on In|formality
Peregrine Schwartz-Shea and Dvora Yanow   *177*

Index   *193*

List of Figures and Tables

Figures

Figure 1.1.	(Left) UK Government Coronavirus leaflet front cover.	25
Figure 1.2.	(Right) UK Government Coronavirus leaflet inside pages.	25
Figure 2.1.	The Temple that identifies the central place of the village studied.	44
Figure 2.2.	A Toggle Lever that would determine whether the household consumption is accounted under the farm or non-farm feeder.	47
Figure 6.1.	Left - The physical infrastructure - overhead water tank; Right - Social infrastructure that enabled access to the resource - in-person relationships. (30/9/2021)	100
Figure 6.2.	Scale shifting photography at OHT. (30/9/2021)	105
Figure 6.3.	(Left) Soni (in blue checked shirt) waiting for the PWD officers. Meanwhile, his team exchanged greetings with PWD's team. (Right) Soni flanked by his men, displaying support and strength. (28/9/2021)	106
Figure 6.4.	(Left) Patel presenting piles of paperwork required for lake notification requirements (21/12/2021); (Right) Jadeja engaging in soil-covered Q&A session while kneeling on the ground (19/12/2021)	107
Figure 6.5.	(Left) The School principal in Bhuj explaining the importance of rainwater harvesting and conservation to his students centred in the photograph (16/12/2021); (Right) A supervisor effortlessly showing WhatsApp-enabled phone to display water kiosk updates in Bhopal's old city (03/12/2021).	108
Figure 6.6.	First series showcasing ordinary objects to tinker the original physical water supply infrastructure. (3/10/21; 3/10/21; 18/11/21) Second series - Mobile phone becoming a norm to access easily. (6/1/22; 6/1/22; 6/1/22)	108
Figure 8.1.	Journey in Kintra.	128
Figure 8.2.	Haith Royal Infirmary – wrapped in carparks.	130
Figure 8.3.	Samuel's Desk.	132
Figure 8.4.	Front and back car parks at Haith Royal Infirmary.	134

x *List of Figures and Tables*

Figure 8.5.	Manager's car park at Kintra Council & Public car park at Kintra Council.	138
Figure 8.6.	Access to the Field.	140
Figure 8.7.	Off on a trip in the snow.	142
Figure 10.1.	First Word Cloud from the first workshop, January 2022.	168
Figure 10.2.	Second Word Cloud from the first workshop.	168
Figure 10.3.	Padlet images, collation from the thematic workshops.	169

Tables

Table 7.1.	Overview of when technical drawings featured during the meeting.	116
Table 7.2.	Overview of how gestures in relation to a technical drawing concentrated discussions on future work.	124

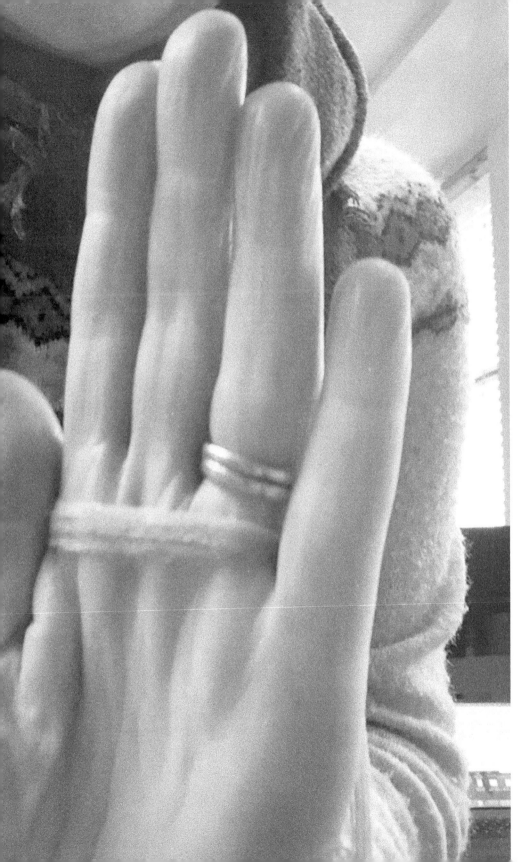

About the Editors

Lindsey Garner-Knapp, University of Edinburgh, United Kingdom. Lindsey's work bridges academia and policymaking and she is committed to building and maintaining connections in both worlds to facilitate research that addresses real-world problems and supports informed policymaking practices. She is a doctoral candidate at the University of Edinburgh in Politics and International Relations and a Researcher at the Centre for Inclusive Trade Policy. Broadly, her work explores international trade policymaking focusing on the multiplicity of heterogeneous actors involved in these entanglements and how they (re)assemble throughout the processes. With her background in anthropology and public policy, Lindsey draws on a variety of qualitative approaches to better understand policymaking in situ highlighting the affects of the human and nonhuman relations. As a practitioner, she has experience in policymaking processes as a policy analyst and policy advisor to multiple regional and city governments in Canada and the United Kingdom.

Joanna Mason, is Research Fellow with the Menzies Centre for Health Policy and Economics, University of Sydney, Australia. Joanna conducts research across the broad fields of public policy, health policy and public administration. Using interpretive and actor-centred approaches – and drawing on her public sector experience in policy – her work contributes to macro policy debates through a focus on the micro-setting and the practical challenges encountered by policymakers. Recent ethnographic work addressed expectations for policy practitioners to utilise academic research in view of the evidence-based policy paradigm which was conducted within the national-level civil service, the Australian Public Service. A recent publication explores how policy ethnography and the sense-making journey that follows can usefully deploy an anthropological orientation that attends to underlying methodological, theoretical, analytical and conceptual precepts and practices. Currently, her work examines health policy and governance focusing on reform to primary care through a comparative study of Australia and Canada.

Tamara Mulherin is a Lecturer in Organisational Studies with the Newcastle Business School at Northumbria University, having completed her PhD in Politics at the University of Edinburgh. She has been a Research Fellow with the Usher Institute at the University of Edinburgh, and the Social Work, Education and Community Wellbeing Department at Northumbria University. Her doctoral research was an inter-organisational, multi-sited ethnographic study into *xiv*   *About the Editors*

health and social care integration in Scotland, exploring how collaborative practices were enacted for the implementation of new legislation. She has more than 25 years of experience in the public and non-government sectors in roles, including management, planning, policy, evaluation, service delivery and community development, across a multiplicity of domains, e.g., mental health, health inequalities, homelessness, social care and domestic violence. She is interested in posthumanist public sector organising, mundane governance and infrastructuring of care, collaboration-as-practice and repair practices in the context of public sector reform.

E. Lianne Visser is an Assistant Professor at the Institute of Public Administration at Leiden University in the Netherlands. Originally trained as an anthropologist at Utrecht University, and with experience as a public policymaker, she is fascinated by the mundane, tacit and often informal practices through which abstract concepts such as policy, governance, and accountability are performed and brought into being. Her research and teaching focuses on customisation and responsiveness by street-level workers; the changing relationship between street-level and policy departments; and mundane aspects of the work of street-level workers, managers and policymakers. She also writes about qualitative, ethnographic methods and practice theory. Her research has been published in leading international journals such as *Journal of Public Administration Research and Theory*, *Public Administration Review*, *Public Administration* and *Public Management Review*.

About the Contributors

Lisa Marie Borrelli works as an Associate Professor at the University of Applied Science – HES-SO Valais -Wallis, Institute of Social Work, Switzerland. Her research interests circle around the broader concepts of exclusion and banishment, including a focus on how non-citizens' rights are restricted by states in the fields of migration law, welfare policies and public administration. She follows an ethnographic approach and is interested in qualitative methodologies to study the decision-making of (non)state actors, bureaucratic practices, policy discourses and legal case work.

Claire Bynner is a Lecturer in Social Justice and Community Action at Moray House School of Education and Sport, University of Edinburgh, Scotland, UK. She has been working in the fields of public policy, democratic innovation and community development as a practitioner and academic for over 20 years. Her academic interests are in participatory democracy, local governance and place-based approaches to poverty and inequality. Her current research examines the community and voluntary sector response to the COVID-19 pandemic in the UK. She is co-editor of the book *COVID-19 and the Voluntary and Community Sector in the UK: Responses, Impacts and Adaptation*, published in 2022.

Kristin Anabel Eggeling (PhD 2019, University of St Andrews, UK) is Assistant Professor at the Department of Political Science at the University of Copenhagen and a Visiting Researcher at the Danish Institute for International Studies (DIIS). Kristin teaches and writes about diplomacy, digitalisation, global tech policy and qualitative and ethnographic methods in Political Science and International Relations. In 2023, Kristin was awarded the *Anthony Deos Early Career Award* for the emerging scholar in the field of Diplomatic Studies by the International Studies Association (ISA).

Evelijn Martinius works as a doctoral researcher at the Department of Organization Studies at the Vrije Universiteit in the Netherlands. Her research examines the management of underground public infrastructures in urban regions in the Netherlands. She is interested in sensory methods such as ethnography and writes about imagination, routines and grassroots pioneering solutions to overcome issues with bounded manageability in societal transitions.

xvi About the Contributors

Neha Mungekar is a PhD candidate at the Dutch Research Institute for Transitions (DRIFT), affiliated with the Erasmus University, Rotterdam, the Netherlands. Currently, she is engaged in the Water4Change project, investigating how to nurture informal governance capacities for transitioning to water-sensitive cities in India. Her professional background encompasses significant roles as an urban designer and environmental photojournalist. Her academic and practice interests are centred on exploring the power dynamics associated with the distribution and allocation of water resources, particularly within the context of the Global South. Her research integrates complex systems thinking and anthropological approaches to provide nuanced insights into water governance and its implications for diverse stakeholders. Her key expertise lies in facilitation, knowledge brokering and consensus building through innovative participatory strategies.

Peregrine Schwartz-Shea is Professor Emerita, Department of Political Science, University of Utah. She published her early research using experimental methods and rational choice theory. Shifting theoretical interests led to research focusing on methodological practices in political science and interpretive methods. With Dvora Yanow, she is co-editor of the Routledge Series on Interpretive Methods, and their coauthored *Interpretive Research Design: Concepts and Processes* (2012) is the first volume in the series. She is past president of the Western Political Science Association (2012–2013) and recipient of two mentoring awards. She received a National Science Foundation grant to co-organise the Workshop on Interpretive Methodologies in Political Science (2009) and served on the Ad Hoc Committee on Human Subjects Research (2017–2020), which produced research ethics guidelines for the American Political Science Association. Since 2020, she serves on the editorial board of *American Political Science Review* and its Advisory Board for Research Ethics.

Meera Sudhakar works as an interdisciplinary researcher studying policy issues in the domain of water and energy. She completed her doctoral studies from National Institute of Advanced Studies, Bengaluru, India in 2022. Her research has focused on tracing changes to policy ideas and institutions that structure energy and water politics in the context of environmental limits.

Larissa Versloot is a Postdoctoral Researcher at the Department of Political Science at the University of Copenhagen and an Associate Fellow at the Institute for Security and Global Affairs at Leiden University. Her research interests are in multilateral cooperation, diplomacy, EU foreign policy and the maintenance of trust in world politics. Her work has been published in *International Affairs* and *Review of International Studies*.

Dvora Yanow is political/organisational ethnographer and interpretive methodologist. Dvora explores the generation and communication of knowing and meaning in policy and organisational settings. Her current project – working title *The Treachery of Categories* – explores category theory and state-created categories for immigrant integration policies and race-ethnic identities. Other interests include social science research ethics and their regulation, work practice studies and science/technology museums and the idea of science. Her most recent work is 'Interpretive policy analysis: Origins and current challenges' (forthcoming, Elgar). With Peregrine Schwartz-Shea, she has co-authored *Interpretive Research Design* (2012), which launched their co-edited Routledge Series on Interpretive Methods, and co-edited *Interpretation and Method* (2nd ed., 2014). She has held fellowships at the Rockefeller Foundation's Bellagio Center and the Käte Hamburger Institute for Global Cooperation Research and visiting positions at the Danish Institute for International Studies, Vienna's Institute for Advanced Studies and Shenyang's Northeastern University (China), among others.

Foreword

What if we began our thinking about public policy here, with conversations in corridors and coffee rooms, with a tap on the shoulder just before the meeting resumes, out on a site visit or with piles of paper on the passenger seat of the car? Not with the political, legislative, ideational, organisational or financial parameters of decision-making but with the physical, material, haptic, affective, familiar, embodied, situated, provisional, contingent and emergent, with the encounter and the casual conversation? For isn't this in fact where policy begins, along with most other human things?

That's not to claim that policy is anything but a public, formal affair, documented and institutionalised – for if it weren't recognisable, repeatable, replicable and communicable in some stable form it would fail in its essential functions. By the same token, however, understanding how something which is none of these things, how something essentially and necessarily informal comes in the end to be formal, must be essential to our understanding of what policy is and the work it does. For policy is not a priori formal but has been made so: it is no more and no less than the formalisation of what has been informally problematised, proposed, argued over and agreed. So why don't we begin with people engaged with each other rather than with that vague, abstract, ultimately ethereal and ephemeral thing we call policy? And then go on in this way, drawing attention to the continued work of informal interaction in sustaining the form and function of policy, in nurturing it, making sense of it, assessing it, perhaps resisting it or putting it into practice.

For that's what's happening here, in this book. Its argument is not that we must now turn our attention wholly to the informal or that we should in any sense look away from what we took to be policy and its principal characteristics. It is, instead, that we might ask how the formal and the informal are mutually constitutive in the making of policy. It's not 'either/or', it's 'both/and' or perhaps 'not only, but also'; it's to say the formal is only part of the story. It's precisely not to construct a new binary, a dualism of formal and informal, but it is to draw new attention to the boundary between the two and to the ways it might be drawn differently in different contexts. Its purpose is to posit a new holism, however hesitant and unsettled, in our thinking about public policy.

There's no surprise that it's these authors who should begin here, with the informal. They were and are themselves first of all practitioners – policymakers and public officials – and they're writing about a world they know from experience, working if not living in it, sharing its values at least in part, having been

xx *Foreword*

socialised into its norms, acquired its assumptions and habits of thought, having become skilled in its established ways of doing things and so able to pass as experts, authorities. They've then entered another world of teaching and research and found the one they came from reflected back to them, represented in theories and models and approaches and frameworks, in carefully crafted case studies, in books and journal papers, that is in relentlessly *formal* ways. This book results at least in part from that friction, from wanting to show and say what their world is really like, how policy really happens.

It's no accident, either, that these stories of the informal should be told by embracing ethnographic methods, by researchers engaging in close and sustained relationships with those around them (more formally known as 'participants'). For those relationships themselves, like those among others we call 'policymakers', are constantly shifting between the informal, sometimes casual, sometimes private and even intimate and varying degrees of legal and professional formality. Nor is it any surprise that their authors should be women, sensitive to the ways different spaces of policy work differently because they are – at least informally – differently gendered.

So we might wonder about the origins and production of this book in the same way we wonder about the origins and production of policy (because of course research, like policy, is a text-based practice). It's been produced by a network of practitioner-researchers with shared if not common interests, that shared interest being in part in discovering what interests they have. It's come from a sense of something missing, first intuited then argued and explicated, in myriad conversations, in the idea for a book, in loose formulations, reformulations and re-visionings, in calls for contributions and expressions of interest, in playing with titles and drafting proposals, in writing and reading the papers themselves, commenting and revising, agonising over an introduction, more writing, more reading and more discussion. And so in the end, a text becomes settled, material and fixed – formal, perhaps – only in order that it should go out in the world, prompting more talk and perhaps more writing.

This book tells us other things about the informal, though they are as germane to social life in general as they are to public policy more specifically. They are that the informal is intrinsically social, always a form of interaction and therefore invariably conventional and rule-bound: that is to say that the informal happens in normal ways. Yet it can also be a source of the new, of the unscripted, critical and questioning.

Richard Freeman
Edinburgh
September 2023

Acknowledgements

Where do we begin to express our gratitude to the people who have seen this endeavour to its completion? Positioned around the 'shareable workbench' (Braidotti, 2019, p. 146), we believe we have much to be thankful for. We are thankful to the people, things, and ideas that have all helped this book materialise, and as a collective accomplishment, it is vital to acknowledge the entanglements with these others through which this book emerged.

To our contributors:
As editors, we welcomed the chapter authors into our community as co-creators of this book and as peers who were equally committed to exploring informality and formality differently. Our approach with all of the authors throughout this book's making was built on multiple forms of engagement along the way. We were fortunate to be a part of the development of such a generative group of authors without which this book would not be possible. In particular, we appreciated their trust in joining with us to work within and expand the universe of the concept of in|formality. We are grateful to them all for the profound ways in which they have thought with and through the concepts, and concomitantly, their diverse perspectives and expertise enriched the construction process and the content of this book.

We want to acknowledge Richard Freeman as the lively conduit through which we came together and are very thankful for his generous and fitting Foreword. He recognises our positionality and our 'pracademic' efforts as producing the conditions for the empirical theorising of the 'both/and' of the in|formal, mutually constitutive making of policy and our embrace of ethnographic methods as a method of inquiry most amenable for 'mak[ing] things visible, audible, tangible, knowable' (Gherardi, 2019, p. 202).

Additionally, we owe a large debt of gratitude to Dvora Yanow and Peregrine Schwartz-Shea for their Afterword reflections and thoughtful consideration of this book's intentions and empirically how it seeks to show this through ethnography. They identify our efforts from the outset to patiently sit in a muddle of the in|formal, not trying to solve it but to take time to consider incommensurability. Their sensitive assessment of each chapter, how they can be read in various ways and the implications are invaluable. We also want to thank them both for their constructive advice regarding the book structure, which we regard as substantively enhancing this book's academic quality. Also for their attentive suggestions which helped us to solve the bumps in the road we encountered during the publication process.

xxii   *Acknowledgements*

To our organisations:
We want to thank our respective universities, as educators and employers, for their flexibility, time and space, both as doctoral students and scholars working on this book. Special thanks goes to Leiden University for providing funding for the purchase of the artwork images used throughout this manuscript.

To the peer reviewers:
We appreciated the anonymous peer reviewers who provided constructive feedback on the initial book proposal, as well as John Boswell and Helen Dickinson's challenging and valuable insights on the introductory chapter. All these comments alerted us to how this book's themes may be received by those within the policy field and ultimately have helped improve the quality of this book and its contribution.

To the editorial team at Emerald:
We are grateful for Emerald Publishers and their support in the development of this book. From the outset, Iram Satti, as the then Commissioning Editor, welcomed and encouraged our efforts. This encouragement continued under the stewardship of Daniel Ridge, Lydia Cutmore, Brindha Thirunavukkarasu and Lauren Kammerdiener as the production process evolved. They took a risk working with us as a group of – at the time – PhD students with little experience as editors but have been invaluable to our development and to what the book has become. Their accommodating and diligent work has helped ensure this book meets academic standards and is ready for publication.

For the artwork:
Emma Weale, as the artist-weaver, has been both open and giving of her time and practice in taking on the commission of creating a tapestry and its accompanying images for our book cover and section breaks. She listened closely to apprehend what we were trying to achieve, capturing a weaving in the making and as a completed work. The images of her work are a testament to the beauty of the weaving, which we think metaphorically aids communicating the in|formal.

And on a personal level:
As we have foregrounded, the making of a book is an endeavour multiplied that emerges from varied collaborative interactions, but it is also underpinned by the support of family, friends, and mentors who have provided encouragement and understanding throughout the process. We want to express our gratitude for their patience, encouragement, and belief in our ability to undertake the project. We also want to share that as doctoral students and early career scholars (ECRs) that *it is possible* to 'grasp the nettle' and collaboratively produce academic texts.

Tamara – Given my feminist praxis, the collective approach to this scholarly project has reaffirmed to me what can emerge when shared interests, curiosity, and collective writing, diffracted through our respective experiences, come together. To have the opportunity to build our writing together as an editorial team of incredible and diverse capabilities has been generative, supportive and creative.

Acknowledgements **xxiii**

Lindsey – There are moments in our lives where we each have the opportunity to do something new and create something amazing – this book has been that for me. As ECRs, we experienced adversity in getting here, but we shared a vision, worked together, and found the most amazing support system with our interlocutors making this collective dream a reality. Together we learned, thought, grew, shared, supported, and wrote – I am grateful for every moment.

Lianne – Making this book has taught me how to do academia differently, write academia differently, present academia differently. To be able to share this book is the culmination of this collective, creative endeavour.

Joanna – Bringing this book to fruition has been a rewarding experience that invigorated, enriched, and extended how I thought about policymaking. The project came about at a crucial stage in my doctoral journey, with the resulting friendships and collegial relationships taking me through this uncertain transition and creating the potential for new, collective endeavours into the future.

As it goes out into the world, we hope we have conveyed through this book what it means to incorporate diverse practitioner sensibilities into scholarly knowledge-making, indicative of what's possible in a collective effort to do academia otherwise. In occupying a feminist standpoint, we attempt to express through the chapters that the ruse of the Eurocentric bifurcated lens through which we encounter the world diminishes our sense of the possibilities and potentialities held within circumstances which unfold. Ours then is the story of relational text work, attuned to the political in the mundane, of co-labouring as a form of care in our writing, that we think brings to life the everyday policy work enmeshed in the in|formal. Accordingly, even as the creation of this book has come to an end, we are all aware that our inquiry into in|formality continues. For, as Donna Haraway (2016) explains,

> It matters what matters we use to think other matters with; it matters what stories we tell to tell other stories with; it matters what knots knot knots, what thoughts think thoughts, what descriptions describe descriptions, what ties tie ties. It matters what stories make worlds, what worlds make stories. (p. 12)

Tamara, Lindsey, Lianne and Joanna
April 2024

References

Braidotti, R. (2019). *Posthuman knowledge* (p. 146). Polity Press.
Gherardi, S. (2019). *How to conduct a practice-based study: Problems and methods*. Edward Elgar Publishing.
Haraway, D. J. (2016). *Staying with the trouble: Making kin in the Chthulucene*. Duke University Press.

Introduction

From Informality and Formality to In|formality: Troubling Absolutism in Policymaking

Joanna Mason[a], E. Lianne Visser[b], Lindsey Garner-Knapp[c] and Tamara Mulherin[d]

[a]*Menzies Centre for Health Policy and Economics, University of Sydney, Australia*
[b]*Institute of Public Administration, Leiden University, The Netherlands*
[c]*University of Edinburgh, UK*
[d]*Newcastle Business School, Northumbria University, UK*

Abstract

This opening chapter introduces key debates in relation to informality in policymaking, laying the theoretical and conceptual groundwork for the individual empirical chapters, beginning with a provocation for how informality can alternatively be understood. Through illustrating where gaps in understanding within current literature exist for how informality acquires meaning, and the physical and material relevance for how it manifests across contexts, this chapter introduces the three thematic clusters that thread through the book's chapters: boundaries, knowledge mastery and networks. In doing so, it briefly positions each chapter in relation to these flexible and overlapping categories, drawing attention to how each chapter presents a different understanding of informality. Key to this chapter is our contention that while informality escapes definition, without binary or fixed conceptualisations of this concept we are better able to take in its fluidity and envisage how it is interwoven in everyday policy work and its human and non-human enactment. Underpinning this contention is a key contribution of this work, a proposition for a re-conceptualising of informality and formality as in|formality. Methodologically, this chapter argues that informality is better 'shown' than 'told' – and that this can be achieved through interpretive and socio-material approaches woven through disciplines that foreground narrative, ethnographic and creative approaches to research.

Keywords: Informality; public administration; policymaking; interpretive research; qualitative research; public policy

---

Informality in Policymaking: Weaving the Threads of Everyday Policy Work, 3–20
Copyright © 2025 by Joanna Mason, E. Lianne Visser, Lindsey Garner-Knapp and Tamara Mulherin
Published under exclusive licence by Emerald Publishing Limited
doi:10.1108/978-1-83797-280-720241001

How and Why Informality Matters

This book is about informality in the policy process, not from 1,000 metres above but from everyday accounts. We invite readers to think differently about informality, particularly through recognition of its entangled relationship with formality. The association of informal with formal plays into how binary relationships narrow and confine the understanding of given concepts through reference to their opposite. Throughout the coming pages, we shed light instead on how policy is made in different contexts from around the globe to explore how and why informality matters – and why this should come to matter – or be of interest to policy scholars, students and professionals. What follows, therefore, is a focus on the everyday policymaking activities from professional policy actors' experiences.

As a collaboration of four female policy scholars and former policy professionals – who all returned to academia to complete doctoral degrees on policymaking using ethnographic approaches – we recognised a gap in the literature that spoke to our previous involvements. The gap we recognised was the lived experiences of policy professionals from across the globe, not as homogeneous but as situated and inclusive of this diversity. Added to this we noticed a dependency on binary thinking within traditional discourses of our disciplines, especially around the concepts of informality and formality. We recognised that our experiences as policy practitioners/academics afforded us unique insights into this matter and skills to work collaboratively to create a text reflective of this.

Why produce a book on informality in public policy and administration? While public policy actors spend considerable time writing policy, advising politicians, eliciting stakeholder views and implementing initiatives – we had witnessed that they also make jokes and gossip during coffee breaks, debrief after meetings at the water cooler or wander outside for a quick word or to avoid prying eyes, thereby creating supportive coalitions with colleagues inside and outside their organisations (Green, 2011; Wagenaar, 2004). Complex emotions also arise in the course of enacting their duties, like doubt or sympathy, and policy actors engage in repeated discussions as a form of therapy (Dorren, 2021) or magical thinking (Boswell, 2022) in which actors cling to seemingly naive ideals in the face of inevitable failure. Furthermore, they engage in tacit, unnoticed work which is entailed in the sensory and aesthetic via materials, bodily movements or voice (Gherardi, 2019). Although scholars have drawn our attention to the informal in policy work (Bevir & Rhodes, 2001; Colebatch, 2014; Lindblom, 2020; Metze, 2010; Yanow, 1996), empirical studies have been limited in exploring these other aspects. A desire to capture everyday accounts and explore how and why they matter provided the impetus for us to bring together a collection on informality in policymaking.

Readers looking for a set definition of informality are encouraged to look elsewhere. This book endeavours instead to show how empirical and theoretical expositions of informality can be threaded together to form a rich tapestry of meaning running across and through policy fields, contexts and situations. As this chapter goes on to argue, little is known about informality without formality as its normative referent. While the term is frequently used generically, purposive framings of informality can also be found within the literature on policymaking across accompanying fields of governance, public administration and bureaucracy.

Here, accounts of informality describe its binary relationship with formality and by what the formal lacks, such as an absence of official rules and procedures or a lack of transparent and accountable processes and decision-making. Through this dichotomisation, the informal acquires a shadowy, dark side coterminous with undesirable qualities of policymaking such as undemocratic, illegitimate and unscrutinised.

How context and local understandings are embedded in the way informality unfolds is conveyed throughout this book. Through immersive engagement so typical of ethnographic approaches (van Hulst et al., 2017), chapter authors unpack the complexities of policy life in the setting under study, capturing the situated intricacies and ambiguities of informality and formality. We argue that with a concerted interest in informality in policymaking and related fields (Boanada-Fuchs & Boanada Fuchs, 2018; Koutkova, 2016) comes a need for a theorisation of *informality* that is robust and attuned to the particularities of discrete cases; one that embraces uncertainty, ambiguity and facilitates conceptual evolution. In keeping with this book's analogy of a tapestry, our claims on why and how to engage with informality can be likened to the *warp* (or vertical) threads running throughout this collection which are subsequently interwoven with the *weft* (or horizontal) threads carried by individual chapters and the insights they bring.

Explaining how and why informality matters is no small feat. In resisting the urge to homogenise the concept, chapters in this book tease out what is unique through contextualising what informality represents, how it manifests and what it affords – bringing into relief the human acts and agency that make the informal possible. Throughout the making of this volume, we have taken informality to be a *sensitizing concept* (Blumer, 1954) that 'merely suggests directions along which to look' as we afford it no 'precise' or 'clean-cut identification' (p. 7). As a lens, the informal draws attention to the fluidity and craft entailed in policy work and how the spaces where this occurs are multiple and creatively established. This book shows how policy is never enacted alone; it is relational, and its engagements are multifaceted, with the informal enmeshed in what actors in policy settings think, do and aspire to. And so, this book seeks to explore how informality emerges in interaction with people, materials and spaces – and how it is intertwined with formality in different contexts.

This chapter proceeds with a discussion of extant literature on informality to demonstrate how we have engaged with and through multiple perspectives to expand our understanding of how different scholars have approached informality over time. This discussion leads towards our novel contribution: a proposition for re-conceptualising the informal/formal as in|formal.[1] Last, but certainly not least, we introduce the chapters within this book using the themes of *boundaries*, *knowledge mastery* and *networks* as supplementary, nested sensitizing concepts to draw together how chapters relate to each other.

---

[1] Both informal and in|formal is used throughout this text. Where the bar is present, this refers to the editors' distinct conceptualisation of this word. Where the bar is absent, this refers to any other usage.

6 *Joanna Mason et al.*

Thinking With the Informal

We are not the first to interrogate the concept of informality, as this concept has featured widely across disciplines and contexts as both a generic term with assumed understanding and as a concept with prescribed meaning. Our engagement with current bodies of knowledge has been iterative, going back and forth between our lived experiences in conversation with these literatures. As a result, our approach is one of weaving our thinking-with and reading-with scholars writing on informality. While focused on policy literature, our enquiry has been eclectic and inclusive of cognate disciplines that explore policymaking with interpretivist and ethnographic sensibilities (McGranahan, 2018). In our aim to assemble insights that would be useful for scholars, students and practitioners to delve deeper into their own policymaking context, we were attuned to what can be borrowed and adapted (Ulmer, 2020) in synthesising what we learned but also to what cannot. Therefore, this section aims to make connections across disciplinary and temporal boundaries to show how informality has been used while creating conduits towards in|formality – our approach to enquiring differently into informality. Put differently, this section involved simultaneously *thinking-with* and *thinking-through* the lens of informality as a 'sensitizing concept' (Blumer, 1954), with what follows best described as a patchwork of literatures that foreground (or background) the informal from multiple disciplines and lines of inquiry.

We recognise that there are already literature reviews on informality which provide rich insights into this concept. We have found value in two particularly, upon which we briefly touch (Boanada-Fuchs & Boanada Fuchs, 2018; Polese, 2023). Writing from a regional studies context, Abel Polese (2023) presents informality as a (weakly) universalisable phenomenon with shared characteristics, suggesting that informality is a performance enacted by individuals or groups that 'bypasses the state' (p. 324). Differently, Anthony Boanada-Fuchs and Vanessa Boanada Fuchs (2018) develop a taxonomy based on the particularities of literature exploring informality and conclude that 'there is no single-dimensional understanding of informality' – yet there are shared, intersecting qualities (transversal relationships) between literatures (pp. 415–416). Like Boanada-Fuchs and Boanada Fuchs' piece, this volume seeks to explore the nuances of how informality emerges and comes to matter in situ, while uniquely focusing on making policy (work). We believe that this volume is unique in concentrating on the informal within the policy domain and within government institutions and organisations. This is now the context to which we turn.

Turning with Informality

As practitioners, the institutions and organisations of government are ever present as the formal locations of policymaking. The discipline of public administration has traditionally treated these structures as rigid and ossified and viewed policymaking as guided by formalised – almost mechanistic – procedures to achieve neutral administrative practice (Koutkova, 2016; O″nday, 2016). In this vision, anything informal is quickly perceived as the opposite of those ideals.

From Informality and Formality to In\formality   7

This vision emerges within distinct Anglo-American and European Public Administration traditions (Lynn, 2006; Ongaro & Van Thiel, 2018) described as the Wilsonian, Westminster and Westphalian traditions based on the application of idealised, consistent and impersonal rules for policymaking and for the design and implementation of policies in response to politically defined objectives. In shifting the analytical focus from the macro structures of the government and their working principles to the administrative actors tasked with enacting policy, commensurate expectations emerge for them to act according to principles such as impartiality, predictability and accountability (de Vries & Kim, 2011; Jun & Sherwood, 2006; Lasswell, 1956; Lynn, 2006; O'Flynn et al., 2013; Simon, 1955). These expectations do not appear out of place when considering that the antecedents of the emphasis on the formal can in part be traced to the influence of Max Weber's theorising of bureaucracy, whereby bureaucracy is the 'organisation and administration *"ohne Ansehen der Person"* (without consideration of the person)' (Weber, 1922/1972, p. 563, in Steenberg, 2016, p. 300). This understanding suggests that informal processes are considered equivalent to state malfunctioning and regarded as illegitimate or undemocratic.

While such perspectives attend sufficiently to the rule-bound interactional conditions among administrators, elected officials and citizens – what actually occupies the time of bureaucratic actors and how they interact with one another appears of lesser interest. Barbara Misztal (2000) reflects on how an understanding of informality developed within social theory, concluding that while '[t]he founding fathers of sociology did not scrutinize ephemeral phenomena such as informality' (p. 23), Weber recognised the role of social relationships, networks and collective action as 'non-instrumentally oriented types of interaction'; concluding that his 'analysis provides a general scheme for the description of informality as a pattern or style of interaction' (p. 23). More recent readings of Weber counter 'the customary view' of bureaucracy (Perrow, 1972/2014, in du Gay & Pedersen, 2020, p. 221) as 'stifling the spontaneity, freedom and self-realization of those in its employ' (du Gay & Pedersen, 2020, p. 221), to suggest rather that Weber regarded the bureaucracy as 'a distinctive "life-order" with its own ethos' to which the authors interpret as expressing 'a casuistical insistence on the necessity of a principle of situation-specific judgement' (p. 227). This transition to exploring situation-specific judgement is a significant pivot towards recognising the role of bureaucratic actors independent of organisational structures.

Erving Goffman's (1969) dramaturgical insights encouraged us to consider a broader arena of where policy activities occur and the different types of doings and sayings that take place in those spaces. Reading Goffman, and using the language of 'convention orders', David Morand (1995) concludes,

> [f]ormality and informality are understood as two different types of interaction orders because each embodies a distinct set of understandings or conventions about how actors are to orient and conduct themselves. One set dictates looser, more casual modes of behaviour and situational involvement, the other tighter, more disciplined modes. (p. 832)

8   Joanna Mason et al.

Goffman's ordering separates that which is formal from informal to recognise that both are performed within their unique set of conventions – or ordering rules. Goffman's orders differ conceptually from those where logic and order are assigned only to the formal category. However, these conceptualisations of informality as forms of interaction maintain a binary understanding of formal and informal, and ascribing certain characteristics to either formal or informal inhibits analysis of how views might change over time or even from situation to situation.

Considering interactional practices from a range of sociological perspectives, Misztal follows Goffman to define informality as a 'form of interaction among partners enjoying relative freedom in interpretation of their roles' requirements' (2000, p. 46). Commenting on the process of societal change and innovation, Misztal (2000) suggests informality has been associated with the private sphere or equated with unstructured, spontaneous, unpredictable and face-to-face interactions. She also maintains that informality contributes to trust, positive emotions and reduced power–distance relations that enable cooperative, quick, flexible arrangements – such that informality is just as necessary for creating order as formality and that a balance needs to be found between the two.

Critically, more nuanced understandings of the informal in public administration theories arose with the emergence of implementation studies. Particularly influential has been Michael Lipsky's (1980) work and his concept of 'street-level bureaucracy' that considered the daily struggle of public servants who mediate between policy directives and the delivery of these policies to government clients. Facing dilemmas of action, he proposed that bureaucratic actors 'at the coalface' develop routines and simplifications to deal with these dilemmas and to maximise control over their work (Lipsky, 1980). Practitioner-initiated routines were perceived as informal when they were contrary to institutional policy – although Lipsky (1980) acknowledged an unclear line between formal and informal due to the tendency for public sector organisations to transform informal practices into formal procedures.

In response to Lipsky, there has been a development of additional scholarship on the use of discretion at the street level in policy (e.g. Evans, 2011; Hupe & Hill, 2007). Evelyn Brodkin highlights that in responding to demands, a lack of resources contributes to 'overdetermining the development of informal practices', inferring this results in 'robbing services of their substantive value and skewing the distribution of benefits' (2012, p. 943). More importantly, although this literature hints at the responsive potential of informal routines, informality poses a risk to upholding impartial and democratic practice (Brodkin, 2012, p. 944). Even though this literature has opened up opportunities to scrutinise the situated enactment of the informal in policy work, the tendency to position the informal in contrast to the formal and to treat the informal as a fixed notion has remained (Visser & van Hulst, 2024).

Augmenting our understanding of who is involved in government (as both elected and unelected officials), 'the governance turn' has been vital to exploring the involvement of non-state actors, non-binding arrangements and voluntary agreements in co-ordinating action (e.g. Christiansen & Neuhold, 2012; Kleine, 2014; Whetsell et al., 2021). Exploring informality across empirical contexts,

From Informality and Formality to In\formality **9**

informal governance theories have highlighted the function of non-government actors in delivering government services. Despite this recognition, informality continued to be conceptualised in terms of occurring with an absence of formal rules, parallel to formal rules, or as a 'systematic departure from formal rules' (Kleine, 2014, p. 304).

Challenging the structure–agency dichotomy, practice approaches present a new way to enquire into how policy is made by exploring the connections between the context and the doings and sayings of policy practitioners. Practice scholars highlight the importance of informal practices as part and parcel of making policy (work) – zooming in on what is said but not written and what is done but not formalised (Bartels, 2018; Cook & Wagenaar, 2012; Freeman et al., 2011). Gatherings, encounters and meetings become microsites of policymaking, fleeting, partly undocumented and uninscribed moments where politics were performed (Freeman, 2019; Freeman & Maybin, 2011). These perspectives illustrate the interactional conditions for actors situated in bureaucratic settings, the *situatedness* of informality in how practitioners make sense of their circumstances and explain how the performances of people and things enable particular orderings associated with formal to become entangled, reproduced and upheld by informal doings. This turn zooms in on 'the everyday experiences of common workers as being part of work in the formal sense', often overlooked in the past as these seemed 'only fleeting events to the invariants of legal rule, organisational structure, bureaucratic procedure, and political accountability' (Wagenaar, 2004, p. 644). This body of work has been highly influential in acknowledging the importance of a grounded account and the role of policy actors in making policy, as well as informing methodologies suited to empirical analyses of informality.

Informality in Relation

Another way of conceptualising informality is in relation to the symbolic othering of a binary term or how it emerges in relation to its context. Several scholars have spoken to the positioning of informality as *the Other* to formality and the work that does in reifying the power asymmetry between the two concepts (Grosz, 1987; Pratt, 2019; van Hulst et al., 2015). Within a binary framework, the two poles are rarely perceived as equal in power or value in a normative sense, and this asymmetric relationship extends into public policy settings (Grosz, 1987; Pratt, 2019; van Hulst et al., 2015). Working in the context of development studies and the north–south divide, Andy Pratt (2019) summarises this in stating,

> Analytically, informality requires a balancing concept of the formal; politically, informality is 'the Other', bound into a teleological relationship with the formal, but unable to ever achieve it. This accounts for the repressive power that the notion of informality has in the contexts of 'development'. (p. 613)

There are two insights that we take note of with Pratt's (2019) contribution: first, that there is a notable power asymmetry between the terms formal and

10   Joanna Mason et al.

informal which allocates greater authority to the former; and second, drawing from the global north-south debates, there is an additional layer of dichotomisation that informs his research context.

Binaries can also be interpreted in the co-dependent relationship forged between opposites. Several authors (Koster & Smart, 2019; Morand, 1995) have noted that in the classic *Seeing Like a State*, James Scott (1998, p. 310) showed how the formal could be parasitic on informal processes – taken to mean that the formal requires the informal to exist. Building on Scott's insights of the dependency relationship of the formal on the informal to legitimise its position, Karla Koutkova (2016) applies this theoretical insight to a local governance setting in Bosnia. She states that in her research she sought to 'debunk the normative assumptions' relating to informality/formality as non-universal, whereby formal procedures and requirements were perceived as 'fake and nonsensical' but informal activities were a 'vehicle of communication' (Koutkova, 2016, p. 233).

Huseyn Aliyev (2015) also highlights the importance of context, specifically the historical context of former Soviet states and the emergence of 'post-Soviet informality' (p. 187). Challenging a universalist notion of in/formality, Aliyev (2015) defines 'post-Soviet informality' as 'a concept that defines the post-Soviet informal sphere as a socio-political, socio-economic and socio-cultural phenomenon intrinsic and peculiar to the former Soviet Union' (p. 191). Here, informality is woven across multiple socio-cultural domains and not reducible to economic, political or social spheres alone (Aliyev, 2015, p. 193).

For Nicolas Lamp (2017) and Colin McFarlane (2012), context is key to their research on informality as well. Lamp's (2017) case study of negotiation processes within the World Trade Organization suggests that formal and informal meetings and documents 'serve essentially different functions' (p. 63). He also highlights how both meetings and documents are equally embedded within overarching working strategies, thus transcending the binary understanding of informal to formal and presenting them as complementary rather than opposite. Similarly, Colin McFarlane (2012) argues from an urban planning position that it is important to analyse how the formal and informal relate to each other in different contexts. People move between formal and informal activities and arrangements over the course of time and place. Entwining the two allows us to see how the relation between the informal and the formal varies temporally and across and between sites.

Looking across disciplinary divides, we noticed that scholars have shown how informality and formality both emerge differently in each context. Thus, this binary understanding of the informal to the formal is being challenged, recognising how officials and scholars counter the dichotomisation of in/formality by highlighting their interconnections (for example, Aliyev, 2015; Koutkova, 2016) but also covertly (for example, Lamp, 2017; McFarlane, 2012) in scholarship that speaks to the entanglement of the concepts.

Summing Up

In this section, we have shown that perceptions of informality appear to be changing. Beginning with strictly binary, and largely negative understandings, there is

From Informality and Formality to In|formality   *11*

increasing interest to analyse the informal and the formal as enmeshed and discerning how they become meaningful in relation (Koutkova, 2016). These efforts highlight the importance of interpretive approaches for revealing the 'myths, rituals and symbols' of bureaucracy (Needham, 2016, p. 348) which shape the shared meaning of informal action and work in favour of the genesis of certain courses of action rather than others.

Thus, approaching formal and informal as dynamic and relational opens up our way of exploring actions that actively connect the two. This recognition constructs informality as knotted in a kind of 'meshwork' in formation – a flow of unfolding relations (Ingold, 2008, pp. 1796–1797). This recognition, treating the informal and formal as imbricated, nonetheless, speaks to a way of conceiving the informal as entangled and in a non-binary manner. As we will explain in the next section, this positions the processual (inter)actions of policy actors as always already in|formal, yet, meaningful effects are often explained in dualistic terms (either/or) in the ongoing daily tinkering (Mol et al., 2010) of policy (making).

Our Approach: In|formality

So, what is our approach to informality? A challenge that we faced while we were working on this book was to avoid generalising and demarcating what informality *is* and *is not*, while not dismissing the concept altogether. Rather, we devote an entire book to theoretically and empirically exploring it in detail. Recognising that there was something coherent within the concept of informal, and refusing to work within a binary framework of what informality is or is not, we instead explored it as a sensitizing concept. As academics or practitioners, we are attuned to practices, spaces, materials and affects that are understood to be informal. Yet, we also sensed that these descriptions were not representative of all contexts and that a critical engagement with the concept of the informal was needed.

Rather than strictly defining informality, we think of it in terms that allow it to be meaningful, situational, relational, contingent, political and entangled with the formal. Our encounters and thinking-with the in|formal as entangled emerge from our engagements with feminist theorising, troubling the 'binary oppositional grid [which] establishes a privileged model of theoretical enquiry by which the identity of a privileged term is guaranteed through the elaboration and expulsion of its opposite or other' (Grosz, 1987, p. 478). As we allude to earlier, conventional ways of reading/knowing policy can also be traced back to these dichotomous, oppositional and hierarchical categorisations founded on binary arrangements which are based on privileged axes of spatial, social, economic and cultural organisation – wherein such binary arrangements 'accord positive value to the primary term and regard the secondary term as its debased counterpart' (Grosz, 1987, p. 480). In this case, formal has been the primary term and informal the secondary one. We are not only questioning this binary positioning but challenging the binary as a fixed relationship.

Formality and informality, consequently, are often conceived as forms of organising action (e.g. structured versus unstructured; rule-based versus unruly; authorised versus unauthorised, legitimate versus illegitimate, etc.) – an

12 Joanna Mason et al.

epistemological demarcation put to work in different ways and contexts. Nevertheless, when it comes to the informal and formal, we

> subscribe to a key set of theorizing moves: (1) that situated actions are consequential in the production of social life, [and] (2) that dualisms are rejected as a way of theorizing, and (3) that relations are mutually constitutive. These principles cannot be taken singularly, but implicate one another. (Feldman & Orlikowski, 2011, p. 1241)

As a result, we employ the term in|formality to highlight the relationality between informal and formal. This | inscription in in|formality is an intentional textual tool to join together the often-dichotomised terms, highlight their mutually constitutive nature and destabilise the normative assumptions often bound tightly to informal and formal. In moving beyond dualisms and polarities, we are working with an ontology of policy enacted that is always already formal and informal, expressed as in|formal, that is constituted through relations, whereby the formal–informal is not readymade but always in formation. Rather than viewing informality and formality as diametrically opposed, they emerge not in advance of action but within its unfolding. There is also a temporality to informal–formal relations, as actors (civil servants, managers, practitioners, etc.) move between formal and informal activities and arrangements through the course of a day. These associations are often invisible in accounts of policy worlds, as we lose sight of the ostensibly mundane, subtle effects of certain actions, whereas the temporal, performative flow of everyday doings become backgrounded, including the role of routine, improvisation and everyday practice in creating 'the gestured, contingent, and shorthand annotation instead of the memorial; exchanged glances and murmurs rather than documents' (McFarlane, 2012, p. 102).

In our efforts to disrupt and vex informal and formal relations, we foreground the in|formal not as either/or rather as both/and, entailing a trail between and among 'more than one, and less than many' partial connections (Strathern in Mol, 2002, p. 82) and

> attempt to occupy the impossible, paradoxical position of the middle ground, the ground left uncovered by the oppositional structure-being both subject and object, self and other, reason and passion, mind and body, rather than one or the other. (Grosz, 1987. p. 480)

Furthermore, we draw from interpretive approaches by emphasising that informality is meaningful. What informality is, is – often tacitly, at other times more explicitly – given meaning in everyday action. Informality is not a property of certain practices, materials and spaces but acquires meaning through enactment and *in situ*. Meaning is also locally and historically situated. Thus, what is perceived to be informal in one context or situation can differ from another. And even within a context, multiple understandings of what is informal can coexist.

In this multiplicity and possible clashes of meaning-making, we can uncover the complexity of informality (Yanow, 2011). How it is perceived is informed by previous actions and by larger historical developments, and in every action it can acquire new meanings. This means that informality is also inherently contingent. This process is not subjective but social, as it happens in interaction between people and with materials.

The challenge of this book was to investigate informality in policymaking from multiple perspectives and contexts while remaining open to the development of the concept itself. The predicament was to be able to observe it, see it, and then share with others that what was encountered was *informality* in policymaking while committing to the intellectual project of holding on to the concept of in|formality as emergent and investigating this from multiple perspectives and contexts. An ethnographic approach or sensibility applied to a policy setting highlights that informality is not opaque or invisible to those who engage in it – this is what our volume offers.

How This Book Proceeds

In this section, we offer brief summaries of the contributions within this volume, along with thoughts on three conceptual themes which authors used in developing their chapter. In the nine empirical chapters, authors describe and analyse the concept of informality by drawing on their entanglements within varied policy domains, contexts and locations. Authors present studies that span rural and urban contexts in diverse geographic locations, illuminating the variety of actors and policy work within these different spaces. While each is uniquely situated, all studies derive from ethnographic or interpretive approaches. Collectively, this assembles scholarship from multiple disciplines and standpoints to foreground the material realities of policy work and the doings and sayings of policy actors. Bookending these chapters is a *Dénouement* on the making of this book and invited contributions from esteemed academics who write about policy and practice in ways that we thought complement the vision we had for this book. A foreword by Richard Freeman and afterword by Peregrine Schwartz-Shea and Dvora Yanow appealingly coax readers to engage with informality holistically and highlight how chapters relate to each other.

While this book is structured according to three onto-epistemological categories, we draw attention briefly to the role of three conceptual themes – boundaries, knowledge mastery and networks – that were instrumental in developing new understandings of informality (see Tamara Mulherin and Lindsey Garner-Knapp's *Dénouement* for more about these themes). *Boundaries* refer to the division between what is formal and informal in the policymaking process between different groups of people or professions, within hierarchies or physical spaces. *Knowledge mastery* denotes understanding a context, process or practice requires mastery of a particular type of knowledge as a skill or capability developed by policymakers. *Networks* refer to how a broad assemblage of actors feed into the policy process including elected officials, civil servants, interest groups and other stakeholders. These themes were brought to bear on authors' conceptualisation

14   *Joanna Mason et al.*

of informality within and through their empirical material, offering both a fruitful heuristic for *thinking with* as chapters took form, and a conceptual tool to transcend normative tropes associated with informality – as nested 'sensitizing concepts' (Blumer, 1954). Themes have consequently been a processual, rather than a procedural, injection into the book's formation as chapters progressed. Most importantly, these themes were chosen for their generative capacity and how they can be associated with both the formal and the informal of policymaking to allow a seeding of ideas about informality without defaulting to familiar but polarising understandings.

It was a challenge to identify threads that tie this book together in a volume that collates diverse scholarship on a concept with wide-ranging meanings. This was compounded by our commitment to resist defining informality. As a result, chapters vary in their stance on informality as in|formality. Describing informality empirically and theoretically without referring to formality and common-usage understandings was not always easy or successful, despite our motivation to do so.

Setting the Stage of Informality

Two authors set the stage and orient the reader to where informality may be situated and how it manifests, inviting readers to perceive informality as a *way of working* or an *arena* – thereby unpacking what informality means in different domains and from different places in the world.

With '"Knowing" the System: Public Administration and Informality During COVID-19', Claire Bynner offers insights into how local knowledge of administrative staff in a local government in the United Kingdom afforded the entanglement of informal and formal *ways of working* for keeping administrative and governance systems going during the pandemic crisis. Working within Westminster conventions, Bynner clearly sets out how the formal and informal binary is framed within this system.

Also speaking to situated knowledge, but from within an Indian context, Meera Sudhakar's chapter 'The Informal Work of Policy Maintenance: Making Space for Local Knowledge in Indian Rural Electricity Governance' examines informality as an *arena* that admits contingent and local knowledge to maintain electricity supply in rural Indian territories. This occurs in the midst of the significant challenge to remain accountable to higher bureaucracy when the measurement of electricity supply and consumption is uncertain.

Informal Practices and Ethnomethodology

Three chapters centre what actors are doing and the meanings of their actions to uncover *practices* of informality and formality via ethnographic and ethnomethodological approaches. Practice-theoretical studies foreground what people do, treating work as situated, spatio-temporal, contingent, ongoing accomplishments (Emirbayer & Maynard, 2011; Garfinkel, 1984; Lynch, 2001), building on the premise that social, organisational and administrative life comes into being – and

From Informality and Formality to In\formality   **15**

can also be challenged and changed – through situated everyday actions (Emirbayer & Maynard, 2011; Feldman & Orlikowski, 2011; Nicolini, 2013). An ethnomethodological approach can be recognised in the three chapters through analysis of what people say and how they make themselves accountable to one another in conversational interactions.

Mapping local understanding to identify where and how boundaries are drawn between informality and formality within the practice of diplomatic work within the European Union, co-authors Kristin Anabel Eggeling and Larissa Versloot speak to the handling of in/formality as a key diplomatic *skill* in their chapter 'Mastering Informality in Diplomacy'. This chapter is a classic example of phenomenological work practice studies, yet offers novel insights into an often-challenging space to gain access to diplomacy in action.

Second in this section is Lisa Marie Borelli's chapter, 'Bureaucratic Hustling and Knowledge Shuffling – Informality within Swiss Public Administration', which zooms in on the interactions of frontline workers and presents in/formality as an *approach*. In line with other ethnomethodologists, Borelli attends to how *knowledge* is shared and decisions are made through informal practices of 'hustling' and 'shuffling' as spontaneous solutions to other work practices.

Rounding off this section is E. Lianne Visser's chapter, 'Catching Up with Catching Up: Collaborative Policy Work, In|formality and Connective Talk', set among public policymakers and semi-public managers in welfare services in the Netherlands. Analysing human interactions, Visser shows how catching up serves to make sense of the participants' identity, relations, and world. As a connective practice, it contributes to overcoming multiple *boundaries* and to entangling the informal and the formal.

Together, by taking an ethnomethodological approach and looking at their accomplishment, these chapters show how informal and formal become meaningful through practical action, be it between diplomats, officials and residents or policymakers and semi-profit managers.

Methods to Study Informality

The following section untangles local meanings of informality and formality and also grapples with how in|formality can be seen or becomes visible – or how authors have been able to 'see and study' informality through ethnographic research. Covering diverse settings from Indian cities to infrastructure meeting rooms, and through rural Scotland, the authors deal with documenting and presenting informality in words, gestures and materials.

To show the underexplored role of informal processes and structures entailed in navigating India's complex water challenges, Neha Mungekar's chapter, 'Visualising Informal Repair: Exploring Photographic 'Routines' in Ethnographic Methodology', outlines her use of photography in a visual ethnography of human and non-human actor *networks*. She reveals through visual methods how informality emerges as a critical element in bridging governance gaps, offering nuanced perspectives on the interconnectedness and relationships among actors within this sector.

16   *Joanna Mason et al.*

Evelijn Martinius' chapter, 'Traceless Transitions: Studying the Role of Drawings and Gestures in Construction Project Meetings', takes on the informal in showing how bodily gestures during meetings become formative to realising plans in the maintenance of a European airport project. Her analysis reveals porous spatial and temporal *boundaries* in the planning process as map lines are not redrawn, yet interpretations change in response to these actions. Martinius shows how informality can be observed through attending to bodily gestures in situ.

Tamara Mulherin's chapter, 'Vehicles of In|formality – the Role of the Car as a Mobile Space of Policy and Relational Work', derived from an ethnography in rural Scotland, foregrounds the role of cars in policy work and what happens while travelling. Car interiors foster social relations through a complex communicative assemblage, a place of work but also a comfort zone for having downtime. The chapter considers cars as informal, threshold spaces, and how the policy work performed in cars was critical for enabling things to go on.

Concluding Thoughts

The remaining two chapters gather loose threads as theoretical and reflective insights through a capstone chapter and a reflection on the making of this book as collaborative endeavour.

The capstone chapter by co-authors Lindsey Garner-Knapp and Joanna Mason, 'Tracing Threads of In/Visibilities: The Knotty Mattering of Policymaking', widens out theoretically to explore the potential of anthropological and ethnographic 'traces' to disrupt conventional understandings of the informal as *bounded* to the formal. Ethnographic vignettes foreground the effects of doings revealed through traces to show the porosities between spatio-temporal policymaking encounters that subverts rigid, dichotomous configurations of the in|formal.

Differently, but also reflecting on this book, Tamara Mulherin and Lindsey Garner-Knapp round off the volume with a reflection of its making in their 'Dénouement: Why the How Comes to Matter'. This chapter chronicles the academic pursuit of producing an edited book and the collaboration upon which it ultimately depends. It is designed as adjunct to the arguments put forward in this chapter, scaffolding how this book came about and from where its aspirations to 'do academia differently' were derived and the impact those 'how' decisions made on the making.

Afterword

Peregrine Schwartz-Shea and Dvora Yanow offer considered thoughts on the book's chapters drawing out key themes and relations between chapters in their 'Afterword: Reflecting on In|formality'. Drawing on their extensive academic experience, these authors support our efforts in locating the scholarship in this volume within the various intersecting, but often siloed, works of literature while simultaneously offering insights into how authors and editors contribute to those diverse scholarships.

From Informality and Formality to In\formality **17**

In closing this chapter as the endpoint of our efforts to explain this book's vision, academic contribution and structure – the informal world of policy awaits readers poised to interrogate these matters across geographic locations, contexts, cultures and policy stages. In reading further, we urge you to ponder on informality and formality as in\formality and invite further scholarship to explore in\formality (or informality) in policymaking from across the globe, particularly using ethnographic, interpretive, practice or socio-material approaches.

References

Aliyev, H. (2015). Post-Soviet informality: Towards theory-building. *International Journal of Sociology and Social Policy*, *35*(3/4), 182–198. https://doi.org/10.1108/ijssp-05-2014-0041

Bartels, K. P. R. (2018). Policy as practice. In H. K. Colebatch, R. Hoppe, & K. P. R. Bartels (Eds.), *Handbook on policy, process and governing* (pp. 68–88). Edward Elgar Publishing. https://doi.org/10.4337/9781784714871

Bevir, M., & Rhodes, R. A. W. (2001). Decentering tradition: Interpreting British government. *Administration & Society*, *33*(2), 107–132. https://doi.org/10.1177/00953990122019703

Blumer, H. (1954). What is wrong with social theory? *American Sociological Review*, *19*(1), 3–10. https://doi.org/10.2307/2088165

Boanada-Fuchs, A., & Boanada Fuchs, V. (2018). Towards a taxonomic understanding of informality. *International Development Planning Review*, *40*, 397–420. https://doi.org/10.3828/idpr.2018.23

Boswell, J. (2022). *Magical thinking in public policy: Why naïve ideals about better policymaking persist in cynical times*. Oxford University Press.

Brodkin, E. Z. (2012). Reflections on street-level bureaucracy: Past, present, and future. *Public Administration Review*, *72*, 940–949. https://doi.org/10.1111/j.1540-6210.2012.02657.x

Christiansen, T., & Neuhold, C. (2012). Introduction. In T. Christiansen & C. Neuhold (Eds.), *International handbook on informal governance* (pp. 1–18). Edward Elgar Publishing.

Colebatch, H. K. (2014). Making sense of governance. *Policy & society*, *33*(4), 307–316. https://doi.org/10.1016/j.polsoc.2014.10.001

Cook, S. D. N., & Wagenaar, H. (2012). Navigating the eternally unfolding present: Toward an epistemology of practice. *American Review of Public Administration*, *42*(1), 3–38. https://doi.org/10.1177/0275074011407404

de Vries, M. S., & Kim, P. S. (2011). *Value and virtue in public administration: A comparative perspective*. Palgrave Macmillan UK. https://doi.org/10.1057/9780230353886

Dorren, L. (2021). *Analysis as therapy: The therapeutic function of ex ante analyses in infrastructure policy processes*. Doctoral dissertation, University of Antwerp.

du Gay, P., & Pedersen, K. Z. (2020). Discretion and bureaucracy. In T. Evans & P. Hupe (Eds.), *Discretion and the quest for controlled freedom* (1st ed., pp. 221–236). Palgrave Macmillan. https://doi.org/10.1007/978-3-030-19566-3

Emirbayer, M., & Maynard, D. W. (2011). Pragmatism and ethnomethodology. *Qualitative sociology*, *34*(1), 221–261. https://doi.org/10.1007/s11133-010-9183-8

Evans, T. (2011). Professionals, managers and discretion: Critiquing street-level bureaucracy. *The British Journal of Social Work*, *41*(2), 368–386. https://doi.org/10.1093/bjsw/bcq074

18 Joanna Mason et al.

Feldman, M. S., & Orlikowski, W. J. (2011). Theorizing practice and practicing theory. *Organization Science*, *22*(5), 1240–1253. https://doi.org/10.1287/orsc.1100.0612

Freeman, R. (2019). Meeting, talk and text: Policy and politics in practice. *Policy and Politics*, *47*(2), 371–388. https://doi.org/10.1332/030557319X15526370368821

Freeman, R., Griggs, S., & Boaz, A. (2011). The practice of policy making. *Evidence & Policy*, *7*(2), 127–136. https://doi.org/10.1332/174426411X579180

Freeman, R., & Maybin, J. (2011). Documents, practices and policy. *Evidence & Policy*, *7*(2), 155–170. https://doi.org/10.1332/174426411X579207

Garfinkel, H. (1984). *Studies in ethnomethodology*. Polity.

Gherardi, S. (2019). *How to conduct a practice-based study: Problems and methods*. Edward Elgar Publishing.

Goffman, E. (1969). *The presentation of self in everyday life*. Allen Lane.

Green, M. (2011). Calculating compassion: Accounting for some categorical practices in international development. In D. Mosse (Ed.), *Adventures in Aidland: The anthropology of professionals in international development* (pp. 33–56). Berghahn Books, Incorporated.

Grosz, E. A. (1987). Feminist theory and the challenge to knowledges. *Women's Studies International Forum*, *10*(5), 475–480. https://doi.org/10.1016/0277-5395(87)90001-X

Hupe, P., & Hill, M. (2007). Street-level bureaucracy and public accountability. *Public Administration*, *85*(2), 279–299. https://doi.org/10.1111/j.1467-9299.2007.00650.x

Ingold, T. (2008). Bindings against boundaries: Entanglements of life in an open world. *Environment and Planning A: Economy and Space*, *40*(8), 1796–1810. https://doi.org/10.1068/a40156

Jun, J. S., & Sherwood, F. P. (2006). *The social construction of public administration: Interpretive and critical perspectives*. State University of New York Press.

Kleine, M. (2014). Informal governance in the European Union. *Journal of European Public Policy*, *21*(2), 303–314. https://doi.org/10.1080/13501763.2013.870023

Koster, M., & Smart, A. (2019). Performing in/formality beyond the dichotomy: An introduction. *Anthropologica*, *61*(1), 20–24. https://doi.org/10.3138/anth.2018-0013

Koutkova, K. (2016). Informality as an interpretive filter: Translating ubleha in local community development in Bosnia. *Journal of Contemporary Central and Eastern Europe*, *24*(3), 223–237. https://doi.org/10.1080/0965156X.2016.1262227

Lamp, N. (2017). The receding horizon of informality in WTO meetings. *Journal of the Royal Anthropological Institute*, *23*(S1), 63–79. https://doi.org/10.1111/1467-9655.12594

Lasswell, H. D. (1956). The political science of science: An inquiry into the possible reconciliation of mastery and freedom. *The American Political Science Review*, *50*(4), 961–979. https://doi.org/10.2307/1951330

Lindblom, C. E. (2020). The science of "muddling through", 19 Pub. Admin. Rev. 79 (1959). *Communication Law and Policy*, *25*(4), 451–455. https://doi.org/10.1080/10811680.2020.1805947

Lipsky, M. (1980). *Street-level bureaucracy: Dilemmas of the individual in public services*. Russell Sage Foundation.

Lynch, M. (2001). Ethnomethodology and the logic of practice. In T. R. Schatzki, K. K. Cetina, & E. Von Savigny (Eds.), *The practice turn in contemporary theory* (pp. 140–157). Routledge. https://doi.org/10.4324/9780203977453-18

Lynn, L. E. (2006). *Public management: Old and new*. Routledge.

McFarlane, C. (2012). Rethinking informality: Politics, crisis, and the city. *Planning Theory & Practice*, *13*(1), 89–108. https://doi.org/10.1080/14649357.2012.649951

McGranahan, C. (2018). Ethnography beyond method: The importance of an ethnographic sensibility. *Sites: A Journal of Social Anthropology and Cultural Studies*, *15*(1), 1–10. https://doi.org/dx.doi.org/10.11157/sites-id373

From Informality and Formality to In\formality   **19**

Metze, T. (2010). New life for old buildings: Mediating between different meanings. In H. K. Colebatch, R. Hoppe, & M. Noordegraaf (Eds.), *Working for policy* (pp. 75–90). Amsterdam University Press.

Misztal, B. A. (2000). *Informality: Social theory and contemporary practice.* Routledge. https://doi.org/10.4324/9780203003626

Mol, A. (2002). *The body multiple: Ontology in medical practice.* Duke University Press.

Mol, A., Moser, I., & Pols, J. (Eds.). (2010). *Care in practice on tinkering in clinics, homes and farms.* transcript.

Morand, D. A. (1995). The role of behavioral formality and informality in the enactment of bureaucratic versus organic organizations. *The Academy of Management Review, 20*(4), 831–872. https://doi.org/10.2307/258958

Needham, C. (2016). Public administration. In M. Bevir & R. A. W. Rhodes (Eds.), *Routledge handbook of interpretive political science* (pp. 338–351). Routledge. https://doi.org/10.4324/9781315725314

Nicolini, D. (2013). *Practice theory, work, and organization: An introduction.* Oxford University Press, Incorporated.

O'Flynn, J., Blackman, D., & Halligan, J. (2013). *Crossing boundaries in public management and policy: The international experience.* Taylor & Francis Group.

Önday, Ö. (2016). Classical organization theory: From generic management of Socrates to bureaucracy of Weber. *International Journal of Business and Management Review, 4*(1), 87–105.

Ongaro, E., & Van Thiel, S. (2018). *The Palgrave handbook of public administration and management in Europe* (1st ed.). Palgrave Macmillan UK. https://doi.org/10.1057/978-1-137-55269-3

Polese, A. (2023). What is informality? (Mapping) "the art of bypassing the state" in Eurasian spaces – And beyond. *Eurasian Geography and Economics, 64*(3), 322–364. https://doi.org/10.1080/15387216.2021.1992791

Pratt, A. (2019). Formality as exception. *Urban Studies, 56*(3), 612–615. https://doi.org/10.1177/0042098018810600

Scott, J. C. (1998). *Seeing like a state: How certain schemes to improve the human condition have failed.* Yale University Press.

Simon, H. A. (1955). A behavioral model of rational choice. *The Quarterly Journal of Economics, 69*(1), 99–118. https://doi.org/10.2307/1884852

Steenberg, R. (2016). The art of not seeing like a state. On the ideology of "informality". *Journal of Contemporary Central and Eastern Europe, 24*(3), 293–306. https://doi.org/10.1080/0965156X.2016.1262229

Ulmer, J. B. (2020). Pivots and pirouettes: Carefully turning traditions. *Qualitative Inquiry, 26*(5), 454–457. https://doi.org/10.1177/1077800419829778

van Hulst, M., Koster, M., & Vermeulen, J. (2015). Ethnographic research. In D. A. Bearfield, E. Berman, & M. J. Dubnick (Eds.), *Encyclopedia of public administration and public policy* (3rd ed., pp. 1–5). Routledge. https://doi.org/10.1081/E-EPAP3-120051222

van Hulst, M., Ybema, S., & Yanow, D. (2017). Ethnography and organizational processes: Studying processes of organizing ethnographically. Studying the complexities of everyday life. In A. Langley & H. Tsoukas (Eds.), *The Sage handbook of process organization studies* (pp. 223–236). SAGE Publications.

Visser, E. L., & van Hulst, M. (2024). The performance and development of deliberative routines: A practice-based ethnographic study. *Journal of Public Administration Research and Theory, 34*(1), 92–104. https://doi.org/10.1093/jopart/muad006

Wagenaar, H. (2004). "Knowing" the rules: Administrative work as practice. *Public Administration Review, 64*(6), 643–655. https://doi.org/10.1111/j.1540-6210.2004.00412.x

20 *Joanna Mason et al.*

Whetsell, T. A., Kroll, A., & DeHart-Davis, L. (2021). Formal hierarchies and informal networks: How organizational structure shapes information search in local government. *Journal of Public Administration Research and Theory, 31*(4), 653–669. https://doi.org/10.1093/jopart/muab003

Yanow, D. (1996). *How does a policy mean? Interpreting policy and organizational actions.* Georgetown University Press.

Yanow, D. (2011). A policy ethnographer's reading of policy anthropology. In C. Shore, S. Wright, & D. Pero (Eds.), *Policy worlds: Anthropology and the analysis of contemporary power* (pp. 300–314). Berghahn Books.

Setting the Stage of Informality

Chapter 1

'Knowing' the System: Public Administration and Informality during COVID-19

Claire Bynner

University of Edinburgh, UK

Abstract

This chapter examines the informal through the accounts of a public official who had a leading role in re-making the administration of community grants in her local authority during the early stages of the COVID-19 pandemic. This chapter explores what happens when there is a rupture to public administration processes, and the rule book is 'thrown out of the window'. The focus is on the early stages of the COVID-19 pandemic and the weeks following the UK government announcement of the 'stay-at-home' order. The analysis draws on practice theory with its focus on the ways in which policy actors engage with concrete situations and negotiate institutional contexts and configurations (Bartels, 2018; Cook & Wagenaar, 2012; Wagenaar, 2004). The analytical framework applies Wagenaar's (2004) four key elements of public administration practice: context, action, knowledge and interaction. This chapter builds on Wagenaar's understanding and explores how the entanglement of [in]formal practices made it possible for public officials to keep administrative systems going during the pandemic crisis.

Keywords: COVID-19; informality; public administration; governance; community grants; practice theory

---

Informality in Policymaking: Weaving the Threads of Everyday Policy Work, 23–38
Copyright © 2025 by Claire Bynner
Published under exclusive licence by Emerald Publishing Limited
doi:10.1108/978-1-83797-280-720241002

24 *Claire Bynner*

Introduction

In March 2020, as the coronavirus COVID-19 spread rapidly across the globe, the UK government was under intense pressure to respond to the pandemic. Prime minister Boris Johnson appeared on television and announced a policy requiring all those who could, to remain at home and only to leave for essential shopping, basic exercise or medical treatment. Essential key workers in the National Health Service (NHS), frontline transport staff and some charity workers were exempt. The lockdown continued until a gradual easing in May, with the lifting of most restrictions occurring in early July 2020. Public spending in the form of a furlough scheme and various grants and loan guarantee schemes sought to mitigate the economic impact of the pandemic, although this had minimal or no impact on some groups. Those who were most negatively affected included younger, lower-earning and less educated people who were unable to work; women and younger adults with poor mental health prior to the pandemic; and children from poorer backgrounds (Blundell et al., 2022). Despite the unprecedented public health measures of lockdown, the UK had one of the worst death tolls from COVID-19 in Europe (World Health Organisation (WHO), 2023). The unequal impact on different population groups exacerbated pre-existing health inequalities and led to extreme anxiety and uncertainty, especially for the most vulnerable individuals and communities (Fancourt et al., 2021; McGowan & Bambra, 2022).

The government stay-at-home order was communicated through public information that arrived through the post (see Figures 1.1 and 1.2). The instruction to 'stay at home in order to protect the NHS [National Health Service] and save lives' (Cabinet Office, 2020, para 1) landed on the makeshift desks of employees who were now working from home, in their bedrooms or in other rooms that had hastily undergone a rapid conversion to temporary offices. With the announcement of lockdown, community organisations began mobilising at speed. The crisis evoked a spirit of social solidarity and community action. With so many people now unable to work, community groups and organisations experienced a sharp increase in potential volunteers. Many community organisations pivoted to deliver their services in new ways, especially using digital technology and working in new collaborations with government, health agencies and other local businesses and voluntary organisations (Dayson & Damm, 2020). This complex landscape of organisations and services scrambled to make sense of the unprecedented situation and worked long hours to get resources such as food and other essentials to vulnerable individuals and communities as quickly as possible (Rees et al., 2022).

For officials working in the local government, the stay-at-home order (lockdown) involved an almost instantaneous shift from a very small number of council staff who could normally work remotely, to most council staff working from home. Nearly all decision-making processes were suspended. The pandemic triggered a reconfiguration of systems and processes. New systems of coordination and control were developed, with new approaches to oversight and authorisation.

Council employees and community workers were working under intense pressure while privately dealing with their own health anxieties, family needs and tragedies. The day-to-day work was intense, and they were struggling with work

Public Administration and Informality During COVID-19

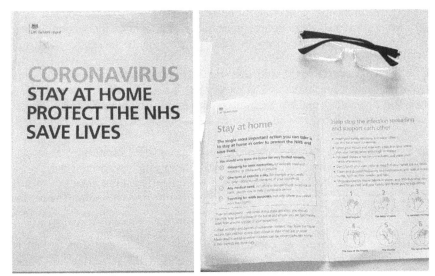

Figure 1.1. (Left) UK Government Coronavirus leaflet front cover.
Source: Original photographs: Claire Bynner.

Figure 1.2. (Right) UK Government Coronavirus leaflet inside pages.
Source: Original photographs: Claire Bynner.

demands and exhaustion. In their efforts to support others, they had little opportunity to pause and reflect on the scale of illness, death and anxiety they were living through, as well as the impact the pandemic was having on their own lives.

Evidence of the increased work demand and stress was repeated across the United Kingdom:

> Staff were [...] also put under great strain, with many re-deployed to work on unfamiliar and ill-defined projects with rapidly evolving objectives; and with illness, shielding, quarantine, home-schooling of children and caring for dependents all diminishing productivity. Simultaneously, demand on council resources peaked as new locally- and nationally-devised policies came into force – from business-support grants to accommodating the homeless, producing shielding lists of vulnerable people and delivering food packages. (Elston & Bel, 2023, p. 9)

Kaye and Morgan (2021) argue that some of the most innovative work that took place during the pandemic was only possible because 'genuine informality was possible' (p. 74). In this account, 'genuine informality' is understood as the absence of formal processes, increased autonomy and 'a fresh culture where people are kind, decent and compassionate towards each other' (p. 74). The informal implies greater flexibility in bureaucratic processes, reduced 'red tape' and more

26 Claire Bynner

trusting relationships. This conceptualisation resonates with sociologist Barbara Misztal's (2002) definition of informality as a form of interaction among partners enjoying relative freedom and contributing to increased trust and positive emotions.

In the literature on community and state responses to the pandemic, informal activity is usually conceptualised as activity that is not officially recognised, small scale and outside normal bureaucratic processes. In this literature, the informal/formal are constructed as a dualism and cast as opposites:

> Formal and informal ways of working are often contrasted as binary opposites – top down versus bottom up – with informal community action characterised as well-intentioned but amateurish at best, or even obstructive to achieving strategic objectives (Wilson et al., 2020, p.4)

Defining what forms of community activity are informal and formal is itself entangled with power relations. Wlison et al. (2020) describe how some 'informal' community groups underwent a 'transition' to the formal during the pandemic:

> Community groups which started out as informal networks of activists are in a process of transition, either by formalising their structures to apply for funding, or developing much tighter eligibility criteria for access to food and services as the crisis has evolved. (Wilson et al., 2020, p. 3).

This 'formalisation' of community activity that was previously below the radar of officials increased the reach and resources of 'informal' community groups, but it also carried the risk that through becoming more visible to officials, these groups would lose their autonomy (Carmel & Harlock, 2008).

Wilson et al. (2020) found that local pandemic responses were characterised by 'a blending and braiding' (Gilchrist, 2016) of informal and formal practices across a spectrum of different types of activity. They conclude that the evidence from the pandemic challenges assumptions underpinning the meaning and enactment of the informal and the formal. In this chapter, I explore how these assumptions are troubled through the everyday practice of one official and her colleagues in a local authority as they worked to rapidly transform administrative and governance systems.

Research Approach

At the time of the announcement of a UK-wide lockdown in March 2020, I was working as a researcher on a university project. Our small research team were forced to suspend our previous fieldwork. Instead, we began to get in touch with our existing contacts in local government and the community sector and attempted to document their experiences of the pandemic. Our pandemic research focused on Scotland, in the United Kingdom and took place in April 2020. One interview stood out in the detailed description of what happened behind the scenes in local government and the changes to administrative and governance practices. This was an interview with a public official, a female senior manager, aged 56, who I refer to here with the pseudonym, Rowan. The interview was conducted using video conferencing software and lasted approximately 60 minutes. All identifiers, including the name of the local authority and the local governance structures, have been removed.

Rowan's role as an official was similar to a role that I had once held, some ten years previously in the same local authority. Despite her lack of time and increased work pressure, Rowan was willing to talk to me and she used the interview as an opportunity to reflect on her experiences. During the interview, Rowan commented that listening to this must be 'as dull as ditch water'; however, with my assurances that this *was* interesting, she provided a more detailed account. My prior knowledge of the working context may have encouraged Rowan to talk about these processes in more detail since as a former local government employee, they were of personal interest to me.

The interview with Rowan reminded me of Wagenaar's paper 'Knowing the Rules - Administrative Work as Practice' (2004) which was also based on a single interview with a public official. In writing this chapter, I revisited this paper from 2004. In the paper, Wagenaar (2004) draws a memorable analogy between the practice of public administration work and the practice of playing the piano. He argues that public administration, just like playing the piano, involves more than just the movement of fingers on the keys. It involves multiple cognitive processes and decisions:

> the hundreds of practical judgments, the everyday, taken-for-granted routines and practices, the explicit and tacit knowledge that is brought to bear on concrete situations, the moving about in the legal–moral environment of large administrative bureaucracies, the mastering of difficult human–emotional situations, the negotiating of discretionary space, and the interactive give and take with colleagues that, taken together, make up every day public administration. (Wagenaar, 2004, p. 644)

Wagenaar (2004) does not examine informality explicitly; however, the informal is suggested in his writing through his interest in the aspects of administrative work that are usually ignored or overlooked by the 'formal' organisation:

> unthinking routines, the informal banter and gossip with colleagues during the coffee break, our sympathies and antipathies, our private doubts about the quality of our work, our affective responses to clients or colleagues, and our recurrent sense of stress or work pressure. (Wagenaar, 2004, p. 644)

28   Claire Bynner

His analysis of these less-visible, tacit, everyday aspects of work was evocative and useful as a starting point for making sense of the informal in public administration practice. Wagenaar's (2004) paper prompted the questions that guided my analysis: What forms of action, knowledge and interaction were made possible during the pandemic? What did the pandemic reveal about the potential for innovating administration and local governance? What does this contribute to our understanding of in[formal] relations between officials and communities? The following sections of this chapter apply the four dimensions of Wagenaar's (2004) analytical framework as a frame for organising with the aim of understanding informal administration practice during the pandemic through the eyes of a public official.

Context – Local Governance and System Breakdown

Rowan described her role and the work of her team as having two main functions. The first role was to manage local partnerships. These were governance structures that involved local government officials, public services and non-government or community actors, working together to agree priorities for local action. The second role was to allocate grant funding from the council budget to address the agreed priorities for each partnership area. With the rise of more participatory and collaborative forms of governance, the range of actors involved had become more complex and diverse over time and now included all political parties and a range of public services in addition to community representatives:

> As a team, we manage a number of local partnerships, across the geography [...] Myself, and my team, are responsible for 12. There is one budget for the authority that is then divided between these [local] partnerships. They then make decisions on the allocation of those grants.

> Interviewer: What would a local partnership look like? Who's on the partnership?

> It's got every elected member from that ward so that that will range from three to four. It's a multi-member award. So that's across all political parties. It's got some core agencies: police, fire and rescue and the NHS [health service] and up to six community representatives [...]

Before the pandemic, partnership meetings were key sites of policymaking where [in]formal social relationships were formed and negotiated.

> These 12 partnerships were meeting about every four to six weeks through the year. There were no virtual meetings at all. All of them met physically, either in their community and their ward or in the [town hall].

Public Administration and Informality During COVID-19   **29**

Rowan's team was responsible for organising partnership meetings and the administration of community grants. Her description of the role of her team aligned with a more traditional understanding of public officials as rational, technical and impersonal. They were tasked with enacting policy, working with formal materials and through official infrastructures, and were held to account through bureaucratic and political oversight.

> What my team were doing as part of that was that they had the core responsibility for grants. The role was to manage that grant process with the ultimate endpoint of taking recommendations to each of those partnerships for approval or rejection. So, their role was to process those grant applications. This included supporting the applicants and coming back to them asking questions, to make sure they fit with the criteria for the grants, and they translate all of that into a report to go to each of these partnerships. So really, then, the decision-making process was the physical meeting of each of these 12 partnerships. They physically meet and the officer presents their report. For example, 'Here's my recommendation, having assessed it and gone back to the applicant, and looked at the fit locally. These are my recommendations'. And the partnership members then would make their decision on those grants.

Rowan's team advised and supported local partnerships on allocations of grant funding to meet the agreed priorities in each local area. Officials in her team had extensive knowledge of the members of their partnership and of the groups and organisations in the local area. The technical side of the job involved the application of a codified set of guidelines or rules on grant funding. At the start of the pandemic, those rules were suspended. After the initial shock of the government-ordered lockdown, there was a need for an adjustment to a new working environment with new digital infrastructures and new management processes.

> Interviewer: in what ways has the pandemic affected you?

> Rowan: Everything had to be looked at in a different light, and new guidance needed to be issued to managers to follow up with their staff. So, there's a huge piece of adjustment for myself as an individual, in terms of working from home and being able to manage from a distance. What that involved, and how we could do that. And we weren't set up with team meetings online. There was a whole lot of stuff there, so I'd say there was a kind of bedding down so that we could do the same jobs effectively from home that we did from at the office and manage some of those core processes like staff support, health and safety.

30   Claire Bynner

With the lockdown, the processes and rules that were the 'core functions' of Rowan and her team were fundamentally ruptured. The in-person meetings, which had been the key sites for decision-making, had disappeared.

> I suppose it then started to become clear that some of our core functions and our ability to deliver those core functions would be significantly affected. We've got money allocated to local partnerships across the city. But they were stopped. The council stopped all of those meetings during lockdown. So, there's no physical meetings happening at all, and those are our means of ensuring that we were able to get decisions, by those members, on those grants.

This rupture to the governance system also meant a breakdown in the democratic norms, infrastructures and processes that provided accountability for decisions, leaving the space open to re-make these systems and relationships.

Action – Re-making and Streamlining

While adjusting to the stay-at-home order and the new context of the pandemic, Rowan and her team were acutely aware of the impact of the pandemic on communities in the local authority area, especially in high-poverty areas. 'The issues of poverty were there already but this crisis pushes things right over the edge' (Rowan). This awareness drove the urgency to get resources out. In practice, this meant re-making, reordering and re-configuring the rules so that new informal processes could act as proxies and mimic the formal processes that normally controlled grant administration. The need for speed and the sense of personal and moral pressure to act provided a rationale and justification for doing things differently.

> Decision-making in the council is a highly structured and focused process. With the Covid-19 lockdown all council structures were told to cease operating with immediate effect. Lockdown meant a suspension of the structures. But we couldn't suspend the grants, so we continued with the grants but put in place a new mechanism to make sure the grants were being awarded in the right way.

> [...] we needed to get money out quickly and make sure we kept the grant system going. And we were under pressure. We felt under pressure at a personal level as well because of the nature of things [...] in an emergency, getting money out. Undergoing some critical analysis of it? We didn't really do that. It was really about getting it up and running quickly.

The council agreed to a new mechanism of delegated authority that allowed officials to take decisions quickly, circumventing normal democratic and administrative processes. This new authorising environment gave official permission for a more informal approach. A key change was simplifying and streamlining the bureaucratic system, reducing the documentation. This also meant changing and circumventing stages of the democratic process and giving more decision-making responsibility to officials.

> We were able to take a bureaucratic system, in terms of grants and shorten it, narrow it down and just make it a lot simpler. Now, there is a bit in terms of democracy there, and the democratic impact of that. It meant that the partnerships were no longer making decisions on the grants. So that was a kind of democratic deficit there. But the benefit of it was that there was a faster assessment from staff. They had to turn things around a bit more quickly, and it didn't go to the partnership, so the team didn't have to produce this big report. But what they did have to do was produce something for consideration by the Chairs [of the partnerships], who then consulted with other elected members locally. And eventually, quite rightly, the community reps expressed annoyance at that.

In this example, the resistance to change came from community representatives (community reps), who were excluded from the new decision-making process. Rowan's account indicates her discomfort with this. At the same time, she justifies the change in terms of streamlining and getting resources out quickly to the most vulnerable communities:

> [...] There is a lot associated with the meetings - agendas, papers getting things out in advance, the physical meeting. All of that it's really bureaucratic, even though it is also democratic. So, we shortened that right down and a physical structure wasn't having to meet, so the Chair and some other members were good enough to make the decision. The decision was made much faster. So, actually a much more limited range of people, but the decision is still based on evidence that each of the officers have collated in the same way [...] We ended up reaching the ultimate goal there even though we didn't have a structured meeting, even though we didn't have all of those democratic processes in place. We wanted to get money out of the door. It was needed quickly. That was basically what it was.

> So, in the absence of those meetings, how can we do that? We came up with a system that enabled us to do that. It enabled us

to continue to maintain and continue the grants system over lock-down, which I think was really important. So that money continued to get allocated to the groups on the ground that knew what people needed, that knew the priorities and they could apply for the money. They had to provide a justification for that and we could get the money to them. They could then spend it supporting the people who needed it in their community.

Rowan identified the community groups 'on the ground' as the key delivery agents and the main source of information she had on local needs and vulnerabilities to inform decisions on where to direct resources. This did not remove the expectation that community groups would need to 'justify' their need for resources through their grant applications, but it enabled Rowan and her colleagues to take action and gather information to inform decisions quickly, without the time needed for more systematic evidence gathering.

Knowledge – Local Needs and Governance Systems

Rowan and her team gained intelligence on the needs of vulnerable people in local areas through their close contacts and communication with community groups, who were often already funded from the budget they managed. Prior to the pandemic, the rules on community grants meant that funds could not be used for the items that were now urgently needed in the pandemic context, such as food, fuel for heating and transport. The officers negotiated and navigated what might be permissible in this unprecedented situation. This resulted in increased communication traffic between officers and reliance on their informal and practical knowledge as they deliberated over what might be normatively acceptable:

> With the relaxation of the criteria and standards protocols for grants, there's been a lot of to-ing and fro-ing on what we should fund.

Changing the community grants administration system involved navigating complex processes and lines of communication between frontline and management, senior council officers and politicians, across service departments and through different stages. In the normal grant administration process, there is a stage which involves manually entering the details of a funding application into a grants management system. This is work done by the 'application inputting team'. With the lockdown, this team had been suspended. Rowan and her colleagues relied on their informal knowledge and contacts with people in different departments to negotiate a solution and get this part of the system moving.

> Staff that input the applications once they're submitted had been told to stop work so we had to negotiate with another department for staff to continue to input the applications for our grants into the system.

'Knowing' the system meant knowing how to get things done in a context of uncertainty and rapid change.

Interaction: Renewing Relationships

The local authority where Rowan worked was characterised by a long history of urban poverty and a complex landscape of community groups, voluntary organisations, networks and collaborations with weak political influence. A decade of cuts to public budgets had increased the competition between community groups for funding leading to growing animosity. Relationships between officers and local community organisations were often strained as less and less community grant funding became available. In March 2020, with the onset of the pandemic and the stay at home order, the Scottish government announced a £350 million fund to support welfare and well-being and an additional £350 million for those most affected by COVID-19. The announcement from the Communities Secretary, Alieen Campbell, stated: 'The funding will be made available to councils, charities, businesses and community groups and designed to be flexible, cutting down on red tape to enable them to respond swiftly and according to local need' (Scottish Government, 2020, para 2). This new funding gave affordance to the officers to renew relationships with community groups.

> The pandemic enabled us to sustain and grow relationships during that difficult period because we had, government money [...] You know that was quite significant money. So, there was a reason and a focus for engaging with groups.

Informal working did not emerge out of the blue. A 'light touch' approach to the application of rules was already an unspoken way of working that was entangled with a more formal and 'business-like' approach. During the pandemic, this informal way of working came to the fore. Rowan's perspective on working informally revealed that her approach to administration was not simply pragmatic. It was driven by a desire to support 'the ones doing the hard work in communities':

> Even without the pandemic, my perspective, my ethos is that these people are applying for money, so let's try and make it as easy as possible for them [...] They are the ones that are doing the hard work in the communities. You don't want to try and tie them in knots, and make things bloody difficult for them. I mean, you need to follow the guidelines and the criteria. They need to be legitimate. We still need a legitimate application. So of course, that goes without saying [...] but it's the light touch, light touch with the applicants, because they've got an awful lot going on, and they are themselves trying to respond quickly in the way that we are trying to respond quickly. As long as they tick all the boxes, let's try and make it as simple and easy as possible.

34   Claire Bynner

However, some members of Rowan's team, who were accustomed to applying the technical rules very specifically, found it difficult to adopt a 'light touch' approach:

> Some people in my team found that really hard and reverted back to 'cross the t's and dot the i's. Back to the ten emails asking for more information, and you are just like, oh God, it's not a two-billion-pound contract. They want to buy tables or food bags!

The pandemic context provided a rare situation where it was more acceptable and safer for officials to flex the rules, to prioritise speed and need over adherence to established processes. Knowing how and when to work more informally, however, required judgement, taking into account the context, the nature of the activity, its economic and public value and the role of social relationships. Working more informally and relationally meant overcoming long-standing habits, beliefs and practices. It meant pushing the formal processes to the background and rendering them less visible or perceptible.

> So, for me, it is about keeping the official stuff under the radar, so they don't experience it. There's something there about the relationship. It's about respect. It's about listening, and meeting people halfway and trying to compromise where you can.

The crisis had revealed the future potential to free up and speed up established bureaucratic processes that were previously regarded as immutable.

> What I would really like to see is a relaxed, flexible, fast process to get money out to folk. That is what I would really like to see for the future. There is a massive opportunity. Isn't there? I feel it really acutely, that this is really, really important.

It also revealed the potential for a more caring and compassionate approach to public administration:

> We have always cared but there have been greater levels of compassion in how we have done this than was possible under the old system.

Rowan hoped that the pandemic experience would change the public administration culture to prioritise community groups and voluntary organisations. Although, given the dominance of the 'business-like model' and the nature of the bureaucracy, this was a fleeting hope.

It needs a clear steer, that our communities are our number one priority. For me, the big object is the people who deliver locally in the communities. They are our number one priority, and we support them as our number one priority. Then that goes down to somebody's behaviour when they're assessing a grant, or they're having a phone call with a group. It's a direct manifestation of that statement.

Our own department doesn't really have that culture, and the council as a whole doesn't have that culture. It's difficult, it is difficult, but it's not part of a bigger picture, it's not a main driver, in managing these grants and assessing these applicants. It is more a business-like model. I mean rightly, you need a business-like approach, don't you? When it comes to money? Of course, you do. But when that becomes the focus, and the process has become the focus, as opposed to the people, that's when you start to lose what it is actually there to do, which is to make a difference in communities. So, it becomes about the process. It's about the assessments, the money. The council back to the council, and that's why I feel, it becomes a bureaucratic process. I think there is some kind of amnesia about what this money is actually for.

Discussion and Conclusions

This chapter has examined the experience of one public official working during the COVID-19 pandemic and her role in innovating local systems of public administration and governance. When the 'rules in use' were temporarily suspended during the pandemic, the official that is at the centre of this account was effectively authorised to re-make the rules and processes. This official worked with her colleagues to adapt their practices to the new context. In re-making the rules, they were acting within shared understandings produced via their histories, knowledges and experiences about what constitutes 'the rules'. They drew on their informal knowledge of the rules and concern for the normative values of the bureaucracy.

Public administration requires the technical knowledge of how to manage complex administrative and communication tasks and how to apply, the rules, to a specific context. Technical knowledge is applied to the tasks of coding, collating and recording decisions, outputs and performance. Working informally requires a different type of knowledge that engages professional judgement, practical experience and relational skills. This practical or phronetic knowledge (Flyvbjerg, 2001) requires experience and skill in thinking deliberatively about the ethic and value of potential actions and their meaning and purpose in a given context (Bynner & Terje, 2021).

36 *Claire Bynner*

The findings from this chapter suggest that public officials are strongly influenced by the need for their actions to be perceived as legitimate and the need to account to the formal governance system. Even during a crisis, these officials remained strongly instrumentally orientated and embedded in the culture and norms of the bureaucracy (even though officers like Rowan viewed this culture critically and found ways to push the formal processes to the background). There was a crisis, but the rules were not abandoned. To enable grant administration to continue, it was necessary to re-make the rules. Informal interactions between officers, other departments and community groups provided a proxy for pre-pandemic partnership meetings and normal rulemaking. Despite the crisis, the requirement for community groups to justify funding requests and for officers to carefully record, document, track and monitor decisions remained.

Yet, in their everyday work with citizens and community groups, the practice of officials during the pandemic was personal, relational, and at times, emotional and empathetic. Informal working was motivated by compassion and a sense of personal commitment to the community groups and activists who were helping vulnerable communities, working for poverty alleviation and social justice. The pandemic gave a renewed moral imperative to act, bringing this ethos to the fore.

Applying feminist political theory, Laura Hand (2021) defines an ethic of care as follows:

> [An] ethic of care is founded on a relational ontology that views people as interconnected and interdependent, values emotion and contextual knowledge, with an orientation toward responsibility and responsiveness in order to promote the well-being of others and focus on preventing harm and suffering. (Hand, 2021, p. 121)

In the context of the pandemic, this ethic of care justified and gave meaning to the informal as a form of knowledge and as a response or action. An ethic of care drove spontaneity, creativity and self-realisation. The informal was meaningful in this context to the extent that it expressed a personal desire to help, beyond the official line. In conveying this ethic of care, the informal gives greater meaning to relationships. This might be particularly relevant in contexts where there are political, social and economic struggles.

This chapter reveals that the informal and formal are not opposites but are entangled in ways that create new conditions and possibilities. In the moment of crisis or rupture, informal activity reveals how entangled the formal and the informal actually are. They enable each other. When the formal is suspended, the informal comes into play. But new practices do not just emerge from nowhere. They emerge from practical knowledge and experience of the formal processes and from an ethic that motivates change.

In the evolution and aftermath of the pandemic, these new possibilities have faded as the sense of emergency has passed. There is now a risk of losing this collective memory and learning, even though the need for support for vulnerable groups remains and the evidence on the long-term effects of the pandemic is still emerging.

Public Administration and Informality During COVID-19   37

Historically, pandemics have forced humans to break with the past and imagine their world anew. This one is no different. It is a portal, a gateway between one world and the next (Roy, 2020, para 47)

Through the 'portal' of the COVID-19 pandemic, we glimpsed the potential for a more caring and compassionate governance system, but this portal has now closed and the opportunity for collective learning and re-imagining the future may be lost.

References

Bartels, K. P. (2018). Policy as practice. In H. K. Colebatch (Ed.), *Handbook on policy, process and governing* (pp. 68–88). Edward Elgar Publishing.

Blundell, R., Costa Dias, M., Cribb, J., Joyce, R., Waters, T., Wernham, T., & Xu, X. (2022). Inequality and the COVID-19 crisis in the United Kingdom. *Annual Review of Economics, 14*, 607–636.

Bynner, C., & Terje, A. (2021). Knowledge mobilisation in public service reform: Integrating empirical, technical and practical wisdom. *Evidence & Policy, 17*(1), 75–91.

Cabinet Office. (2020). *[Withdrawn] Staying at home and away from others (social distancing)*. https://www.gov.uk/government/publications/full-guidance-on-staying-at-home-and-away-from-others

Carmel, E., & Harlock, J. (2008). Instituting the 'third sector' as a governable terrain: Partnership, procurement and performance in the UK. *Policy & politics, 36*(2), 155–171.

Cook, S. N., & Wagenaar, H. (2012). Navigating the eternally unfolding present: Toward an epistemology of practice. *The American Review of Public Administration, 42*(1), 3–38.

Dayson, C., & Damm, C. (2020). Re-making state-civil society relationships during the COVID 19 pandemic? An English perspective. *People, Place and Policy Online, 14*(3), 282–289.

Elston, T., & Bel, G. (2023). Does inter-municipal collaboration improve public service resilience? Evidence from local authorities in England. *Public Management Review, 25*(4), 734–761.

Fancourt, D., Steptoe, A., & Bu, F. (2021). Trajectories of anxiety and depressive symptoms during enforced isolation due to COVID-19 in England: A longitudinal observational study. *The Lancet Psychiatry, 8*(2), 141–149.

Flyvbjerg, B. (2001). *Making social science matter: Why social inquiry fails and how it can succeed again*. Cambridge University Press.

Gilchrist, A. (2016). *Blending, braiding, balancing: Strategies for managing the interplay between formal and informal ways of working with communities*. TSRC Working Paper 136. University of Birmingham, Birmingham.

Hand, L. C. (2021). A virtuous hearer: An exploration of epistemic injustice and an ethic of care in public encounters. *Administrative Theory & Praxis, 43*(1), 117–133.

Kaye, S., & Morgan, C. (2021). *Shifting the balance: Local adaptation, innovation and collaboration during the pandemic and beyond*. New Local.

McGowan, V. J., & Bambra, C. (2022). COVID-19 mortality and deprivation: Pandemic, syndemic, and endemic health inequalities. *The Lancet Public Health, 7*(11), e966–e975.

Misztal, B. (2002). *Informality: Social theory and contemporary practice*. Routledge.

38   Claire Bynner

Rees, J., Macmillan, R., Dayson, C., Damm, C., & Bynner, C. (2022). *COVID-19 and the voluntary and community sector in the UK: Responses, impacts and adaptation*. Policy Press.

Roy, A. (2020). *The pandemic as portal*. Available at https://www.ft.com/content/10d8f5e8-74eb-11ea-95fe-fcd274e920ca (Accessed: 31 July 2024)

Scottish Government (2020). *Helping communities affected by COVID-19*. Available at https://www.gov.scot/news/helping-communities-affected-by-covid-19/ (Accessed: 31 July 2024)

Wagenaar, H. (2004). "Knowing" the rules: Administrative work as practice. *Public Administration Review*, *64*(6), 643–656.

Wilson, M., McCabe, A., & Macmillan, R. (2020). *Blending formal and informal community responses*. Local Trust.

World Health Organisation (WHO). (2023). *WHO health emergency dashboard*. WHO (COVID-19) Homepage. Retrieved June 8, 2023, from https://covid19.who.int/region/euro/country/gb

Chapter 2

The Informal Work of Policy Maintenance: Making Space for Local Knowledge in Indian Rural Electricity Governance

Meera Sudhakar[a,b]

[a]National Institute of Advanced Studies, Bengaluru, Karnataka, India
[b]Manipal Academy of Higher Education, Manipal, Karnataka, India

Abstract

Informality, particularly in the context of the global south, has been understood as deviations from the formal rules of the state. It is therefore often associated with illegality and weak governing capacity. This chapter examines informality as emerging in the dynamics of how change is accommodated in the practices of the sub-division, the lowest administrative unit of the state-owned electricity-supply company in the southern Indian state of Karnataka. It locates informal as an arena that admits contingent and local knowledge to guide its practices that organize accountability relations.

Keywords: Accountability relations; policy maintenance; ethics of measurement; data gaps and ignorance; local knowledge

Introduction: Accountability Relations and Data

If I can reduce the losses in the network to 14%, I would be given a PhD! See, we measure [electricity] supply at the beginning of

---

Informality in Policymaking: Weaving the Threads of Everyday Policy Work, 39–49
Copyright © 2025 by Meera Sudhakar
Published under exclusive licence by Emerald Publishing Limited
doi:10.1108/978-1-83797-280-720241003

40   Meera Sudhakar

> the feeder[1] and sometimes at the distribution transformer before supplying [to consumers]. In some feeders, we measure only at the start of a feeder, after this, we don't know where it is going.

This response regarding the lack of data came up early in my conversation with the assistant engineer at the rural electricity sub-division office in Karnataka. This was not entirely a surprise – a narrative of absence of data and a discourse of blame directed towards the lower levels in the bureaucratic hierarchy has characterised policy discourse in the governance of the electricity sector in India (Chatterjee, 2012). The note of humour in his mention of PhD reflected the immediate context of our interaction. Like most other office staff at the sub-division, he knew I was there to study the recently implemented rural feeder separation programme, which he had already evaluated positively. A key goal of the programme was that of improving transparency and accountability within the electricity bureaucracy using measured 'data', a policy goal I contextualise in the next section. The response came when the conversation turned to whether these changes improved the sub-division's capacity to meet the performance standards stipulated by the electricity regulator. While he indicated a state of continuity regarding limitations of data in rural feeders, he also indicated that the sub-division knew how to respond to this context. After all, he was located in the middle of a gradual process of changing rules and norms of governance, having served in several rural sub-divisions in the district in this role for close to seven years, managing a team of about 20 field staff who were in charge of daily maintenance and repair of the rural electricity network.

Data are central to how formal accountability is organised within public bureaucracies. Data gaps lead to a weakening of hierarchical relations of accountability. In this chapter, my aim is to turn analytical attention. This chapter draws on research work undertaken during 2017–2019 as part of my doctoral studies. The study sought to understand the process and outcomes of implementation of the rural electricity feeder separation programme in the Indian sub-national state of Karnataka. While this chapter draws on data from official documents and key informant interviews conducted at multiple levels of the state bureaucracy, it relies primarily on ethnographic methods, undertaken at one of the rural electricity subdivisions, the lowest administrative unit in the electricity-governance hierarchy in Karnataka, and a village it supplies to, as the main sites of observation. 'Rural' is used to capture the geographic, demographic and economic characteristics of these territories – a) they are located from far away from offices of electricity administration, often located in towns, b) they have low population densities and c) they serve territories in which irrigated agriculture continues to be the main economic activity driving electricity demand. I collected ethnographic data while staying in the village for a period of four months in 2018 and building rapport

---

[1]Rural feeders are network infrastructures that carry electricity from the sub-station, usually located in towns, closer to consumption points in the countryside where they are stepped down before distribution to individual installations.

with several farming households. This provided opportunities for observing irrigation practices in the village closely. The sub-division staff became informants through informal conversations, formal interviews and opportunities to accompany sub-division field staff during revenue collection and maintenance operations in several villages for which permission was granted at the sub-division.

This chapter begins with a brief historical account of how an organisational context for deviations from formal accountability was created in the practices of state-owned electricity-supply companies (ESCOMs). It then presents empirical vignettes showing how the sub-division relies on very different forms of knowledge to negotiate its accountability relations with two of its stakeholders: formally measured data are how the sub-division's accountability with the higher bureaucracy is organised; however, a parallel domain of more personal and practical knowledge co-exists in order to maintain informal practices of electricity supply to rural territories. The final section reflects on informality as emerging in the practices of how state institutions are required to be responsive in these two different domains of knowledge.

Limits to Formal Accountability Relations: A Historical Context

Rural electrification in the global south has been a domain of policy interventions by national governments and multilateral development organisations due to its proven ability to considerably improve the quality of life and productivity in rural areas. Much like the experience of other countries, these efforts have been driven by imaginaries of modernisation, progress and development with the goal of transforming socio-economic relations in rural peripheries (Pellegrini & Tasciotti, 2013). Recent analytical attention towards electricity networks as important sites of understanding power relations and negotiations between the state and its citizens reveals how this has been far from a predictable and smooth process, often deviating from ideal notions of governance-necessitating practices that are geographically and culturally specific (Abram et al., 2019; Gupta, 2015). The present rural electricity-governance context can be summarised as one in which electricity grids have been extended to most villages in India; however, several hamlets and households continue to be excluded from the grid; even when connected, rural households continue to get limited duration of electricity supply. The poor quality of supply and the governance challenges in the sector are often broadly diagnosed as the malfunctioning of state-owned electricity-supply companies. 'Unaccounted' or non-revenue-yielding electricity consumption in various forms is common and is often characterised as theft (Sharma et al., 2016; Smith, 2004), corruption (Jamil & Ahmad, 2013) or as political patronage to win elections (Min & Golden, 2014). What appears common is that the challenges of supplying at affordable rates to sparsely populated rural territories, where low-income agriculture continues to be the major source of livelihood, have generated a set of governance dynamics that is vastly different from the experience of more developed countries. This section briefly sketches this historical context that has necessitated deviations from formal bureaucratic accountability in the governance practices of state-owned ESCOMs.

42   Meera Sudhakar

A significant driver that required deviation from formal accountability was a deliberate and formal government policy in support for the agriculture sector in the past. Most Indian sub-national states have a policy of unmetered and free electricity supply to agriculture since the early 1980s, driven by farmers' movements in several regions seeking state support and subsidies for agriculture. While there was a diversity of demands from these political movements from the countryside, each specific to its agro-ecological context, subsidised and often free electricity for irrigation was a deliberate policy response from most sub-national governments in order to support agricultural modernisation (Varshney, 1998). It is impossible to attribute whether this unaccounted consumption is indeed consumed for irrigation, lost in distribution networks or simply stolen through unmetered uses for other purposes. They were all accounted under aggregate technical and commercial losses incurred by the electricity-supply company. When the unmetered consumption was low compared to the total electricity supplied by the electricity distribution company, it was easier to overlook the misattribution of this unaccounted consumption in the network.

By early 2000, this unaccounted consumption amounted to almost 40% of the total power supplied in the network in Karnataka. Several changes in the sector have contributed to this: the rural electricity grid infrastructure has extended spatially in order to meet the goals of universal electricity access often through ad hoc extensions of the low-voltage infrastructure, leading to increases in technical losses. Mechanised irrigation and demand for electricity from farms have also increased in the past two decades as more farmers switched to groundwater-based irrigation. As the size of unaccounted consumption increased, the inability to attribute responsibility for it became a point of public contention. A series of organisational reforms in the electricity sector, including corporatisation and the creation of a new regulatory agency, focussed on reducing these losses and improving the operational efficiency of state-owned electricity distribution companies through annual performance reviews, transparency of reporting and reduction of distribution network losses have been the focus of policy since 2000. As part of these public management reforms to delineate accountability, the regulator stipulated that the ESCOM be reimbursed by the government for the cost to subsidise agricultural consumption as per tariffs set by the regulator. In short, as agricultural installations continued to remain unmetered, an acceptable estimate of agricultural consumption on the rural feeder would form the basis for how much the government needed to pay the ESCOM in the form of an annual subsidy bill. On the other hand, responsibility for technical losses incurred in the network and losses due to theft or incomplete revenue collection would be the responsibility of the ESCOM. The lowest units of administration of the ESCOM, the sub-divisions, have become crucial actors in these accountability discourses.

As the agricultural consumption and the subsidy bill for the government steadily increased over the years, the higher bureaucracy in the state – comprising the state electricity regulator and the finance department – had been demanding more transparent measures to calculate electricity subsidies to agriculture. This goal of accurate measurements and transparency of agricultural subsidy has been a main policy goal for the state bureaucracy from the rural feeder separation programme undertaken in 2011. The programme sought to separate the rural electricity feeders into two – a new feeder that could provide electricity exclusively to non-agriculture consumers in rural areas and an older feeder that would supply all agriculture installations in rural areas. In the next section, I turn to how the sub-division functions as a mediator in this changing context using both formal and informal knowledge to negotiate accountability relations with its two stakeholders – formal relations of accountability based on measured data to respond to the state bureaucracy and informal relations of accountability to respond to the local norms of electricity consumption in the village.

The Sub-Division and Its Work Across Knowledge Boundaries

Unlike schools, health centres and post offices in rural areas that provide access to public services through more direct and face-to-face interactions with the citizens, relations of providing electricity are mediated through infrastructures – wires, poles and electricity transformers. Sub-division offices are typically located in the nearest town where junior engineers and a small team of field staff in charge of billing, revenue collection and maintenance of infrastructure venture out into the villages on a two-wheeler, often driving by through the roads from the town to inspect, repair and maintain the electricity infrastructure. Close daily interactions with the citizens are not necessary if the accountability relations in the sector were organised through metering and formal tariffs. This ability to govern from afar is often organised through a familiar form of bureaucratic accountability – practices that require an account giver to measure and assume responsibility for losses in the rural feeder, the role an assistant engineer with responsibility for a rural feeder is formally assigned to do. However, as the vignette above illustrates, this responsibility is often delegated to the sub-division engineering staff in the form of performance standards with very little ability to respond to it.

Figure 2.1 represents the entrance to the village as the office staff would approach it from the nearest town. The maze of loosely hanging wires haphazardly criss-crossing overhead as the last arm of the rural electricity infrastructure is extended ad hoc in order to provide services to a new habitation or a structure is a common sight. When I went to the village, my focus was on the additional set of wires that were installed over the old electricity poles, as part of the feeder separation programme. This new parallel infrastructure is meant to supply a higher duration of electricity to non-farm consumers. This created a new set of wires that needed to be more strictly monitored against theft. Like several other distribution utilities in India, a large part of the electricity supplied on a rural feeder often goes unaccounted, mainly due to illegal hooking from agricultural and domestic installations (Sharma et al., 2016). Many decades of functioning in the presence of large numbers of unmetered connections in the rural feeder has required the sub-division to evolve practices that rely on informal relations with the villages they serve in order to regulate unaccounted consumption. While they are usually interpreted as collusion and corruption, I provide

44 *Meera Sudhakar*

Figure 2.1. The Temple that identifies the central place of the village studied.

a reading of these practices as 'informal' bargaining relations. These practices respond to, and accommodate the authority of local norms and are evolving in response to new policy instruments and rules implemented, such as the one attempted through feeder separation. The vignettes in this chapter attempt to show that these informal negotiations are mediated by the sub-division through more efficient and less adversarial ways of vigilance and monitoring undertaken by sub-division 'field staff' – meter readers and linemen – who serve as important intermediaries in monitoring and implementing the changing norms of who can access the now-separate rural feeders and for what purposes. An outcome of such a locally negotiated practice is that structures by the road, which can be easily monitored, such as the temple, are connected to the new infrastructure, while other non-farm installations are excluded from connection to the higher-duration infrastructure.

The field tasks are undertaken by a fleet of long-term, non-transferable employees who interact closely with a village for extended periods and are familiar with the spatial-social practices of the village and their inhabitants. This is in contrast to the 'office staff', engineers at the sub-division who work not more than a few years at a particular sub-division. The field staff serve two important organisational tasks of the sub-division that require knowing the place, and its changing consumption practices. The first is the more formal task of billing and revenue collection from metered installations. This includes visiting individuals, households and fewer small commercial establishments that used electricity for low-power loads such as lights, fans, television sets and small equipment.

These formally mandated visits can be undertaken with minimal interpersonal interactions. However, the personal knowledge and relations that are built during these repetitive daily visits are important for their second task – the more unstructured task of monitoring and regulation of feeders that run through the village. An intimate knowledge of the location of households, and close interactions with several members in the village, has become crucial to the gradual evolution to the local norms regarding what kind of consumption, even if unmetered, was permissible and acceptable in rural feeders. I now turn to how the sub-division has responded and also shaped the electricity consumption practices in the village in the absence of more formal means of monitoring and control.

Informality of Electricity Consumption Practices

One of the farmers justified deviations from the formal registration procedures of the sub-division in terms of the immediacy of electricity consumption practices in the village:

> In the village, we first dig a borewell and start drawing [ground] water when the first well fails; we do the paperwork later.

Doing paperwork meant that the irrigation equipment used to draw groundwater need to be formally registered at the sub-division office in the town. Formalisation takes time and could wait given the contingency of responding to local changes to farming practices: his father had taken a formal registration number for the irrigation equipment almost two decades ago, since then, he had to replace the borewells twice when a higher power machine was needed to irrigate. There was no need to formally register these upgrades in capacity, once a registration number was allotted. Several other farmers in the village also reported that their bore wells often dried up and they installed back-up equipment to respond to these episodes. The field staff understood this need for increasing irrigation equipment in response to contingencies of farming needs. It was a common and acceptable practice therefore to take a single formal registration number and run two or three bore wells depending on each farm's requirements. The field staff never checked if irrigation equipment was formally registered as they were all unmetered anyway. Formalisation conferred some benefits by enabling the farmers to access other supports for agriculture – such as dedicated transformers that provide voltage support and prevent equipment burnout in the rural feeder.

Another source of informal consumption in the village was also a result of past policies that targeted poor households who could not afford to connect to the grid. The policy had sought to connect all households irrespective of their ability to pay as long as their consumption was below 30 units of electricity. These households remained unmetered as long as they did not use anything more than a light bulb or two. It was a common practice for new housing structures to start using electricity for lighting and apply for a formal registration only if they added more appliances later on.

46   Meera Sudhakar

Limiting, Yet Accommodating the Informal

Even if informal consumption practices are tolerated, it is important to limit informality in order to achieve the performance benchmarks of the sub-division. The first practice of limiting informality involved a close knowledge of the spatial activities in the village – the meter reader or the feeder maintenance staff would drive by the road from the town to the village at least once in a couple of days in a two-wheeler. In one of our interactions, the meter reader said that his main job was revenue collection from metered installations. He was therefore cordial with the households and never showed his 'power' even if he saw an unmetered connection. He would overlook it if the household was poor and used no more than a couple of lights and a fan. If he felt the house was adding more appliances, he would report this to the engineer at the sub-division office instead of a direct confrontation with the consumers. The sub-division engineers relied on reports from the field staff to monitor these changes, after which they would initiate a formalisation process for the household.

A second and more effective practice for limiting informal consumption was achieved not through monitoring and controlling access to feeders but by limiting the temporal duration of supply. Such a practice of rationing in rural feeders has evolved to match the local irrigation practices. While the government has stipulated a state-wide policy of providing seven hours of day-time electricity to rural feeders, the sub-division has evolved local schedules of supply to match the local irrigation practices, often varying the duration according to the season and in response to irrigation requirements in the village. These are communicated through in-person interactions between farmers and the engineers at the sub-division office. The engineer mentioned how the members of the local farmer organisations had requested, counter-intuitively, to restrict agriculture supply to no more than three hours in order to adapt electricity supply to the use of micro-irrigation practices. By undertaking deviations based on local contingencies, the sub-division has evolved a new supply schedule that attempts to limit informal consumption in the rural feeder.

When the metered and unmetered consumption was supplied through a single electricity infrastructure, the most effective way of limiting the informal – the practice of rationing supply to rural feeders – also constrained the growth of formally metered consumption. This constraint was the primary driver for the programme of rural feeder separation that sought to create a separate electricity feeder to supply exclusively to non-farm consumers and limit the older feeder to supply only to agriculture consumers. In contrast to the discourse of having completed rural feeder separation in all sub-divisions, the sub-division engineers admit that a full separation of farm and non-farm installations cannot be achieved in practice in the field. Several practical concerns of grid-based electricity provision in rural territories prove to be a limitation: first, the new non-farm feeder had to be drawn along the road from the town to the village in order to allow for easy monitoring. This was necessary to prevent the informal practices of unauthorised connections getting replicated in the new feeder. Second, because of this limitation, households that were metered, yet located farther away from the main habitations in the village, had to continue in the agriculture feeder unless they drew a private cable from the new feeder to their household.

My first encounter with the contradiction between the policy discourse of complete separation of farm and non-farm consumption and the practices in the village was when a farmer told me he could switch between the new and the old feeder for his household consumption as long as he is metered. Figure 2.2 depicts the lever at the domestic electricity meter that allowed him to choose which of the two feeders his household would consume from. The only change in norm was that irrigation equipment could only be run in the agriculture feeder while a few households continued to be in the agriculture feeder. Several households could not be served from the new feeder due to their isolated location. Several other practices of temporary informality continued on the agriculture feeder without penalty. The feeder that is deemed to be 'agriculture feeder' has thus become a hybrid domain that allows unaccounted practices of electricity consumption to continue as long as they remain within the informal norms of consumption referred to in the last section.

While this arrangement creates incoherence between policy discourse and practice, it has allowed the sub-division to negotiate and maintain two parallel domains of accountability. First, it has created a new domain of formal accountability through the creation of a new feeder. The sub-division can be subject to performance standards using measured data on this. The sub-division in turn ensures that only metered consumption is allowed on this feeder. The programme has also entrenched and legitimised a parallel domain of informality that allows for continuity of unaccounted consumption as long as its size is limited, acting as a form of strong social control. Since programme implementation, the ESCOM has made a submission to the regulator that 'losses' do not have any meaning on

Figure 2.2. A Toggle Lever that would determine whether the household consumption is accounted under the farm or non-farm feeder.

48   Meera Sudhakar

the agriculture feeder as 'the entire reading at the input end of the feeder is considered as receivables towards electricity subsidy for agriculture'.[2]

Informality as a Response to Imperfect Knowledge

Informality is a term that is used in multiple ways in policy contexts, the concept itself carrying a long history (Guha-Khasnobis & Kanbur, 2006). The main
purpose for invoking it has been to describe and evaluate practices that deviate
from idealised and abstract forms of organising governance, such as through the
market or bureaucratic forms. Particularly in the context of the global south,
informality has been discussed as a central feature of the development process,
associated with difficult to govern peripheries (Radnitz, 2011). It is also often
associated closely with deviations from legality and with the weak capacity of the
state. For instance, informal housing or the labour sectors are used to describe
arrangements through which marginalised social groups secure a living or access
to services when these services are obtained in the shadow of the law or by escap-
ing full payments. As noted by others, this treatment of informality as a residual
seems to be based on a view of the development processes as a path of increasing
modernisation and formality in state-society relations in the process of transition from agrarian societies to industrialised ones (Radnitz, 2011). Those who
have paid attention to the fuzziness of the formal–informal boundary show how
informal politics operate through practices that sometimes subvert and at other
times co-exist alongside the formal in the process of negotiating multiple values
(Goodfellow, 2020).

As this chapter seeks to show, the work of operating across the formal–
informal boundary is closely linked to knowledge boundaries and therefore to the
ambiguities in the policy context. Formal policy arenas often limit the types of
knowledge that are admitted into policy deliberations during decisions regarding
which policy goals are to be prioritised, what needs to be done about them and
how their outcomes are to be evaluated. The main aim of this chapter has been to
make visible informal as an arena that can admit a broader conception of knowledge while accommodating policy change. The empirical vignettes presented in
this chapter suggest that there are no easy responses to the practice of managing
multiple forms of legitimacy that are demanded from public institutions while
co-ordinating socio-economic change in multi-stakeholder settings. However,
both in the contexts of urban politics (Banks et al., 2020) and in the politics of
rural peripheries, attention to the dynamics of how the formal–informal boundary is negotiated seems to offer new insights into how the modern democratic
state seeks legitimacy.

---

[2]Written response of the ESCOM to the Karnataka Electricity Regulatory
Commission in response to a question regarding estimate for technical losses in the
agriculture feeder.

References

Abram, S., Winthereik, B. R., & Yarrow, T. (2019). *Electrifying anthropology: Exploring electrical practices and infrastructures*. Bloomsbury Academic.

Banks, N., Lombard, M., & Mitlin, D. (2020). Urban informality as a site of critical analysis. *The Journal of Development Studies*, 56(2), 223–238. https://doi.org/10.1080/00220388.2019.1577384.

Chatterjee, E. (2012). Dissipated energy: Indian electric power and the politics of blame. *Contemporary South Asia*, 20(1), 91–103. https://doi.org/10.1080/09584935.2011.646072

Goodfellow, T. (2020). Political informality: Deals, trust networks, and the negotiation of value in the urban realm. *The Journal of Development Studies*, 56(2), 278–94. https://doi.org/10.1080/00220388.2019.1577385

Guha-Khasnobis, B., & Kanbur, R. (2006). *Linking the formal and informal economy: Concepts and policies*. OUP Oxford.

Gupta, A. (2015). An anthropology of electricity from the global south. *Cultural Anthropology*, 30(4), 555–568. https://doi.org/10.14506/ca30.4.04

Jamil, F., & Ahmad, E. (2013). *An economic investigation of corruption and electricity theft*. PIDE-Working Papers.

Min, B. & Golden, M. (2014). Electoral cycles in electricity losses in India. *Energy Policy*, 65(February), 619–25. https://doi.org/10.1016/j.enpol.2013.09.060.

Pellegrini, L., & Tasciotti, L. (2013). Rural electrification now and then: Comparing contemporary challenges in developing countries to the USA's experience in retrospect. In *Forum for development studies* 40(1), 153–76. doi:10.1080/08039410.2012.732108.

Radnitz, S. (2011). Informal politics and the state edited by H. Farrell, V. I. Ganev, S. Hertog, and L. L. Tsai. *Comparative Politics*, 43(3), 351–371.

Sharma, T., Pandey, K. K., Punia, D. K., & Rao, J. (2016). Of pilferers and poachers: Combating electricity theft in India. *Energy Research & Social Science*, 11, 40–52. https://doi.org/10.1016/j.erss.2015.08.006

Smith, T. B. (2004). Electricity theft: A comparative analysis. *Energy Policy*, 32(18), 2067–2076. https://doi.org/10.1016/S0301-4215(03)00182-4

Varshney, A. (1998). *Democracy, development, and the countryside: Urban-rural struggles in India*. Cambridge University Press.

Informal Practices and Ethnomethodology

Chapter 3

Mastering Informality in Diplomacy

Kristin Anabel Eggeling[a,b] and Larissa Versloot[a]

[a] *University of Copenhagen, Denmark*
[b] *Danish Institute for International Studies, Denmark*

Abstract

Diplomats are often considered to be masters of informality. Scholars and practitioners alike have long suggested that the real work of diplomacy happens in the corridor, during the coffee break and cocktail parties. But while everyone agrees that informality is a key ingredient of diplomatic work, few have explicitly explored it, and we lack a conceptualisation of how informality becomes meaningful. In this chapter, we unpack the question: through which spaces and practices is informality performed in diplomacy? Based on thick descriptions generated through ethnographic research in and around the institutions of the European Union (EU), we make two key contributions. First, we map local understandings of the term and give a grounded account of how diplomats use informality and interpret its functions. Second, we take these 'tales from the field' (van Maanen, 2011[1988]) and consider them in the light of theoretical debates on informality, particularly through the concept of boundary. Where and how is the boundary between the formal and informal constituted? Who has the power to draw and move these boundaries? How does it matter, politically, if something is 'formal' or 'informal'? Based on our analysis, we find that informality comes in many forms and can be both politically productive and disruptive. In diplomacy, handling informality is a key diplomatic skill that is learned over time to be, eventually, mastered.

Keywords: diplomacy; informality; practice; European Union; boundary; ethnographic research

---

Informality in Policymaking: Weaving the Threads of Everyday Policy Work, 53–66
Copyright © 2025 by Kristin Anabel Eggeling and Larissa Versloot
Published under exclusive licence by Emerald Publishing Limited
doi:10.1108/978-1-83797-280-720241004

Introduction

The Trilogue working group meets on Wednesdays at 9 a.m. in a room with five doors and no windows.[1] Today's meeting is chaired by Karina, a slim woman in her mid-30s and is attended by Commission, Council and Parliament colleagues, 22 people in total. Karina walks into the room at 10 past 9 and greets various people with hugs, cheek kisses and handshakes, speaking both English and French. *Okay, good morning, shall we start?* Karina says to the room. *According to Item 1 on the agenda – does anyone have anything to say? Yes, good morning,* a man's voice says from across the table, *we are not very happy with the formulation here.* From this point, the conversation about how to amend the text jumps back and forth, without any words, names or rounds of introduction. As the chair works through the agenda, some colleagues lean in across the table and listen carefully, some stand and rest on the back of someone else's chair chatting to them, some speak to no one and focus on their computers or phones and some take phone calls out into the hallway. The attendees sit in three camps around the table, moving the negotiation back and forth between institutions. A voice says: *Maybe the Commission could remind us here? What is the Council's position? Does anyone from the European Parliament (EP) have an opinion?*

Agreements are passed on Articles 4, 4.16, and 7.

The clock moves to 11. There are no breaks, and none seem to be considered. A small blue chocolate bar is passed around among the Commission colleagues. *So, what can we all agree to put in Column 4 of the document? We have been talking about this for a year and four months; we really need to make a decision now if we ever want to move on with our lives,* someone says in a slow smirking voice and others laugh. They eventually get to Article 9a. *I need to say something from our side,* Marco, a Commission representative says, *and to clear the way for possible misunderstandings, we know very well that this point is important for the Council, but we have some legal concerns here and we're surprised to see this in.* Before he can finish his point, Barbara, a Council rep with deep lines forming on her forehead, interrupts with a statement that catapults the conversation into a 20-second screaming match. The air thickens. Those not directly involved exchange quick nervous looks, some smile shily and others look down into their laps.

This is just, this is just – Barbara says with a hissing voice and then she is at a loss for words. The discussion gets heated, and voices get raised. *We are surprised by the strong negative comments,* Marco counters, *and would welcome if such comments would come in a more timely fashion next time.* He turns to Karina and says *apologies, Chair, we will need to discuss this internally. I will tell you as soon as we have a common agreement and then we can put it on the agenda again.* Barbara makes a similar statement about having to check again with colleagues in

---

[1]The opening vignette is based on observations of an informal Trilogue working group meeting attended by Kristin Eggeling in November 2019 in Brussels. All names used in the account are pseudonyms. A Trilogue is an inter-institutional deliberation between the European Commission, the European Parliament and the Council of the EU, where representatives from each institution meet in the late stages of the negotiation process around a legislative file before proposals can be adopted by the member states and made into EU law.

Mastering Informality in Diplomacy   55

Council, and the conversation calms down. Some people leave the room, including Marco. It is now close to noon. He returns 10 minutes later with a paper coffee cup in his left hand and sits back down in his spot. A split second after he sits down, he stands up again and walks over to Barbara. *It was not personal*, he says in a calm voice, placing his hand on the back of her chair. She turns around, smiles politely and taps his arm. *Of course not*, she says, *we will just take it up again next time. And just – where did you get that coffee?*

≪≫＞≪≪＜≫≫

Diplomats, as well as many other professionals, intuitively know that mastering the line between formality and informality is important. Managers take time and effort to go on business trips despite the possibility of virtual meetings, and doctors know that building a good relationship with patients is part of doing their work well. A large body of scholarship in sociology, psychology, law and management studies (Goffman, 1983; Minzberg, 1974; Roger, 2020; Seligman, 1997) supports this intuition and has demonstrated the relevance of informal practices for the emergence of social bonds and trust, often key in the delicate tasks that need to be performed by managers or doctors, such as negotiating or operating (Misztal, 1999, pp. 2–3). Yet whereas social skills may not be the first thing that comes to mind when thinking of managers or doctors, they are often presumed to be key responsibilities of the practitioners we focus on in this chapter: diplomats. Diplomats are commonly seen as the 'masters' of informality (Cornut, 2018). In the description of the diplomatic negotiation above, Marco knows when he needs to walk over to Barbara to reassure her personally despite professional disagreement. Beyond this example, much diplomatic work is said to be done through small gestures – like passing chocolate – or at social gatherings away from 'the office', such as at cocktail parties, in hallways and by the coffee machine. Such informal work is what diplomats are *supposed* to do and what is often considered by themselves as a crucial part of their job.

Starting from the assumption that informality is key in diplomacy, we take this chapter to explore how it *is practised*. To do that, we first map local understandings of the term and give an account of how diplomats use informality in their work and interpret its function in different ways. Second, and based on this, we focus on how and by whom a *boundary* between the formal and informal is constituted and how it matters politically, if something is formal, informal or something in between. We draw on ethnographic fieldwork material obtained in the context of EU diplomacy from 2018 to 2022.[2] Throughout this chapter, we

---

[2] This research was done by Authors 1 and 2 independently in the context of a postdoc and PhD project, respectively. It included interviews with ~100 diplomatic actors in Brussels at various professional levels, including ambassadors, attachés, seconded experts, civil servants, interpreters and institutional interns; as well as participant observations at diplomatic training, formal and informal meetings, walks, lunches and coffees in and around the institutions of the EU in the European Quarter in Brussels, as well as in online webinars, social media and chats, in particular during the COVID-19 pandemic in 2020 and 2021. For a lack of space, we cannot explain the research methodology in detail here but have written about this elsewhere (see Eggeling & Versloot, 2023).

56   Kristin Anabel Eggeling and Larissa Versloot

quote this material either by reference to observations ('O') or interviews ('I'), followed by the date the research was done. Theoretically, we ground our work in scholarship that approaches diplomacy as 'social practice', focusing on tacit rules, everyday performances and ordinary sayings and doings (Adler-Nissen, 2016; Neumann, 2002; Pouliot, 2008).

We find that diplomats draw boundaries of informality and formality both when it comes to the work that they do and the community that they consider themselves part of. Over time, diplomats learn how such boundaries are drawn, as competently navigating these boundaries is a key diplomatic skill. The process of drawing these boundaries, moreover, is a contested one due to the political consequences of such boundary work (Gieryn, 1983). Within the field of diplomacy, calling something formal or informal has important political and legal implications. This chapter furthermore contributes, theoretically, by developing a practice approach to informality in diplomacy.

This chapter has three parts. We start with an introduction to debate the question of informality in diplomatic studies and some contextual information on the EU diplomatic scene in Brussels. Second, we turn to what we call, following John van Maanen's (2011[1988]), 'tales of the field', that is, thick ethnographic descriptions of how EU diplomats understand and work with the concept of informality. This is followed by a third section that relates the findings from the field back to theoretical debates on informality. Throughout, we develop our key argument that in the diplomatic world, recognising, redrawing and possibly resisting the boundaries of formality and informality is a professional skill that is learned over time to be, eventually, mastered. Our evidence from Brussels shows that even in complex international organisations that rely on clear goals and formal rules, its professionals retain considerable freedom in the ways they act out their roles. When asked about such seeming digressions, EU diplomats skilfully present their informal actions to follow logically from and positively contribute to formal procedures.

Diplomats as the 'Masters' of Informality

The diplomatic world is an intriguing setting to study informality, as it casts the conflicts and complexities of international politics onto the bodies of living individuals.[3] It is a place where big political questions meet small personal actions. In the above, for example, the deepening lines on Barbara's forehead signal the dissatisfaction of the Council towards the other institutions' propositions, and Marco's decision to leave the room diffuses the heat of the moment. What is

---

[3]We only focus on the kinds of diplomatic actors that can be considered part of the 'formal' international diplomatic world in this chapter. All the individuals we draw on here are representatives of recognised states in international relations. There is also scholarship on so-called informal diplomacy conducted by representatives of liminal or non-recognised states (for example, Lutfi, 2022) or citizen diplomats acting in their own or their communities rather than a state's interest (Tyler & Beyernick, 2016).

Mastering Informality in Diplomacy **57**

further interesting is that while the aims and end goals of diplomacy may always remain unreachable – it is, after all, the 'estrangement' between polities that diplomacy seeks to mediate – there are strong normative and procedural constraints that limit what diplomats can legitimately do. This task has long fallen to the notion of diplomatic protocol, which has brought order into a messy world by prescribing not *what* needs to be done but *how* to go about the search for a compromise. Diplomats, classical accounts of the profession note, are to act with respect, patience and tact (Nicolson, 1961), and those who can hold this line even when confronted with critical problems are the ones who become diplomatic virtuosos (Cornut, 2018, pp. 714–715).

The opening vignette gives a glimpse into the diplomatic protocol at work in an EU working group, readable from how people address each other, work through an agenda, take breaks and approach each other after it is all over. What it shows is a mixture of formal and informal interactions, some scripted by the institution's fixed rules such as the fragmentation of the conversation into articles or the need to reach intra- before inter-institutional agreement; and others that spontaneously arise in the encounter, such as the passing of the chocolate or the reassurance that nothing that happened was meant to be taken personally. Highlighting the mixing of formal and informal practice has long been part of scholarship on diplomacy and often features in practitioner accounts of their own practice.

Different conceptual boundaries that speak to the relation between formality and informality have been mapped onto diplomatic practice, including that between scripts and improvisation (Cornut, 2018), the public, the personal and the private (Neumann, 2013), real work, sociability and distractions (Adler-Nissen & Eggeling, 2022; Nair, 2020), hierarchies and professional status (Adler-Nissen & Eggeling, 2022; Nair, 2020) or performativity and genuineness (Danielson & Hedling, 2022; McConnell, 2018). Most of this work has approached diplomacy as a 'social practice', a study of what the practitioners of it do (Kustermans, 2016, p. 177).

In this chapter, we build on this scholarship and introduce work by sociologist Barbara Misztal (1999) as a starting point for our conceptualisation of in/formality. At its core, Misztal writes, the relationship between formality and informality is a more specific expression of the relationship between predictability and unpredictability, where the predictable is normally linked to the formal and the unpredictable to the informal. Thinking about it in this way can partly correct a normative bias attached to the concept of informality. This often shows the concept of informality in stereotypical uses of the term to refer to relaxed, casual or non-ceremonial approaches to social encounters, fun diversions from rule-based activities, gossip or 'just' small talk (Misztal, 1999, p. 17–18). Yet cast in the context of unpredictability, Misztal argues, informality also carries with it a darker side of nepotism, favouritism or patronage (1999, p. 18). The appeal of formality then lies in adding predictability in the form of transparency, accountability and rights (Misztal, 1999, p. 4). Informality and formality, she argues, should therefore not be regarded as mutually exclusive options 'but rather as two tactics, each providing a partial solution to the unpredictability of the [social world]' (Misztal, 1999, p. 9).

58 *Kristin Anabel Eggeling and Larissa Versloot*

Both formal and informal forms of interaction are thus important for sustaining social environments. The essential issue for Misztal is how to synchronise and 'strike the optimal balance' between formality and informality so that they sustain a sense of order and cohesion that allows for 'the improvement of the quality of social life' (1999, pp. 9–10). The task of the social scientist then is to understand how social actors mix formality and informality in ways so that they 'manage to treat others with tact or "the right touch"', which, according to her, always 'depends upon particularities of a given type of interaction' (Misztal, 1999, p. 10).

While Misztal wrote about managers and doctors, two of her propositions are particularly relevant to the study of diplomacy. First, the continuous balancing act between formality and informality is prominent in diplomatic practice. It is in and through practice that the boundary between the formal and informal is (re-)constituted. Practices are recognised as socially meaningful when performed 'competently' (Adler & Pouliot, 2011) and one way to think about competence is the performance of diplomatic tasks with just 'the right touch' (Misztal, 1999, p. 1).

A competent Brussels diplomat, in this sense, is someone who knows how to achieve the requirements of the job (the need to reach the twenty seven member states of the EU (EU27), as well as inter-institutional agreement on a legislative file) by balancing the formal and informal steps along the way, regardless of whether they come in the form of adversity or support. In the EU diplomatic setting, the formal rules for how to work on and close a file are extensively spelled out. There is a whole institutional architecture that defines how a legislative proposal is initiated and then passes through working group, diplomatic and political levels to become law. This formal process is accompanied by centimetres thick (internal) documents outlining the protocol of how diplomatic actors are to interact with and in the Council. Around these formalised rules and protocol, however, exists a whole informal world that plays out in and around the cafes of the European Quarter, in email and text message threads, in phone calls and face-to-face encounters between diplomats that happen serendipitously before, after and during formal negotiations. The boundaries between these spaces and kinds of interaction, as we will show below, are constantly being redrawn. During the COVID-19 pandemic, for example, videoconferences between heads of state were more informal ways of engaging than any physical meetings between ambassadors and diplomatic representatives, even if they happened as walks in the park. This is because the face-to-face format trumped the political status of the attendees of the meeting as a requirement of formal decision-making as stipulated in the Treaties of the EU (Barigazzi, 2021).

Examples like this show that diplomats have to adapt and learn over time what 'counts' as formal and informal work in Brussels. They do so reflexively but also tacitly as they gain a practical sense of the 'rules of the game' (Pouliot & Cornut, 2015). The longer they are in town, the more they know. For example, we observed more seasoned EU diplomats know when it is time to pick up the phone or invite someone for lunch as additional informal ways to get a

Mastering Informality in Diplomacy   **59**

sense of what the other(s) have gathered from a meeting or are going to argue about; just as much as they learn when it is time to really put one's foot down during the speaking time one is assigned in the formal meeting. In interesting and head-spinning ways to an outsider, moreover, the members of the diplomatic field in Brussels mix formal and informal engagements in the same spaces and almost the same slots of time. For example, formal meetings of the Council of Ministers, attended by Ministers or other high-level national political representatives and/or Ambassadors, always have an 'informal breakfast' meeting before the first agenda part of the meeting is called, which happens in the same room and with the same people present (O: 5 December 2019). The only difference between formality and informality in this case is a written and pre-published agenda for the formal part of the meeting and the opportunity for more free and serendipitous conversations in the informal pre-meeting. The informal breakfast, in turn, was prepared through 'informal-informal' meetings in smaller groups and so on.

Second, and following from this, diplomats do not only learn but also negotiate and contest what constitutes 'formal' and 'informal' in their professional field. Gaining competence thereby not only refers to learning about the 'rules of the game' but also to knowing how and when to bend or disregard them (Cornut, 2018; Kuus, 2015). For example, bringing up a formal agenda point is not what is supposed to happen in the informal pre-meetings. Rather, this time it is supposed to be used for smaller pre-negotiations, often among 'like-minded' states that want to try out their negotiation position before going on the record in the formal meeting. What the 'right touch' is when it comes to the synthesis of, and the boundary between, formal and informal work in diplomacy is constantly renegotiated. As the field of diplomacy is inherently political, such 'boundary work' (Adler-Nissen & Eggeling, 2022) has important consequences: some win and some lose when some practices are competently pushed in, or pulled from, the informal to the formal domain and vice versa. This is how questions of political status and professional hierarchy arise, as it is normally those actors who work in senior positions that enjoy more 'freedom in interpreting their roles' requirements' (Misztal, 1999, p. 46). In the Brussels diplomatic scene, this may explain why, for example, it is often the interns and lower ranked diplomats who wear the most formal clothes (O: 5 December 2019).

Practising Diplomatic Informality at the Council of the EU

Diplomats in Brussels do lots of things that can be considered informal. Thinking back to the vignette in the beginning, they interrupt set agendas to take phone calls in the hallway, eat candy during meetings and walk with each other to takeaway coffee spots. Rather than surveying any activity that could be considered informal, in this section, we are giving examples that highlight the recognition and (re)drawing of *boundaries* around what is considered in/formal. While additional dynamics of such boundary work could be identified, we focus on three examples.

60   Kristin Anabel Eggeling and Larissa Versloot

The first section concerns how diplomats intuitively invoke the concepts of in/formality when asked about their daily work routines. The tales we retell show that while the formal requirements of their job give purpose to their practice, they see much of their 'real work' to lie in the surrounding informal activities. The second set of tales concerns the drawing of a boundary around questions of belonging to the diplomatic community and what kinds of activities are to be performed by a diplomat, and which ones are not. The drawing of this boundary relates in/formality to dynamics of professional status, hierarchy and gender and may lie at the core of why diplomacy is often considered to be an exclusionary and elitist profession (Towns, 2022). Third, we include tales that highlight the materiality of the boundary between formality and informality that shows itself primarily in the making of formal rules such as guidelines about who should (not) be part of closed-door meetings or the legal difference of calling a meeting formal or informal.

Tales From the Field: The Boundaries of Informality

Drawing Boundaries: What Is In/formal Work

What does your everyday work look like? What do you do on a daily basis? When asked such questions, diplomats intuitively answer by drawing a boundary between what they call their formal and informal work.

What diplomats describe as formal work are activities related to official meetings: attending them, preparing them, negotiating and then reporting new information back to the capital. When diplomats talk about informal work, they often mention that this is their 'real' work. It contains staying 'in the loop' about positions of other member states, the content of an upcoming draft document or the 'script' for the next meeting (e.g., I 27 June 2019, 12 February 2021, 05 March 2021). Especially diplomatic meetings tend to serve as the theatre where agreed-upon scripts are 'played out' (Juncos & Pomorska, 2011, p. 1105). These scripts are decided upon and negotiated informally. Diplomats at permanent representations have been considered 'professional gossipers' (Pouliot, 2016, p. 128): they have to stay informed about the state of play so that they can transfer that information back home, thereby preventing their governments from having to deal with unwelcome surprises. Much of this informal work takes place in the margins of formal meetings, for instance, during breaks, at the coffee machine, during lunch or in the hallway.

Proper conduct of formal work in diplomatic practice is inherently connected to doing informal work. Indeed, 'without having had any kind of informal contacts well in advance or without having formed a coalition ahead of meeting', diplomats would likely 'not succeed' in terms of getting a message across properly or gaining enough support for a certain proposal during the formal meeting (I 20 June 2019). These dynamics became apparent during the COVID-19 pandemic when such informal work became more difficult. Picking up gossip and rumours is, after all, and according to one diplomat, why they are in Brussels in the first place: 'If you don't hear the rumours or can chat in between the formal meetings, or in the lunchbreaks – what is the point? What is the point of us being here? What is the added value?' (I 29 January 2021).

Thus, though diplomats draw a reflexive boundary between formal and informal work, these activities are always 'meshed together' in practice (see also Pouliot, 2016, p. 42). This diplomatic boundary work is nonetheless significant, as the synchronisation of informal and formal work fosters a sense of social order: informal work makes formal work meaningful and vice versa. Diplomats would not be able to properly fulfil their formal duties without doing the informal work, yet doing such informal work is pointless without formal work. Scheduled, formal meetings make a diplomat's work predictable, but there is a need for informal unpredictability to create 'wiggle room' – to break free from the rigidity of protocol and explore what it is that others really need or want, so that a compromise can be found. How these boundaries are drawn and who gets to be part of informal spaces – a place at the lunch table or a chat at the coffee machine – has significant consequences for the formal negotiations.

Bounding the Community: Who Gets to Be a Diplomat

Diplomats are a global 'community of practice' (Adler, 2008; Hofius, 2023). Such communities are constituted by 'like-minded groups of participants [that are] linked informally and contextually by a shared interest in learning and applying a common practice' (Græger, 2016, p. 479). The EU diplomatic community in Brussels is linked in a myriad of ways, from the physical proximity of their workplaces in the European Quarter, to shared weekly formal meetings in the Council and to intranet platforms, social media followings and different message and email threads. While the physical arrangement of most permanent representations in walking distance from Place Schuman, the Brussels square on which the headquarters of the European Commission, the European External Action Service and the Council of the EU sit side by side, and the weekly working groups and ambassadorial meetings formally structure the spaces and calendars of EU diplomatic actors, the latter, more informal practices, fill the spatial and temporal gaps in between.

To try out a negotiation position for an upcoming Council meeting, for example, diplomats 'test the waters' by writing positions into WhatsApp chats to see who and how the colleagues react (Eggeling & Versloot, 2023, p. 11). This may lead to the conclusion that communicating through a tool like WhatsApp, per se, is considered an informal activity. Yet, when one asks the diplomats about their use of text messaging apps, a more complicated picture emerges. As one ambassador explains: there are various groups that include the same selection of people but that are used for different purposes and in different ways. Giving the example of the Ambassadors sitting on the Political and Security Committee (PSC), he explained that there are indeed two ambassador chat groups, one more 'leisure-oriented' group where the latest football matches and results are discussed, and one more 'serious' group in which agenda items and negotiation positions are discussed (I: 19 March 2019). Drawing this boundary has been a purposeful choice so that colleagues can better use their scarce time and not get overwhelmed by information that may be uninteresting to them. Still, having the informal WhatsApp group is considered important if only to retain a 'personal touch' (I: 19 March 2019). Another example is a network among women ambassadors in Brussels, playfully referred to as 'COREMER'.[4] Across political affiliations, group activities such as luncheons or receptions to which only some colleagues are invited bounds the diplomatic field along gender lines. This practice can be observed in other diplomatic settings as well and is generally explained as an act of informal female-to-female solidarity in an otherwise masculine field (Towns, 2022).

In addition to such horizontal boundary drawing between diplomatic sub-communities based on serious work, fun diversion or gender relations, diplomatic actors also use reference to in/formality to draw boundaries along vertical power hierarchies. For example, many mid-level diplomats do not consider it to be part of their job to casually keep the public informed about what is going on, for example, by tweeting or speaking publicly to journalists (O: 15 November 2028). This, rather, is either the job of a spokesperson or technical intern at one extreme or, indeed, the political duty of the minister or Head of State on the other. Another example of such 'vertical boundary work' (Adler-Nissen & Eggeling, 2022, pp. 18–20) is the freedom with which diplomatic actors of different ranks can move around the buildings and meeting rooms of the EU institutions. While higher ranked actors, such as ambassadors and their sherpas, enter formal meetings across formal doorsteps and red carpets, interns, attachés and working group diplomats have to show their identification badges and may have to pass security at the main gates (field notes 5 December 2019). Once in the meeting room, then, those of lower access rank need to visibly display their badges or ID cards and hold themselves to the back of the room, while Ambassadors have more freedom in how they present themselves and approach others. Such examples illustrate the stickiness of the diplomatic world's 'international pecking orders' (Pouliot, 2016) in which practical know-how about how to relate to the formal rules of interaction is crucial to blending in and doing one's work well.

The Materiality of the Boundary: Rules, Access and Legality

The changed working conditions of the pandemic served as a contrast fluid and illuminated the materiality of some 'hard' boundaries between the formal and informal in EU diplomacy. For instance, whereas many negotiations moved online during the period of lockdowns and in turn became 'informal videoconferences', some meetings *had* to be given special 'formal' status in order to continue in person. This included the weekly meetings of the EU ambassadors and those meetings in which decisions had to be made about the EU's military and civilian missions. For the latter meetings, one diplomat reports, 'there need to be bodies in

---

[4]This name is a play on the abbreviation of COREPER (Comité des représentants permanents; Council of Permanent Representatives) and the French 'pére' (father), which is replaced by 'mére', mother. See https://mobile.twitter.com/heidiguerer/status/1279152495848275969 (last accessed March 2, 2023).

the room' (I 1 February 2021). They continued to say that this is due to 'Council procedures – we cannot accept procedures [on these matters] when we are not in the room' (I 1 February 2021). This example shows the limits of the materiality of the formal and informal. The Treaties of the EU clearly state that formal conclusions can only be adopted as the outcome of physical meetings. During COVID-19, this legal requirement bestowed essential importance on resident ambassadors in Brussels (Barigazzi, 2021; cf. Eggeling & Adler-Nissen, 2021). This example shows how some diplomatic rules are formalised via material requirements, which may be difficult, if not impossible, to redraw. When the legal requirements are clearly stated, there was no informal way around the formality attached to the physicality, and eventually, to the diplomatic body.

Another material expression in our field that speaks to the boundary between formality and informality is the enforcement of rules surrounding the presence – or absence – of mobile devices inside the meeting room. Diplomacy is a practice predicated on restraint, patience and, crucially, confidentiality, and diplomatic work can be seriously harmed if internal information is leaked or prematurely shared with outsiders. A central concern in this context surrounds the virtual ubiquity of digital devices in diplomatic work settings today, particularly laptops and smartphones. While these devices can be used to work more efficiently by reading the news or replying to emails while the meeting is in session (O: 22 November 2018; 14 October 2021), they can also be used in ways that undermine the purpose of diplomatic work by sharing opinionated and partial information on what is going on behind closed doors (O: 13 November 2018). These and other digital disruptions are an issue for concern in EU diplomacy and the Office of the General Secretariat of the EU Council specifically. The Office of the General Secretariat of the EU Council is the institution charged with arranging the diplomat's meetings and ensuring good working conditions and has worked out a range of formal use guidelines to regulate the informal use of digital devices while on the job. For example, many meetings in the EU now happen under 'no tech' or controlled tech rules, meaning that delegates and meeting attendees need to lock their personal mobile devices into storage facilities outside of meeting rooms; or, as a more extreme measure, an institution 'jams the internet connection' to limit all information sharing that is physically happening on site (I: 18 October 2021). The installation of storage lockers, in this example, shows how the formality and confidentiality of the meeting are being protected by, first, the drawing, and, second, the enforcing of an otherwise invisible tech/no-tech boundary.

Conclusion

In this chapter, we have shown that balancing formality and informality is a professional skill that diplomats learn over time and can, eventually, practically master. The interaction between Marco, Barbara and Karina at the start of this chapter shows that many of the things diplomats do are productive for upholding the balance between the formal and informal. In their formal role as representing one of the EU's institutions, both Marco and Barbara defend their institutions'

64 *Kristin Anabel Eggeling and Larissa Versloot*

interests as best as they can, knowing that the exact wording of the text they negotiate can have important legal consequences. Similarly, both Marco and Barbara acknowledge, informally, that what they do 'as representing their formal institution' is not necessarily how they appreciate each other as colleagues and human beings.

In the analysis, we mapped local understandings of informality in diplomacy by distinguishing three sets of tales from the field that show how diplomats constitute boundaries between the formal and informal. First, we discussed how diplomats intuitively invoke the concept of in/formality when asked what they do on a daily basis. Diplomats distinguish between tasks they feel they need to perform – such as taking part in meetings and writing reports – and tasks which are deemed 'essential' to properly do their job – activities labelled as informal work, such as going for lunch with colleagues. Second, a boundary is constituted between those who are part of certain diplomatic communities and those who are not. This matters, as being part of certain in/formal communities allows for particular information and activities to become available. We find that boundaries are constantly, informally, renegotiated, during which hierarchies based on professional status or gender in part determine which diplomatic privileges or most sensitive information may be available to some and not others. Third, we discuss how the boundary between the formal and informal is at times materially expressed and defined in diplomacy. Some material requirements can be attached to formal meeting spaces – such as the need to have bodies in the room or the prohibition of technological devices – without any informal way around this.

A delicate balance between predictability and unpredictability is upheld in and through what diplomats do. On the one hand, formal rules and set meeting agendas provide expectations in the diplomatic field: in the end, being a diplomat at the EU means working towards producing texts that become EU laws. Yet as diplomats tell us, the 'essential' part of their job is expressed informally – it is navigating the unpredictability of *how* this goal is reached that takes up much of a diplomat's time. Being a diplomat means expressing 'the right touch' of informality and formality (Misztal, 1999). While diplomats aim to master this skill, they also renegotiate boundaries between what in/formal work is and who can be part of the diplomatic community. Balancing and challenging the formal and informal by learning how to 'master informality' is important for maintaining social order, as Misztal (1999) reminds us. By unpacking how this is done in diplomacy, this chapter has shown that the ways diplomats practice (in)formality oftentimes reinforce existing boundaries and (gendered) hierarchies in the diplomatic field.

References

Adler, E. (2008). The spread of security communities: Communities of practices, self-restraint, and NATO's post-Cold War evolution. *European Journal of International Relations, 14*(2), 195–230. https://doi.org/10.1177/1354066108089241

Adler, E., & Pouliot, V. (2011). International practices. *International Theory, 3*(1), 1–36. https://doi.org/10.1017/S175297191000031X

Mastering Informality in Diplomacy   65

Adler-Nissen, R. (2016). Towards a practice turn in EU studies: The everyday of European integration. *Journal of Common Market Studies*, *54*(1), 87–103. https://doi.org/10.1111/jcms.12329

Adler-Nisen, R., & Eggeling, K. A. (2022). Blended diplomacy: The entanglement and contestation of digital technologies in everyday diplomatic practice. *European Journal of International Relations*, *28*(3), 640–666. https://doi.org/10.1177/13540661221107837

Barigazzi, J. (2021). *How ambassadors took over the EU – POLITICO, POLITICO*. Retrieved March 1, 2023, from https://www.politico.eu/article/eu-ambassadors-coreper-power-center/

Cornut, J. (2018). Diplomacy, agency, and the logic of improvis9ation and virtuosity in practice. *European Journal of International Relations*, *24*(3), 712–736. https://doi.org/10.1177/1354066117725156

Danielson, A., & Hedling, E. (2022). Visual diplomacy in virtual summitry: Status signalling during the coronavirus crisis. *Review of International Studies*, *48*(2), 243–261. https://doi.org/10.1017/S0260210521000607

Eggeling, K. A., & Adler-Nissen, R. (2021). The synthetic situation in diplomacy: Scopic media and the digital mediation of estrangement. *Global Studies Quarterly*, *1*(2), 1–14. https://doi.org/10.1093/isagsq/ksab005

Eggeling, K. A., & Versloot, L. (2023). Taking trust online: Digitalisation and the practice of information sharing in diplomatic negotiations. *Review of International Studies*, *49*(4), 637–656. https://doi.org/10.1017/S0260210522000559

Gieryn, T. F. (1983). Boundary-work and the demarcation of science from non-science. *American Sociological Review*, *48*(6), 781–795. https://doi.org/10.2307/2095325

Goffman, E. (1983). The interaction order: American Sociological Association, 1982 presidential address. *American Sociological Review*, *48*(1), 1–17. https://doi.org/10.2307/2095141

Græger, N. (2016). European security as practice: EU–NATO communities of practice in the making? *European Security*, *25*(4), 478–501. https://doi.org/10.1080/09662839.2016.1236021

Hofius, M. (2023). *European Union communities of practice: Diplomacy and boundary work in Ukraine*. Routledge.

Juncos, A. E., & Pomorska, K. (2011). Invisible and unaccountable? National representatives and council officials in EU foreign policy. *Journal of European Public Policy*, *18*(8), 1096–1114. https://doi.org/10.1080/13501763.2011.615197

Kustermans, J. (2016). Parsing the practice turn: Practice, practical knowledge, practices. *Millennium: Journal of International Studies*, *44*(2), 175–196. https://doi.org/10.1177/0305829815613045

Kuus, M. (2015). Symbolic power in diplomatic practice: Matters of style in Brussels. *Cooperation and Conflict*, *50*(3), 368–384. https://www.jstor.org/stable/45084295

Lutfi, A. (2022). 'Pretenders, entrepreneurs, and mercurians: An ethnohistorical approach to conceptualizing diplomacy', *History and Anthropology*, *33*(3), 407–429. https://doi.org/10.1080/02757206.2021.1946047

McConnell, F. (2018). Performing diplomatic decorum: Repertoires of "appropriate" behavior in the margins of international diplomacy. *International Political Sociology*, *12*(4), 362–381. https://doi.org/10.1093/ips/oly021

Minzberg, H. (1974). *The nature of managerial work*. Harper and Row.

Misztal, B. A. (1999). *Informality social theory and contemporary practice*. Routledge.

Nair, D. (2020). Emotional Labor and the Power of International Bureaucrats. *International Studies Quarterly*, *64*(3), 573–587.

Neumann, I. B. (2002). Returning practice to the linguistic turn: The case of diplomacy. *Millennium: Journal of International Studies*, *31*(3), 627–651. https://doi.org/10.1177/03058298020310031201

Neumann, I. B. (2013). *Diplomatic sites: A critical enquiry*. Oxford University Press.

Nicolson, H. (1961). Diplomacy then and now. *Foreign Affairs*, *40*(1), 39–49. https://www.foreignaffairs.com/articles/1961-10-01/diplomacy-then-and-now

Pouliot, V. (2008). A logic of practicality: A theory of practice of security communities. *International Organization*, *62*(2), 257–288. https://doi.org/10.1017/S0020818308080090

Pouliot, V. (2016). *International pecking orders. The politics and practice of multilateral diplomacy*. Cambridge University Press.

Pouliot, V., & Cornut, J. (2015). Practice theory and the study of diplomacy: A research agenda. *Cooperation and Conflict*, *50*(3), 297–315. https://doi.org/10.1177/0010836715574913

Roger, C. B. (2020). *The origins of informality: Why the legal foundations of global governance are shifting, and why it matters*. Oxford University Press.

Seligman, A. B. (1997). *The problem of trust*. Princeton University Press.

Towns, A. E. (2022). WAW, no women? Foucault's reverse discourse and gendered subjects in diplomatic networks. *Global Society*, *36*(3), 347–367. https://doi.org/10.1080/13600826.2022.2052021

Tyler, M. C., & Beyernick, C. (2016). Citizen diplomacy. In C. Constantinou, P. Kerr, & P. Sharp (Eds.), *The SAGE handbook of diplomacy* (pp. 521–529). Sage.

van Maanen, J. (2011[1988]). *Tales of the field: on writing ethnography*. Chicago University Press.

Chapter 4

Bureaucratic Hustling and Knowledge Shuffling – Informality within Swiss Public Administration

Lisa Marie Borrelli

HES-SO Valais-Wallis, Switzerland

Abstract

States retain (socio-political) tools to govern the lives of their population and beyond. Such governing takes place in various offices, where frontline staff need to implement policies that are created at higher levels of the administrative and political hierarchy. This chapter proposes an in-depth view on work that is being done in Swiss resident registration offices, through an ethnographic lens. Following caseworkers in their daily work routines over an extended period allowed me to trace their practices and (in)formal approaches to their work. This chapter delves into longer field note extracts that allow for deeper contextuality. Two key themes that will be engaged with, hustling and shuffling, explore the presence of informality and the consequences that such informal practices have for institutional functioning. First, insights show that a high workload combined with a lack of resources, creates an air of hustling that pushes frontline staff to make up for shortcomings in resources by inventing new and more efficient ways to implement their work. Hustling goes beyond individual coping mechanisms; often embedded in collective routines and practices that are, however, not codified. Second, given the high amount of information, policies and laws frontline workers need to be familiar with, they shuffle around with knowledge and devise productive ways to communicate with each other while remaining able to process cases. As such, informality is neither the opposite to formality nor simply uncodified but can range

---

Informality in Policymaking: Weaving the Threads of Everyday Policy Work, 67–80
Copyright © 2025 by Lisa Marie Borrelli
Published under exclusive licence by Emerald Publishing Limited
doi:10.1108/978-1-83797-280-720241005

68   Lisa Marie Borrelli

from spontaneous solutions to established sets of practice that blur the boundary between formal and informal.

Keywords: Knowledge production; migration governance; informality; knowledge shuffling; bureaucratic hustling; street-level bureaucracy

Policymaking Through Routinised Informality

States retain (socio-political) tools to govern the lives of their populations and beyond. Such governing is facilitated by documentation (Kosciejew & Hugh, 2015) and organisational routines, and includes more or less formal practices which take place in various (political and legal) fields, including ministries as well as public administrative offices. Within such bureaucratic action, traditional Weberian ideals call for formal sets of rules that are predictable and transparent (Townley, 2008; Weber, 1947), automatically placing informal practice at the negative end of administrative practices. Yet, policy implementation is done by frontline staff who are often in direct contact with those 'to be governed' and, as such, also negotiate and contest policies and thus affect outcomes (Meyers & Lehmann Nielsen, 2012). They maintain certain degrees of discretion (Tummers & Bekkers, 2014) which are embedded along a continuum of formal and informal practices.

Based on prior work arguing that street-level bureaucrats (Lipsky, 1980) and frontline workers (Brodkin, 2012) are being crucial actors of policy implementation, this chapter provides an in-depth view on Swiss public administration, particularly focused on residents' registration offices viewed through an ethnographic lens. These bureaucrats are in charge of keeping track of the municipal population and registering those who move to their municipality and re-register those who leave. Following caseworkers in their daily routines, this work seeks to advance scholarship exploring how knowledge is shared and decisions made through an understanding of informal practices in the observed field.

Organisational practices, entailing working knowledge, are often informal; based on experiences and learning by doing (Borrelli, 2019; Dahlvik, 2017; Fenwick, 2014). Yet, importantly, this does not happen in a vacuum (Fenwick, 2001) but in a field that is 'characterized by multiple sources, strategies and concerns' (Fenwick et al., 2012, p. 2). These practices are heavily based on an interrelationship between formal structures, routines (Fenwick et al., 2012; Pentland & Feldman, 2008) and informal processes that can be productive and enabling (Mason, Visser, Garner-Knapp & Mulherin, 2024), as well as unpredictable. The tension and also symbiosis between informality and formality (Eggeling & Versloot, 2024; Misztal, 2002) include aspects of discretion within decision-making (Ellis, 2011), for example, where frontline workers retain a more or less broad 'marge de manoeuvre' but also recognise structural gaps caused by laws and policies that need to be filled with informal practices and procedures (Eule et al.,

2019). Yet, in contrast to scholarship that discusses informal policymaking at a senior bureaucratic level (Borén & Young, 2021; see also the chapter on diplomats by Eggeling and Versloot, 2024; Pernegger, 2021), fewer works focus on frontline staff and how informal practice shapes everyday office work.

This chapter thus attempts to redraw a picture of bureaucratic work as a lively hub of knowledge exchange and ad hoc solutions at the street level. Here, informal practices are characterised by routine just as much as formal practices are, with the potential to become formalised or at least as established as written-down rules and regulations. I therefore apply the terms 'hustling' and knowledge 'shuffling' that – as I argue – are characteristic for public administration and relate them to practices of documentation that are impacted by, but also guide, informal practices within Swiss administration.

Underpinning this, I wish to broaden an understanding of informality beyond 'a means of decision-making that is uncodified, non-institutional and where social relationships and webs of influence play crucial roles' (Harsh, 2013, p. 481; see also Ayres, 2017). Instead, informal practices can indeed be codified (internally) and institutionalised, yet not written down. This definition does not automatically ascribe informality to a realm of full discretion outside of policies and laws. Instead, it highlights a much broader realm where informality appears in spaces where a codified way of acting may not be present and where it introduces a change and thus brings formalisation but also enables, advances or trumps formal practices, e.g., when informal ways seem more feasible. At the same time, this definition highlights networks in which different procedures happen, and discourses exist, and where social relationships matter. This understanding allows informal practices to be routinised, socialised, as well as individually shaped, while not officially announced and/or openly propagated.

Informality as (Un)codified and Routinised Ad Hoc Practice

Studies of public administration and policy work have highlighted that bureaucratic systems often rely on street-level bureaucrats who implement policies but also contribute to the actual policymaking and breaking (Hill & Hupe, 2002; Lipsky, 1980). Street-level bureaucrats, also called frontline actors, are often in direct contact with clients who are targeted by policies or who take immediate decisions on cases, thus contributing to the actual shaping of a policy. Given the discretion that is embedded in public administration (Bouchard & Carroll, 2002), and the (often excessive) changes that occur in policies and laws (Borrelli & Wyss, 2022; Eule et al., 2019; Huke, 2021, on migration law), formality and informality have been acknowledged to be inherently part of everyday work in administration (Dahlvik, 2016) operating as complementary to each other rather than in opposition (Dahlvik, 2017; Lueger & Froschauer, 2015). They are in fact bound to each other in the way that formality creates a framework that stabilises social processes which are then regulated by informality, e.g., through producing flexibility and reducing complexity (Dahlvik, 2016; see also Zérah, 2020). Research within the field of asylum practices, for example, depicts tensions between standardisation versus discretion, unambiguousness versus uncertainty, individualisation

70   Lisa Marie Borrelli

versus generalisation, and finally responsibility versus distancing which mirror the binary of formality and informality (Dahlvik, 2017). These insights hold true for various fields of bureaucracy and public administration given that the state per se is a non-unified actor consisting of manifold entities and thus, at times, with diverging interests interests (Bevir & Rhodes, 2010; Das, 2004).

Yet, most research studies policymakers and the level of informality when shaping policies, rather than frontline work (Borén & Young, 2021; Pernegger, 2021). Taking on an understanding of street-level bureaucrats as (active) policymakers, I expand on prior works by focusing on how informal practices make up street-level bureaucrats' everyday practice and mundane case handling, often in harmony with formal practices. This goes in line with scholarly work that analyses coping strategies,[1] supported by the often high caseload and lack of resources that bureaucracies experience.

This chapter underlines the contention that informal practices are not solely ad hoc decisions taken by an individual but may equally be engrained in the everyday life of organisations, since social life is an ongoing production of (recurrent) actions (Feldman & Orlikowski, 2011) which do not need to be codified in regulations or laws entirely. Instead, informal procedures can resemble routines, the product of an attempt to design efficient or effective work practices (Pentland & Feldman, 2008). Understanding informal practices therefore as part of a dynamic process, being both spontaneous decisions and routines, allows us to explore how individuals practising such routines learn from experience and therefore transform them over time. Informal practice can thus be defined as 'generative systems that produce repetitive, recognizable patterns of interdependent action carried out by multiple participants' (Pentland & Feldman, 2008, p. 236). Yet, such informal (routinised) practices also present aspirations to create additional accountability while being enacted within the affordances of discretion (Fenwick et al., 2012). Nevertheless, there are also dead routines, rigidly put in place, stored (both remaining quite literally on the shelf, noted down somewhere, unused, but also held in a repository where procedures can be retrieved to read and apply) and often executed mindlessly (Fenwick et al., 2012).

To help grasp such informal moments and structures, I wish to introduce the notions of *hustling* and *shuffling* to convey an atmosphere of action that characterises each office and that influences the way informality is dealt with and actively used by frontline workers. This expands the notion of active routines by foregrounding the informal elements of the former. Both terms maintain a certain air of improvisation and urgency that imply informality. Hustling, as multivocal word, retains many definitions: to proceed or work rapidly or energetically; to convey or cause movement, especially to leave, roughly or hurriedly; to speed up, or an urge to push or force one's way; to be aggressive, especially in business or other financial dealings; finally, it can be slang for describing that someone earns their living by illicit or unethical means. I want to highlight that hustling,

---

[1]Coping includes cherry-picking cases that are easily solvable or foot-dragging cases that seem difficult until someone else finds a solution, to name some examples (Lipsky, 1980; Tummers et al., 2015).

as a rapid way of acting, is part of most if not all bureaucracies (Borrelli & Wyss, 2022; Das, 2004; Hoag, 2010) and is partly created by gaps in laws and policies.

Simultaneously, frontline workers rush around with various printed documents and files, shuffling around papers (Wissink & van Oorschot, 2020) but also using the forms wrongly at times, exchanging and controlling them. More importantly, knowledge and information are shuffled around, either in the form of materials, e.g., documents, emails or notes, or through communication. Given the many tasks of frontline staff and the bustling atmosphere in public administration offices, a loss of information can occur (see Borrelli, 2018, on whispering down the lane effects), yet also a potential dragging of files (e.g., physical shuffling to change their order to process easier cases). Here, informality, though often studied through discretion (Dahlvik, 2017), also becomes a matter of judgement, a weighing up by bureaucrats for deciding what practice to make use of. Hence, informal practices are a result of, and contribute to, the creation of formalised processes. Informal collaborations between bureaucrats circumvent or realise otherwise ineffective formalised collaborations due to their bottom-up approach (Cohen & Cohen, 2021).

Context and Data

Switzerland, as a federal state, is divided into 26 cantons in which municipalities each have a residents' registration office. As their name already implies, their function is to register individuals, both citizens and non-citizens, in each municipality. If people move, change their type of residence permit, marry, need proof of their address or for many other reasons, they come to their respective office. The office staff mostly consist of trained clerks with vocational training in public administration, yet some of the employees have a background in logistics or arrive from other administrative professions. 'Clients' who pass by the offices either need to bring documents (for registration) or do so because they need documents (e.g., to receive their residence permit or an attestation of their registration to submit to their employer or another agency).

The following data derived from fieldwork including semi-structured interviews with professionals in two registration offices, and six weeks of observations conducted at one office and one day at the other. Empirical material was collected between 2019 and 2021 and was based on agreements with each office. All employees were informed about my role as a researcher who was interested in the everyday life of their office and the particular ways bureaucrats handle cases of non-citizens who become dependent on social assistance (see Achermann et al., 2021).[2] I participated in required work for staff in both offices, allowing me to follow their everyday work and practices. To maintain anonymity, I adhere to a data confidentiality

---

[2] The research originally set out to study the consequences of social assistance dependency and the use of integration criteria directed towards non-citizens (see https://nccr-onthemove.ch/wp_live14/wp-content/uploads/2018/11/IP29_Governing-Social-Cohesion-Migration.pdf and https://nccr-onthemove.ch/projects/governing-migration-and-social-cohesion-through-integration-requirements-a-socio-legal-study-on-civic-stratification-in-switzerland/).

72 Lisa Marie Borrelli

agreement that was signed by all involved, omits the name of canton(s) in which research was conducted, and make use of aliases to refer to individual participants.

Bustling Bureaucratic Offices: An Entry Point to Informal Practices of Knowledge Production

The first hour of the day at the resident registration office is marked by zealousness which is followed by a period of idleness – a dynamic pattern that continues throughout the day. One of the caseworkers I am sitting with looks at me with curious excitement, asking: 'Are you ready?'. I nod. Then the door to the residents' registration office opens: a queue has already built up in the hallway, and one of the employees designated to become 'floorwalker' (someone designated to walk around and not working from a fixed desk) approaches each waiting individual to briefly get a sense of what they are here for, assessing also whether the matter will be quickly resolvable. Later, this same person remains in charge of 'scouting' cases: to see if clients took the correct 'number', having been divided into different support categories and potentially also trying to process 'easy cases' to reduce the burden on colleagues sitting in their booths.

Most employees had arrived far in advance of the official opening, hoping that they would find the time to respond to some emails, or process some of the cases that arrived electronically. During the office's public opening hours, work in this office is entirely dependent on the uncontrollable arrival of clients. This means that by the end of the day, work might have piled up in email inboxes, during which time clients have continued to enter the premises, taking numbers handed out by the one employee doing the 'floorwalker' for the day.

Most days are busy, and there is always a melange of easy and more difficult and time-consuming cases that require various forms to be filled out, signed and assessed. The floorwalker continues to run around the room, at times walking back to the entrance and a high table where they can sign and stamp forms, thus processing the easiest cases so that they do not clog the waiting room.

The number system is connected to a board on which numbers pop up; navigating people to the correct booth. Each employee has a button that can be pressed which shows their availability. The number system is threefold, differentiating between letters A for 'brief tasks', B for cases that include foreign nationals and C for cases involving citizens, with a number added to each letter to indicate the number of cases that came before (e.g., Client A15 is the 15th client in Category A of that day). Caseworkers can select the preferred category or ask for random selection; however, they never know for sure what kind of case will come before them.

> A seemingly simple case might end up becoming complicated, a person might have several questions or might also have taken a wrong number. Staff therefore estimate the time needed for each case carefully before going on a break or ending their shift, e.g., selecting a brief case when time is short (field notes, residents' registration office, 2020).

These lively, ad hoc, moments connect to a more stable set-up of practices, routines and exchanges between caseworkers, clients and superiors that reveal the many layers that create decisions and organisational structures.

Hustling as Informal Response to Workload, Lack of Resources and Established Relations

Given that workload remains unpredictable and client needs manifold, the differentiated number system works as a form of categorisation that allows a first selection to be made by caseworkers who assesses the complexity of cases. Brief cases (for which clients select 'A' on the digital number system) are those where one simply needs to verify the address of a client who might need it for their employer or to buy a discounted ticket for public transportation. New caseworkers, for example, often only process quick or citizen cases since non-citizen cases often require a broader knowledge of various databases and forms that can only be acquired over time. This system of handling has been established informally since learning-by-doing is common in the registration office. It also presents a way to cope with the complex set of tasks new caseworkers face, hence making coping a mechanism engrained in a structure, rather than an individual strategy of stress management. Placing a 'gatekeeper' at the door allows for an overview of cases and thus becomes a second collective effort to deal with the uncertainty of client needs. This collective coping endeavour represents one set of practices that – despite being individually decided from office to office, thus being informal – can become a routine and stable practice for those working in the respective office. The hustling happening in the office therefore allows bureaucrats to collectively find ways to cope and orchestrate human and non-human interactions that constitutes a workflow. While facilitating their work, this set-up also benefits clients who can avoid long waiting times if their need is easy to process. The number system also allows for individual decisions on who to take. More advanced caseworkers can freely choose which category they select allowing them to manage their time and workload, deciding for one or two 'quick' cases shortly before a break or end of a shift, or to reduce the number of people in the waiting room when other desks are blocked by 'more difficult' cases. This seemingly small area of autonomy has significant effects as caseworkers regain some ability to plan their cases (at least in theory). However, this results in an uneven selection that can frustrate clients who can see a quicker processing of certain groups than others but are unaware of the process that lies behind it.

At the same time, the office is characterised by information (e.g., documents) that arrives by post, electronically as some tasks can be done on the office's website, or in person through client services. This requires a system capable of both

74 Lisa Marie Borrelli

in-person and online case processing. This parallel system increases the number of possible tasks that each caseworker must learn, making the office seem messy at first glance, characterised by manifold forms, procedures and databases which heighten the feeling of hustling that an outsider might get when observing everyday work life. Informal and formal practices are thus often blurry.

> Today is one of those busy days. I decide to follow the floorwalker who shuffles back and forward between his standing booth and clients, quickly moving from one client to the next, to the desk and back to clients. Trying to handle several cases at the same time to keep waiting times low and juggling various documents that he took from those waiting, I realise at some point that some information gets lost (the floorwalker being unable to remember all the information or clients' questions). While in other more quiet moments, the floorwalker becomes obsolete, thus taking on regular cases, too. But today, it is exceptionally crowded. This is one of the moments when more pragmatic choices need to be made so that caseworkers are able to save time through being more lenient, e.g., by accepting simple explanations from their client than they would be during calmer periods, where more questions would be asked or forms more carefully looked at. During calmer periods, caseworkers would check forms more carefully or ask more questions, such as on the exact location of an apartment, someone wishes to register in.

> I am told by some of the staff that they are planning to change the system so that people can make appointments online so that their workload will become more foreseeable, thus giving them time to engage with the (not so) slowly overflowing email inboxes. Yet, they also mention that with the new system, people may still show up unannounced and I wonder for whom the system is really designed (field notes, residents' registration office, 2020).

While some informal practices are the result of lacking resources, the number system that appoints clients to case workers within the three categories has also been created to avoid the establishment of excessively familiar client–caseworker relations. This is to avoid client preferences and prevent clients from learning which caseworker is lenient. It is an example of an 'informal' practice that upholds certain formal normative principles of procedural fairness and thus reduces the prevalence of another information practice (nepotism). However, at times, caseworkers recognise clients and might ask them for their number and carefully time their next push on the button (field notes, residents' registration office, 2020). They also circumvent organisational rules: for example, through a willingness to speak a language other than those spoken in the respective canton (being German, Italian or French). Yet, caseworkers maintain that a certain familiarity helps with case processing because it takes time to gain understanding and 'know' the case. As such, social relationships between co-workers and between caseworkers and clients influence practice, while constituting informality (Harsh, 2013).

Thus routines, existing both formally and informally, become established by office structures but are also challenged in moments of restricted time when more pragmatic solutions take over to keep a system running. Therefore, I do not find a linear picture of informality constructing formality but understand administrative offices as blurred places of improvisation and routines. Informality, thus, becomes a way of mastering, and at times coping, on the job, and which are both collectively created and individually practised. Making use of hustling helps to move beyond a notion of coping that is framed around individualised behaviours in public administration. It is a collective activity in which individual strategies have as much space as collective actions.

Informality as Knowledge Shuffling – An (Un)productive Way of Professionalising Work

A high workload combined with a lack of resources push frontline staff to make up for administrative shortcomings by inventing new and more efficient ways to communicate with each other, while remaining able to process cases. Here informal, but mundane, practice makes up for unpredictable and high workload which 'work-to-rule' procedures cannot handle (as has been shown in many other fields, see Lord, 2022). Floorwalkers can check the system to see who worked last on a case and ask colleagues for clarification or updates or also navigate clients to the respective booth. Here, documentation facilitates tracing of caseworker responsibilities and the procedures they utilised to understand the case but also to (re)gain knowledge about it. On the one hand, this includes formal paperwork received by clients. On the other hand, it can also include case notes that are made as remarks in the online system. As such, instead of always asking the head of the team, who has more authority and is supposed to be the most knowledgeable, employees often exchange questions and potential solutions informally between each other or read through a file. They quickly walk over to someone else's booth, ask their question, explain their case and receive feedback by their peers (field notes, 2020, see also Cohen & Cohen, 2021, on informal collaborations between street-level bureaucrats). The ability to quickly inquire on how to file a case or which box to tick in the online forms and databases, is of great value to create a workflow that does not overburden the head of the team. As staff know the team leader is highly stressed, they collectively avoid approaching them unless necessary. This approach has been established informally over time and is learned by newcomers.

Within these offices, knowledge is produced, shaped and neglected but also shuffled (around), creating an air of hustling. Clients arrive to either hand over or receive information and need to obey a vast set of rules, including filling out certain papers (in specific ways), making copies or bringing signed forms. They do not always understand why certain documents are needed, and given the sheer number of forms, caseworkers also make mistakes. Yet, at times, untransparent decisions and shuffling of documents, and thus information, can be at the clients' advantage.

> A woman arrives with her daughter, both are from Cuba. They need a permit prolongation for their F-permit (temporally admitted foreign nationals). The caseworker mentions: 'Oh this [permit]

76   Lisa Marie Borrelli

> has long expired, since March 2020'. We are now in September, and the woman explains that they could not have come earlier, first because of COVID and then because of her work. She works as a cleaning professional. The caseworker investigates the national database ZEMIS (central migration information system), where all seems in order; so the permit can be prolonged. Because the woman has worked since March 2020 and the registration with the State Secretariat for Migration is missing, the caseworker hands her the necessary form and adds: 'I've got to tell you, you also have time to go shopping and so on, so you could have come by earlier'. She continues to lecture them for coming in late, since usually one needs to bring specific supporting documents if the permit has expired for more than six months. But the caseworker will do an exemption in this instance because of COVID (field notes, residents' registration office, 2020).

Initially checking online databases, the caseworker decides to disobey part of the procedures that exist for renewing a residence permit which would have required her clients to bring more documentation for the prolongation. This indicates a certain pragmatism but also shows leniency. Accordingly, informal practices may also shine a light on categories of deservingness.* At the same time, informal practice can seem absurd and be in opposition to pragmatism.

> The first case in the morning is a relocation within the city. A Swiss woman moved into a condominium with her two children and mentions that she moved on the third of the month, seemingly an easy case. The caseworker, however, explains that usually one moves on the 1st or 15th of a month. I feel irritated, not seeing the point of when one moves and amazed by the pettiness of the caseworker who shows unease about putting in the actual date of the relocation. The woman agrees to enter the 15th to appease the caseworker and the exchange ends (field notes, residents' registration office, 2020).

The ability to engage in ad hoc discretionary practice and informal routine can also support formal practice. Here, informality enforces formal rules to bring into line what is perceived as out of the ordinary. The pedantic nature of documentation that allows for allocating people to a specific apartment (rather than an address), and thus making them readable to the state, is afflicted with a blend of formal and informal procedures. For example, in the case of relocation, the caseworkers inquire about the floor and apartment number (or location, being, e.g., on the left or right). However, apartments are often 'occupied' by other tenants (in the system) who may have forgotten to deregister or have given wrong information. This blocks new clients from moving in, on paper. Documenting everything, and

---

*A feature of the Resident Registration Offices, and recognised in social policy literature, not discussed further here.

in detail, makes cases easier to trace but is also fraught with mistakes which can have an effect on clients later on. In the case of wrongfully assigned apartments, it is then up to the caseworker to either 'kick out' old tenants from the system or to ask the clients to return with some statements written by the landlord, also asking for the names of the other tenants. While documentation plays a key role in creating knowledge within offices and about clients, informality is a key element for being able to properly document procedures and process client information. As such, caseworkers make use of and organise different sorts of knowledge. They rely on their formalised knowledge of procedures based on regulations, as well as on routinised informal practice – knowledge that is received by learning-by-doing and in collaboration with colleagues. They further document, and thus transform, client information into knowledge that becomes relevant for the state (and various other institutions), shuffling it around the office and between colleagues and clients.

Conclusion

Informal practices can be fuzzy and often operate in grey areas between formal regulations and potentially uncodified and highly untransparent acts. Yet, frontline workers depend on these practices because administration is complex and ambiguity is purposefully written into policy to allow flexibility, which in turn is used by caseworkers to handle their caseload. It is often assumed that individuals seek order and a fixed structure, yet my observations also demonstrate how flexibility not only creates moments of stress but moments in which caseworkers enjoy their autonomy and ability to decide on their own.

The presented material shows how informality is both uncodified, happening in the moment, and codified through long-standing organisational routines that have been established. Such an interplay is created through hustling – as I described in the introductory field note – and refers to the fluctuating pace of administrative work in which quick changes appear and caseload increases. It also partially stands for a pushing through of work and, at times, rather an undiscernible (and potentially illicit) way of making policies work (or contesting them). At the same time, studying practices and exchanges through the lens of (in)formality discloses how knowledge is distributed among practitioners. While this exchange retains a sense of improvisation, it can become a routine that is institutionalised and therefore socialised through socio-material interactions. This shuffling includes a mixing of knowledge between staff (resulting in certain practices) that allow them to act beyond written-down pathways and guidelines.

Prior research has discussed discretion within bureaucracy, arguing both for and against it, problematising the uncertainty that comes with discretionary decisions, while also acknowledging the need to adapt to individual cases that frontline staff need to process. (Borrelli et al., 2023, e.g., see as a review in migration studies) An understanding of discretion ranges from an avoidable evil that should be reduced to a necessary tool to keep the system running. In this context, formal structures and standardisation are contrasted with informal procedures and practices, creating a binary of 'correct' versus' 'wrong' behaviour. This chapter has addressed informality in street-level bureaucracy and argued that it remains a crucial part of any organisation. It is impossible to regulate all possible outcomes

78 Lisa Marie Borrelli

and imagine all scenarios that frontline staff face. What is considered informal should not be understood as only and always directed against the law or standing in contrast to it but also characterised as (routinised) practices that enable policies to work and that fill in legal and procedural gaps and bring to life bureaucratic work. Informal practices are pragmatic and consist of lived bureaucratic procedures that necessarily consist of less formalised practices and thus facilitate quick action.

However, it is also important to acknowledge that (un)codified informal practices can increase social inequality and reproduce as well as normalise privilege and oppression (Feldman & Pentland, 2022; see also the chapter by Eggeling and Versloot, revealing the different power structures in diplomatic informal relations). Clients who do not find friendly caseworkers who speak their language will continue to face exclusion at the nexus of practices and socio-material arrangements, as not all forms cater to the diverse population. This ethical dilemma opens discussions about who is punished or supported by (in)formal practices and who has the resources to learn the rules of the game and potentially bend them.

References

Achermann, C., Borrelli, L. M., Kurt, S., Niragire Nirere, D., & Pfirter, L. (2021, March 3). Die zunehmende Verschränkung von Migrationskontrolle und Sozialhilfe. *Solidarité sans frontières*. https://www.sosf.ch/de/themen/migrationspolitik/informationen-artikel/die-zunehmende-verschraenkung-von-migrationskontrolle-und-sozialhilfe.html?zur=41

Ayres, S. (2017). Assessing the impact of informal governance on political innovation. *Public Management Review, 19*(1), 90–107. https://doi.org/10.1080/14719037.2016.1200665

Bevir, M., & Rhodes, R. A. W. (2010). *The state as cultural practice*. Oxford University Press.

Borén, T., & Young, C. (2021). Policy mobilities as informal processes: Evidence from "creative city" policy-making in Gdańsk and Stockholm. *Urban Geography, 42*(4), 551–569. https://doi.org/10.1080/02723638.2020.1735197

Borrelli, L. M. (2018). Whisper down, up and between the lane – Exclusionary policies and their limits of control in times of irregular migration. *Public Administration, 96*(4), 803–816. https://doi.org/10.1111/padm.12528

Borrelli, L. M. (2019). The border inside – Organizational socialization of street-level bureaucrats in the European migration regime. *Journal of Borderlands Studies, 36*, 579–598. https://doi.org/10.1080/08865655.2019.1676815

Borrelli, L. M., Hedlund, D., Johannesson, L., & Lindberg, A. (2023). *Border bureaucracies: A literature review of discretion in migration control*. Working Paper 32. https://nccr-onthemove.ch/wp_live14/wp-content/uploads/2023/01/WP32_Borelli-et-al.pdf

Borrelli, L. M., & Wyss, A. (2022). Informing for the sake of it: Legal intricacies, acceleration and suspicion in the German and Swiss migration regimes. *Citizenship Studies, 26*(7), 1–17. https://doi.org/10.1080/13621025.2022.2137941

Bouchard, G., & Carroll, B. W. (2002). Policy-making and administrative discretion: The case of immigration in Canada. *Canadian Public Administration, 45*(2), 239–257. https://doi.org/10.1111/j.1754-7121.2002.tb01082.x

Brodkin, E. Z. (2012). Reflections on street-level bureaucracy: Past, present, and future. *Public Administration Review, 72*(6), 940–949. https://doi.org/10.1111/j.1540-6210.2012.02657.x

Cohen, G., & Cohen, N. (2021). Understanding street-level bureaucrats' informal collaboration: Evidence from police officers across the jurisdictional divide. *Public Management Review, 25*(2), 1–19. https://doi.org/10.1080/14719037.2021.1963824

Dahlvik, J. (2016). Asylanträge verwalten und entscheiden: Der soziologische Blick auf Verborgenes: Eine Forschungsnotiz. *Österreichische Zeitschrift für Soziologie, 41*(S2), 191–205. https://doi.org/10.1007/s11614-016-0226-6

Dahlvik, J. (2017). Entscheiden über Asyl: Organisationssoziologische Überlegungen zum Zusammenspiel von Formalität und Informalität im österreichischen Asyl-Verwaltungsverfahren. In C. Lahusen & S. Schneider (Eds.), *Asyl verwalten. Zur bürokratischen Bearbeitung eines gesellschaftlichen Problems* (pp. 117–143). Transcript Verlag.

Das, V. (2004). The signature of the state: The paradox of illegibility. In D. Poole & V. Das (Eds.), *Anthropology in the margins of the state* (pp. 225–252). School of American Research Press; James Currey.

Eggeling, K. A., & Versloot, L. (2024). Mastering Informality in Diplomacy. In L. Garner-Knapp, J. Mason, T. Mulherin, & E. L. Visser (Eds.), *Informality in Policymaking: Weaving the Threads of Everyday Policy Work* (pp. 53–66). Emerald Publishing Limited.

Ellis, K. (2011). 'Street-level bureaucracy' revisited: The changing face of frontline discretion in adult social care in England. *Social Policy & Administration, 45*(3), 221–244. https://doi.org/10.1111/j.1467-9515.2011.00766.x

Eule, T. G., Borrelli, L. M., Lindberg, A., & Wyss, A. (2019). *Migrants before the law: Contested migration control in Europe.* Palgrave Macmillan.

Feldman, M. S., & Orlikowski, W. J. (2011). Theorizing practice and practicing theory. *Organization Science, 22*(5), 1240–1253. https://doi.org/10.1287/orsc.1100.0612

Feldman, M. S., & Pentland, B. T. (2022). Routine dynamics: Toward a critical conversation. *Strategic Organization, 20*(4), 846–859. https://doi.org/10.1177/14761270221130876

Fenwick, T. J. (2001). Work knowing 'on the fly': Enterprise cultures and co-emergent epistemology. *Studies in Continuing Education, 23*(2), 243–259. https://doi.org/10.1080/01580370120101993

Fenwick, T. J. (2014). Knowledge circulations in inter-para/professional practice: A socio-material enquiry. *Journal of Vocational Education & Training, 66*(3), 264–280. https://doi.org/10.1080/13636820.2014.917695

Fenwick, T. J., Nerland, M., & Jensen, K. (2012). Sociomaterial approaches to conceptualising professional learning and practice. *Journal of Education and Work, 25*(1), 1–13. https://doi.org/10.1080/13639080.2012.644901

Harsh, M. (2013). Informal governance of emerging technologies in Africa. In T. Christiansen & C. Neuhold (Eds.), *International Handbook of Informal Governance* (pp. 481–501). Edward Elgar.

Hill, M. J., & Hupe, P. L. (2002). *Implementing public policy: Governance in theory and practice.* Sage.

Hoag, C. B. (2010). The magic of the populace: An ethnography of illegibility in the South African immigration bureaucracy. *Political and Legal Anthropology Review, 33*(1), 6–25.

Huke, N. (2021). *Ohnmacht in der Demokratie.* Das gebrochene Versprechen politischer Teilhabe.

Kosciejew, M., & Hugh, R. (2015). Disciplinary documentation in Apartheid South Africa: A conceptual framework of documents, associated practices, and their effects. *Journal of Documentation, 71*(1), 96–115. https://doi.org/10.1108/JD-10-2013-0130

Lipsky, M. (1980). *Street-level bureaucracy: Dilemmas of the individual in public services.* Russell Sage Foundation.

Lord, J. (2022). Quiet quitting is a new name for an old method of industrial action. *The Conversation.* https://theconversation.com/quiet-quitting-is-a-new-name-for-an-old-method-of-industrial-action-189752

80 Lisa Marie Borrelli

Lueger, M., & Froschauer, U. (2015). Informalität als organisationaler Basisrhythmus. Beobachtungen in Familienunternehmen. In V. von Groddeck & S. M. Wilz (Eds.), *Formalität und Informalität in Organisationen* (pp. 191–213). Springer VS.

Mason, J., Visser, E. L., Garner-Knapp, L., & Mulherin, T. (2024). From Informality and Formality to In|formality: Troubling Absolutism in Policymaking. In L. Garner-Knapp, J. Mason, T. Mulherin, & E. L. Visser (Eds.), *Informality in Policymaking: Weaving the Threads of Everyday Policy Work* (pp. 3–20). Emerald Publishing Limited.

Meyers, M. K., & Lehmann Nielsen, V. (2012). Street-level bureaucrats and the implementation of public policy. In B. G. Peters & J. Pierre (Eds.), *The SAGE handbook of public administration* (2nd ed., pp. 305–318). SAGE Publications Ltd.

Misztal, B. (2002). *Informality* (1st ed.). Routledge. https://doi.org/10.4324/9780203003626

Pentland, B. T., & Feldman, M. S. (2008). Designing routines: On the folly of designing artifacts, while hoping for patterns of action. *Information and Organization, 18*(4), 235–250. https://doi.org/10.1016/j.infoandorg.2008.08.001

Pernegger, L. (2021). Effects of the state's informal practices on organisational capability and social inclusion: Three cases of city governance in Johannesburg. *Urban Studies, 58*(6), 1193–1210. https://doi.org/10.1177/0042098020910111

Townley, B. (2008). Bureaucratic rationality. In B. Townley (Ed.), *Reason's neglect* (1st ed., pp. 46–65). Oxford University Press. https://doi.org/10.1093/acprof:oso/9780199298358.003.0003

Tummers, L. L. G., & Bekkers, V. (2014). Policy implementation, street-level bureaucracy, and the importance of discretion. *Public Management Review, 16*(4), 527–547. https://doi.org/10.1080/14719037.2013.841978

Tummers, L. L. G., Bekkers, V., Vink, E., & Musheno, M. (2015). Coping during public service delivery: A conceptualization and systematic review of the literature. *JPART, 25*, 1099–1126. https://doi.org/10.1093/jopart/muu056

Weber, M. (1947). *The theory of social and economic organizations*. Free Press.

Wissink, L., & van Oorschot, I. (2020). Affective bureaucratic relations: File practices in a European deportation unit and criminal court. *Environment and Planning C: Politics and Space, 39*(5), 239965442097747. https://doi.org/10.1177/2399654420977475

Zérah, M.-H. (2020). The street-level bureaucracy at the intersection of formal and informal water provision. In M.-H. Zérah (Ed.), *Oxford research encyclopedia of environmental science*. Oxford University Press. https://doi.org/10.1093/acrefore/9780199389414.013.676

Chapter 5

Catching Up with Catching Up: Collaborative Policy Work, In|formality and Connective Talk

E. Lianne Visser

Institute of Public Administration, Leiden University, the Netherlands

Abstract

In this chapter, I ask what catching up means in the practice of collaborative policymaking. During ethnographic fieldwork among municipal policymakers and semi-public managers in child and family services in the Netherlands, I found the central actors constantly catching up. These are not interactions that we generally see in accounts of public policymaking, nor has this 'mundane' activity been systematically analysed. Based on many hours of participant observation, and illustrated through a composite narrative, I demonstrate how catching serves to construct the participants' identity (who am I in this meeting), and relationship (what is our relation in this meeting), and to make sense of the specific situation of the meeting (what is it we are doing here) and of the larger 'world' beyond (what has happened and might structure what we will be doing here). I argue that catching up is a connective practice, connecting temporalities, spaces, knowledge and people. Within its actions, the informal and the formal are entangled.

Keywords: Informality; institutional talk; policy work; collaborative governance; ethnography; relationality

Before entering the meeting room, two municipal policymakers and two managers from a local child and family service provider, the CJG, walk towards a coffee machine in the hallway. After a quick introductory handshake with a new manager, Charly, the

---

Informality in Policymaking: Weaving the Threads of Everyday Policy Work, 81–93
Copyright © 2025 by E. Lianne Visser
Published under exclusive licence by Emerald Publishing Limited
doi:10.1108/978-1-83797-280-720241006

82 E. Lianne Visser

managers have been 'picked up' by the policymakers at the reception downstairs, where modern entrance gates separate those who have access passes to the municipal building from those who do not. The beautiful ancient building which is used only for policy work and meetings, separated from other municipal buildings with public functions, has recently been modernised on the inside. A sleek, white spiral staircase leads guests up to a mezzanine in the otherwise largely open-plan hall that has a canteen, coffee bar and several flexible workspaces. Upstairs in the mezzanine three meeting rooms face a central coffee area, separated only by large glass walls that enable what happens inside the meeting rooms to be displayed, materially representing the new 'transparency' of 'public' buildings.

While pushing the button for a caffe latte, policymaker Emma asks whether everybody has read the article about the effects of the recent decentralisation of child and family services in the local newspaper. Manager Natalie says she has not, while policymaker Amy and manager Charly noddingly confirm they have. Emma starts to explain the article to Natalie, stating the negative depiction of the decentralisation efforts. She says she recognises parts of the story. Many errors are being made, and some things still are not properly organised even two years later. But, she argues, here in Dunetown, we have positioned ourselves closer to the actual provision of child and family services. We collaborate closely with providers and monitor what happens. Amy and Natalie nod. Charly asks Emma what she thought of the comments on the number of children in 'isolation treatment'. Emma, with an expression of dismay, responds that it is terrible to read. Children with problems should not be isolated but instead receive necessary care and support that helps them. The thing is, she argues, we do not contract providers at the lowest possible cost. If you do, then providers might not have the capacity to do otherwise, to not put them in isolation. Our approach to providers is more relational.

Before starting their meeting, the municipal policymaker engages in a conversation with her colleagues and CJG managers that – although related to their work – is not part of the purpose of their gathering, nor does it obviously contribute to decision-making. Not only do they discuss the newspaper article, but the policymaker seems keen to position her organisation and her organisation's work in relation to the article.

During my ethnographic research among municipal policymakers and managers of the semi-public child and family service organisation CJG,[1] these kinds of

---

[1] The organisation is semi-public as it is organised exclusively to provide public services and is non-profit. CJG is a general acronym used in the Netherlands, for anonymity the name that follows the acronym has been deleted.

interactions were not an exception, nor were they limited to coffee breaks. Before, during, and after collaborative meetings, actors were catching up on personal concerns, on developments that influenced their policy goals or tasks, on developments that happened parallel to their meetings and on developments that were seemingly completely detached from what they aimed to do in those meetings.

Such interactions are generally absent in accounts of public policymaking or collaborative governance. Scholars have highlighted the importance of network creation, trust, mutual goals, engagement and shared motivation (e.g., Ansell & Gash, 2008). Yet, these elements are treated as static once they are in place, with attention rarely paid to how relationships are built and sustained (Bartels & Turnbull, 2020; Visser & van Hulst, 2024). In response, various studies have shown the complexities of organising and reconciling the differences between actors in multistakeholder collaboration (Blijleven & van Hulst, 2022; van der Woerd et al., 2024; van Duijn et al., 2022; Waring & Crompton, 2020). Recently, scholars have proposed to analyse ongoing – mundane – *actor positioning-processes* in which actors strive for different, actor-based understandings of the nature of the issues discussed, the purpose of the collaboration and its rules of engagement as an important part of understanding collaborative policymaking (Bannink et al., 2024; La Grouw et al., 2024). Yet, empirical studies that scrutinise mundane interactions and their meaning in processes of collaborative policymaking remain scarce.

In this chapter, I ask what catching up means in the practice of collaborative policymaking. To do so, I draw from theories of institutional conversation and sensemaking (Gherardi, 2012; Goffman, 1959) and argue that catching up as a part of collaborative policymaking serves to both construct participants' identities and relationship among them. It informs how participants make sense of the specific situation of the meeting and of the larger 'world' beyond. This way, catching up is in essence a connective practice. Furthermore, I argue that given the plurality of action contexts and authorities, collaborative policymaking is inherently relational and requires different kinds of encounters and forms of communication.

This chapter opens with a composite narrative of typical interactions of catching up in a policy meeting between public policymakers and external, semi-public managers. In this account, I have merged the characters and events from multiple ethnographic observations into a single composite narrative (Jarzabkowski et al., 2014). Following this is an outline of the local context of the policy meeting and the ethnographic methods with which data have been collected, before I analyse the functions of catching up and reflect on how this connective practice is a particular, yet vital, aspect to collaborative policymaking.

Typical Interactions of Catching Up

'I'm sorry I'm late', Kate exclaims as she enters one of the three meeting rooms that had been left open in anticipation of her arrival. She has just hung up one mobile phone before entering the room but is still finishing an email to an Alderman[2] – while walking – on another. Kate joins the two municipal policymakers and two managers already in the room. She closes the glass door in the glass wall with a bang and briefly lifts her shoulders in response to the sound, puts the two phones in a shoulder bag now placed on the table in front of the last free chair and sits down. She sighs, 'I do not know how I can do this anymore', while she takes a notebook and pen out of the bag and removes the bag to the floor. The others had stopped their conversation having just observed the scene and laughed in response to Kate's comment. It is crowded in the small meeting room which fits no more than a rectangular table and six chairs around it. All of those present at the meeting have a bundle of papers, a notebook and pen or a tablet in front of them along with the takeaway coffee cup. The two visitors to the building had hung their coats over their chairs. They all seated themselves around the table intuitively as there is no meeting chair, nor a secretary to make the minutes.

There is also no agenda to steer the meeting and the 'official' start of these biweekly meetings between the municipality and the CJG is lowkey. Sometimes it happens when one of the participants makes a comment proposing to start the meeting but just as often the conversations from the coffee machine naturally evolve into conversations about new topics. After Kate settles down, the others look at her expectantly. She brings an energy of excitement with her, she is busy and one can feel and see her enthusiasm for her work, not least because of the enormous smile she has on her face whenever she starts talking about it. Kate leans towards Charly and rhetorically asks: 'So you're the new recruit?' 'Yes, I'll introduce myself', Charly responds, explaining that he has recently joined the CJG management team and will manage the relationship between child and family services and schools. He goes on to describe his previous work experience and expresses his excitement to have started. Manager Natalie responds that 'they', at the CJG, are happy that Charly has come to strengthen their management team and are back at full capacity now, expecting to be able to pay more attention to specific developments as they arise. 'Good to hear', Kate responds, 'and good to have you back as well. How was your holiday?'. 'Oh, it was wonderful, I had such a relaxing week', Natalie responds, with a soft, friendly voice, but a – seemingly reserved – straight posture and a small nod with

---

[2]In the Netherlands, an Alderman (*wethouder*) is part of the municipal executive, comparable to the Office of Minister at the national level.

her head. 'Where did you go again', Emma interrupts. 'Greece', Natalie replies, 'two weeks. I lay on the beach, read books, and just relaxed'. 'That sounds lovely', Kate responds, 'I feel I have not read a book since Zoe was born'. The lower part of Natalie's face folds into something between a smile and a grimace. 'Well deserved', Kate continues, 'after the year we've had'. 'We have, have we not?', Natalie replies. 'So, what have I missed, how has it been here'?

'Yes, let's continue, we have some points we would like to discuss and decide upon, but we also need to catch up and look ahead today', Kate says. Kate and Amy start by explaining the procurement trajectory with regional child and family service providers. Their summary feels improvised by the way that they complement each other's stories and switch between topics and storylines. There has been a lot of technical back and forth with providers, they explain, and yesterday the results were published in the digital procurement system. They both talk quickly and with varying pitches, sometimes disapprovingly shaking their heads while at other times smiling. They give the impression of finding it frustrating and exciting at the same time. One of the larger providers has not enrolled in the procurement process, they reveal, which is problematic as the welfare services they deliver cannot be stopped. Many children are receiving treatment from the particular provider. The municipality will either be required to prolong the existing contract and its associated conditions or a temporary contract will have to be drawn up. Manager Natalie is bent over her tablet, taking down notes for herself. She continues for a couple of seconds after Kate and Amy have stopped talking and then looks up and responds while rolling her eyes: 'That will cause us a lot of extra work', referring to the possibility of having to draw up a temporary contract every time a CJG professional refers a family to that provider. They continue to discuss why the provider might not have enrolled, followed by ten minutes of detailed discussions about the enrolment and conditions that particular providers must adhere to.

The discussion almost seamlessly morphs into talk about related topics, until Natalie brings up the situation of a family that is in need of a personalised solution, one that would require involvement beyond contracted providers. 'I am not involved in the substance of cases', Kate says while her upper body bends further over the table towards the managers, her voice both pronounced and soft as if to indicate annoyance in a friendly manner. 'I keep being contacted and consulted on many complex cases'. Contrary to her statement, she continues with her views on the case, arguing the solution the CJG has proposed is good, and that she likes the fact that the family can receive tailor-made support. Charly, being new to the collaboration, nods and asks who must be contacted to ask questions about the substance of specific cases. Kate confirms that most people ask her but argues that she does not have the time to spend much of the meeting discussing cases. Together, they will need to find a new way of working between them. Natalie nods with a serious face, saying pensively, 'Yes, working together requires regularly evaluating our communication processes. This will take some time to restructure and get right, though'. A large smile forms on her face which is reciprocated by the others.

Next, municipal policymaker Emma introduces another topic for everyone to catch up on, introducing the change by shifting in her chair. In a meeting she participated in, somebody from the municipality had complained about the CJG. The person was frustrated that a specific youth-focused team had not offered proper 'streetwork' for the local young people. 'It's because of the image they have of the CJG's tasks', she says. Kate shakes her head, stating: 'We have to do something about this. They still don't have the right understanding of our task'. Manager Natalie has been nodding and responds: 'Streetwork is completely different than what we do. People should know that. But we are not there yet. We have to clarify the different roles and tasks because they seem to fade away when we do not communicate them actively'.

As the participants continue their meeting, they switch between catching up on developments discussing solutions and making decisions. Topics are introduced by all those present which gives the impression of an equal relationship between the participants. The way the meeting progresses appears familiar to the participants, although unexpected topics or tones sometimes throw participants off briefly. Their meeting ends as it had started, a bit scattered, with its final conclusion having been understood spontaneously by the participants. Some summarising of what had been discussed re-affirms tasks that have come out of the meeting. They each pick up their bag from the floor and put away their tablets and notebooks. The managers put on their coats while Amy gathers the empty coffee cups, and all participants proceed to walk back into the coffee area towards the stairs. In front of the stairs, they pause one last time for some final exchanges before they say goodbye and walk their separate ways: the managers go down the stairs, while the policymakers enter a hallway towards another meeting room.

Locating Policy Practices in Local Child and Family Services

The above narrative is situated in policy and governance meetings between a municipality in the Netherlands and a local child and family service provider which the municipality has outsourced local access to care to. Key to the collaboration between the two organisations is the aim of experimenting together in their search for the best possible child and family service provision. This approach requires trust, regular deliberation, negotiation and continuous adaptation. The collaboration between the two organisations is based on mutual dependency. The municipality is the commissioning party, is financially and politically responsible and plays a large role in developing the operating policy framework. In turn, the service provider receives a subsidy to allocate to services and also delivers primary services, having a legal mandate to make allocation decisions and corresponding expenditures. The service provider has the professional expertise and everyday experience to potentially improve service provision. These policymakers and managers have been working together for several years, regularly holding this type of meeting.

I followed everyday encounters between the municipal policymakers and semi-public managers between December 2016 and December 2017 to understand how they governed and adapted policy in this context. This fieldwork resulted in 71 hours of observation of meetings, many hours of additional observations of informal policy work and interactions, 27 interviews (all between one and two hours duration) in addition to many informal conversations with policymakers and managers about their work and their policy and governance practices. I supplemented these activities with an analysis of associated documents such as policy plans, performance contracts and meeting minutes. This chapter is the result of my curiosity being sparked by the practice of catching up that I observed so often. Why did they engage in this practice that seemed so mundane, so irrelevant, so inefficient from the perspective of an outsider, a layperson? Catching up seemed to flow by, yet it was repeated often. Inspired by the advice of organisational ethnographer Huising that reads 'If it's happening all the time and it seems boring, it's likely gold. There's a puzzle here' (CIPA workshop Writing ethnographic field notes, 7 October 2020), I decided to delve deeper into the practice.

To do so, I first compiled a list of all events and quotes in which actors catch up. Then, I consulted literature on the role of talk and conversation in work and on the role of organisational meetings in search of possible explanations. I systematically compared and analysed whether the data I had on catching up fit with the explanations and categories I found in the literature. This allowed me to compose an explanation from different bodies of literature. Finally, I strived to present the data in a way that would render my fieldwork experiences and interactions with my research participants accessible. The collected data form a composite narrative in which the characters and events from multiple ethnographic observations are merged together (Jarzabkowski et al., 2014). The narrative above encapsulates typical interactions that I encountered across multiple observations of meetings.

88   E. Lianne Visser

This device allows for one vivid, unified tale, in a 'slice-of-life' fashion to make the tale as meaningful as possible for the reader, while at the same time presenting a tale that is more conceptually transferrable in revealing the patterns at work.

Analysing the Work of Catching Up

In this section, I analyse the purposes that catching up serves for the participants. The literature on institutional conversation and sensemaking offers multiple explanations of talk and conversation at work. Institutional conversation, also called discursive practices, enables the performance of work. That is, everyday organisational action can be achieved through talk-in interaction (Llewellyn, 2008). In work contexts, people also use ordinary conversation, which can, for example, be used to create the work climate. Institutional conversations are oriented to a goal, task or identity associated with the institution concerned (Gherardi, 2012). It is a professional activity that draws on specific competence. Institutional conversation is distinguishable from ordinary conversation by different lexical choices. These tend to evoke the institutional context through specialised knowledge, the use of 'we' to denote the institutional identity and universalistic expressions that sanctify institutional discourse. Institutional conversations are structured by standard procedures and certain sequences and turns in interaction, for example, defined by meeting chairs, a meeting agenda or the setting in which the conversation unfolds. The conversations (re)produce social relations. Participants (need to) have specific knowledge about how to manage and construct those relations. Often, it is argued, institutional social relations tend to be asymmetrical, for example, in the case of doctors and patients or managers and street-level bureaucrats. These social relations can be uncovered by identifying who is addressing whom, who is listening, and who is present but not listening as indicated by body posture, tone of voice, direction of the gaze and turn-taking (Drew & Heritage, 1992). Looking into these characteristics, I identify four functions of catching up in collaborative policy work.

Catching up does not serve to 'get work done' in the sense of drafting an implementation plan, deciding on regulatory measures or a similar aspect of policy work. Looking more closely at the tale above, catching up can be understood as exchanges that do not entail discussing possible solutions or making decisions. The CJG and municipality regularly catch up on national policy developments, new professional regulations and changes among child and family service providers. They catch up on political gossip, the alderman's reactions to developments and the reorganisation of management structures and responsibilities. And they catch up on relevant newspaper articles or documentary releases, personnel changes and holidays. Catching up cannot only be recognised in what is being said. It is also present in how it is being said: in changing tone, speed and loudness of voice. In reciprocating smiles and other facial expressions or leaning towards other actors. Catching up unfolds when the groups of actors meet: with actors catching up before, during and after collaborative meetings. Generally, this starts already before a meeting begins, as they are walking towards a room, making a stop to get some coffee, and there is a realisation, albeit tacit; 'we are about to have a meeting'. Although they are not oriented towards drafting a plan or making a decision, the interactions of catching up that unfold can partly be characterised as institutional as they are oriented towards institutional goals, tasks and identities. More specifically, one of the functions is to (re)construct a situated social or organisational identity (Gherardi, 2012). That is, to define who a certain individual is in a specific interaction. Sometimes, individuals do not speak on their own behalf but represent a specific institution or a 'user' of that institution (Drew & Heritage, 1992). The identity construction can then invoke the institution's identity and consequently reproduce the institution through interaction.

Looking closer at the narrative, once the involved actors have realised that they are about to have, or are already, in a meeting, they need to define who am I in this meeting and what am I doing here? Who is sitting in front of me and what are they doing here? In other words, they need to define their identities. We see this happening in the narrative when new manager Charly introduces himself. When his colleague Natalie responds that 'they' (as an institutional we) are at full capacity. When policymaker Emma responds to the newspaper article by saying 'they' do it differently. The actors are generating an identity that defines who they are and how they should be perceived in the meeting. In that sense, the first purpose of catching up is the formation of a situated social identity.

This does not have to start from scratch when the participants have participated in multiple meetings together. Some previous understandings remain, as we see in the narrative above. They know which organisation one represents, what that organisation aims to do in general terms and even some private details about the meeting participants. Yet, every new meeting represents a new situation as external developments might have unfolded, so new topics need to be discussed and agreed upon. Thus, even after sequences of meetings, participants need to validate their identities and possibly adjust them. Therefore, the meeting participants engage in identity formation continuously, and every time they develop a situated social identity, and – in part – this is done through catching up.

Second, scholars have argued that talk in organisations can contribute to the expression and construction of a sense of community (Gherardi, 2012). Stories are told that construct the categories that give names and meanings to events. Such talk not only maintains, develops and distributes practical knowledge within groups but also maintains, transmits and changes a code of behaviour, a professional competence and a community memory. All in all, this contributes to a group's identity and the attachment of actors to each other (Gherardi, 2012). I transport these insights from within organisations to participants in collaborative policymaking across organisations; they also need to define who they are in relation to one another.

In the composite narrative, the actors are constructing their relationship, which is a dynamic process with provisional outcomes. The actors smile, try to put each other at ease and discuss their personal lives. They need to check: we agreed we were close and friendly, or perhaps we agreed to be more professional or even very formal. But this is a new situation, a new meeting. Are we still on good terms, are we behaving in the same way, is our 'social' relationship maybe progressing towards something else? They have to re-enact the relationship they think they have. At times, the two groups of actors form a temporary collective identity, when they talk about how 'we' and 'our' tasks are misunderstood.

In addition, there is a political component to (per-)forming the relationship. They need to establish who has the authority to define what happens in the meeting and beyond. This can be partially structured through, for example, an agenda and a person who chairs the meeting. Still, in practice, the authority can be challenged, (re-)negotiated, disrupted or, just simply, momentarily performed differently. In the case described above, there is largely a mutual dependency, yet this is constantly re-enacted, for example, by checking whether they have each other's back, by informing the other early on about important developments or by sharing their assessment of a situation (Visser, 2024). Simultaneously, their positioning is often changed and challenged but is acceptable enough that it does not impact their overall relationship. Contrary to existing work on institutional conversation (Drew & Heritage, 1992), the social relations between the commissioning policymakers and implementing managers are not necessarily asymmetric to begin with, as policymakers have the power to end the subsidy, but the managers have knowledge of how to organise access to care and have the practical experience that allows improving and restructuring both policy delivery and procurement. The practice of catching up is one of the ways in which the actors negotiate and challenge their relationship.

Third, through talk, actors can define the situation and make sense of what they are doing in the meeting (Goffman, 1959; Schwartzman, 1989). They need to do so to decide how to make speech appropriate to the situation but also to define how to act, what to do and what to expect from the other. To be able to act, participants need to put circumstances together and transform them into a situation which is, or can be, verbalised and used as a coordinated system for action (Taylor & Van Every, 2000). Sensemaking can be understood as a process of situation-building (Gherardi, 2012). Actors need to define: what kind of meeting are we in, what is it about, what will or can or should we do and how? There is a need to 'build' the situation in order to be able to act in the meeting and to collaborate as far as that can occur within the meeting. Moreover, everybody in the room must understand what they are doing there.

In the narrative, we can see how catching up serves to make sense of the meeting. Kate explains that she will not discuss the substance of individual cases in the meeting. Interestingly, in the past, she did engage in case discussions, but she argues that they need to change this part of their collaboration, indicating the need to re-establish this over time. If the process of sensemaking fails, there is a chance that the meeting will not accomplish anything as people are working towards different goals. Again, this is a political process, as participants have to agree on a shared understanding (Freeman, 2019). There is a possibility that claims concerning the definition of the situation are disagreed with, that they are challenged or imposed. The definition can be partly institutionalised through having a meeting agenda. Yet, an agenda does not exclude the necessity to discuss and negotiate the agenda items to the larger meaning of what the meeting is about. In this sense, catching up is forward-looking, aimed to be able to provide conditions for future action.

Finally, beyond the meeting, there are developments occurring that impact what can and has to be done. Sensemaking and consecutive action also concerns the situation external to the encounter or an account of the world to which it is deemed to relate in some way (Schwartzman, 1989). There are numerous developments that might have preceded the meeting, ranging from regulatory changes to discussions that took place in concurrent meetings. There is a need to capture what has been agreed upon and ensure continuity between interactions in collaborative policymaking. In the narrative, the actors discuss the developments in procurement to make sure they know everything needed to make future plans or decisions. Catching up then serves to construct the context beyond the meeting, to understand the 'world order' in which they are acting. In this sense, catching up is also backward-looking, ensuring that they know what has happened that might structure what they are doing, ensuring that there is nothing else they need to know about before engaging in new actions.

Catching Up as Connective Practice

What I have purposely left in the middle thus far is whether or how catching up could be understood as informal. The analysis above helps to shed light on this. Catching up conjures an image of an informal practice, not part of the structures, legal rules, lines of authority and accountabilities that are deemed part of formal policy (Wagenaar, 2004). However, we cannot draw such a clear dividing line between catching up and seemingly formal policy practices. It does not have a clear boundary or demarcation. As policymakers and managers run the course of pre-meeting, meeting and post-meeting proceedings and move from the entrance to the lounge area, meeting room and back, they shift between different forms of interaction, between events and between spaces. The performance of catching up is not separated by time or place. The shift between catching as a type of interaction and other types (and forms) of interaction is not consciously or strategically made. In his argument that informality is a practice, geographer McFarlane (2012) has argued that there is a temporal aspect to informal–formal relations. Following those insights, we can recognise actors within catching up moving between formal and informal actions and arrangements over the course of time and place.

Sociologist Misztal (2000) characterised informality as a mode of interaction wherein participants possess a degree of latitude in interpreting the expectations of their roles. Traditionally, it has been linked with the realm of personal relationships, often denoted by its lack of structure, spontaneous nature and unpredictability. Catching up is not defined by written rules or outlined in policy tasks. What is said and done is not documented or inscribed and as such leaves no trace (Freeman, 2019). Yet, contrary to Misztal's definition, catching up is not as unstructured. It is recognisable and intelligible to its participants, skilfully and knowledgeably performed in the narrative. Catching up is 'remarkably organized', and this order matters (Llewellyn, 2008).

92   E. Lianne Visser

To better understand how informality and formality are entwined, anthropologist Koster (2019) has proposed to understand community leaders as connective agents who connect the institutional with the personal and the official with the unofficial. Similarly, I argue that catching up can be understood as a *connective practice.*

Catching up connects events as it involves discussions of what has happened, what is happening and what will be done. It also connects what happens in the meeting with what happens preceding and following the meeting, as an intertext. By being both forward- and backward-looking, it overcomes – imaginary – boundaries between the past, present and future. It makes encounters, gatherings and meetings intelligible as part of 'a series of interactions of similar and different kinds' (Freeman, 2019), in relation to other events and to other forms of interaction. Furthermore, catching up connects knowledges between people and time, building a provisional collective knowing that is necessary to act.

Catching up also connects people by establishing temporary identities of, and relationships between, collaborative partners in policymaking. It contributes to the building and sustaining of relationships of understanding, commitment and reciprocity that are vital to collaborative policymaking and that have been so often overlooked (Bartels & Turnbull, 2020; La Grouw et al., 2024). As such, it also exposes that there is no singular network or process of collaboration to be understood (Bannink et al., 2024). Rather, it is in interaction that collectives can be temporarily formed but also broken down, that action imperatives can develop but also fail to do so. Given the plurality of action contexts and authorities (Misztal, 2000), collaborative policymaking is inherently a relational practice that needs different kinds of encounters and forms of communication. Catching up is one of them. It connects the formal and informal within its actions and interactions.

References

Ansell, C., & Gash, A. (2008). Collaborative governance in theory and practice. *Journal of Public Administration Research and Theory, 18*(4), 543–571.

Bannink, D., Sancino, A., & Sorrentino, M. (2024). Governance without we. Wicked problems and collaborative governance. *Public Policy and Administration, 39*(3), 1–23.

Bartels, K., & Turnbull, N. (2020). Relational public administration: A synthesis and heuristic classification of relational approaches. *Public Management Review, 22*(9), 1324–1346.

Blijleven, W., & van Hulst, M. (2022). Encounters with the organisation: How local civil servants experience and handle tensions in public engagement. *Local Government Studies, 48*(3), 615–639.

Drew, P., & Heritage, J. (1992). Analyzing talk at work: An introduction. In P. Drew & J. Heritage (Eds.), *Talk at work: Interaction in institutional settings* (pp. 3–65). Cambridge University Press.

Freeman, R. (2019). Meeting, talk and text: Policy and politics in practice. *Policy & Politics, 47*(2), 371–388.

Gherardi, S. (2012). *How to conduct a practice-based study: Problems and methods*. Edward Elgar Publishing.

Goffman, E. (1959). *The presentation of self in everyday life*. Penguin Books.

Jarzabkowski, P., Bednarek, R., & Lê, J. K. (2014). Producing persuasive findings: Demystifying ethnographic textwork in strategy and organization research. *Strategic Organization, 12*(4), 274–287.

Koster, M. (2019). Assembling formal and informal urban governance. *Anthropologica, 61*(1), 25–34.

La Grouw, Y., van der Woerd, O., Visser, E. L., & Blijleven, W. (2024). Mundane dynamics: Understanding collaborative approaches to 'big' problems through studying 'small' practices. *Public Policy and Administration, 39*(3), 1–30.

Llewellyn, N. (2008). Organization in actual episodes of work: Harvey Sacks and organization studies. *Organization Studies, 29*(5), 763–791.

McFarlane, C. (2012). Rethinking informality: Politics, crisis, and the city. *Planning Theory & Practice, 13*(1), 89–108.

Misztal, B. A. (2000). *Informality: Social theory and contemporary practice*. Psychology Press.

Schwartzman, H. B. (1989). *The meeting: Gatherings in organizations and communities*. Plenum Press.

Taylor, J. R., & Van Every, E. J. (2000). *The emergent organization: Communication as its site and surface*. Routledge.

van der Woerd, O., Janssens, J., van der Scheer, W., & Bal, R. (2024). Managing (through) a network of collaborations: A case study on hospital executives' work in a Dutch urbanized region. *Public Management Review, 26*(5), 1299–1321.

van Duijn, S., Bannink, D., & Ybema, S. (2022). Working toward network governance: Local actors' strategies for navigating tensions in localized health care governance. *Administration & Society, 54*(4), 660–689.

Visser, E. L. (2024). Permanently provisional: An ethnographic analysis of responsive governance practices in and through meetings. *Public Administration*, 1–18.

Visser, E. L., & van Hulst, M. (2024). The performance and development of deliberative routines: A practice-based ethnographic study. *Journal of Public Administration Research and Theory, 34*(1), 92–104.

Wagenaar, H. (2004). "Knowing" the rules: Administrative work as practice. *Public Administration Review, 64*(6), 643–656.

Waring, J., & Crompton, A. (2020). The struggles for (and of) network management: An ethnographic study of non-dominant policy actors in the English healthcare system. *Public Management Review, 22*(2), 297–315.

Methods to Study Informality

Chapter 6

Visualising Informal Repair: Exploring Photographic 'Routines' in Ethnographic Methodology

Neha Mungekar[a,b]

[a]Dutch Research Institute for Transitions (DRIFT), Erasmus University Rotterdam, Rotterdam, Netherlands
[b]Erasmus School of Social and Behavioural Sciences (ESSB), Erasmus University Rotterdam, Netherlands

Abstract

In this chapter, I illustrate the use of visual ethnography to uncover the nuanced role of informal processes and structures, henceforth referred to as informality, in navigating the complex challenges of water governance in India through enabling repair. By repair, I refer to the ability of informality to act as a transformative approach, adept at navigating and addressing the multifaceted governance challenges faced by Indian cities. The mapping of informality in repair within urban water governance uncovered three dilemmas: 1) the difficulty of documenting transient oral narratives, 2) the discrepancies between verbal accounts and observed practices and 3) ethical concerns associated with documenting illicit activities. To address these dilemmas, I coupled ethnographic approaches with photographic methods. Ethnography provided reflection, clarity and a documented record, although it introduced a delay in capturing observations. Photographic methods compensated for this by offering an immediate visual record and facilitating live analysis alongside textual notes. I outline five routines of conducting visual ethnography, applied in the cities of Bhopal and Bhuj, to shed light on how various actors enact informality in addressing the gaps

---

Informality in Policymaking: Weaving the Threads of Everyday Policy Work, 97–112

Copyright © 2025 by Neha Mungekar. Published under exclusive licence by Emerald Publishing Limited. These works are published under the Creative Commons Attribution (CC BY 4.0) licence. Anyone may reproduce, distribute, translate and create derivative works of these works (for both commercial and non-commercial purposes), subject to full attribution to the original publication and authors. The full terms of this licence may be seen at http://creativecommons.org/licences/by/4.0/legalcode
doi:10.1108/978-1-83797-280-720241007

within urban water governance. These routines served as a photographic praxis to critically engage with both human and non-human actors in these locales. Through these routines, I illustrate how informality results in two types of repairs: reactive and reparative. Reactive repair serves as a temporary measure to restore the status quo. In contrast, reparative repair aims at fostering long-term change, illustrating the dynamic ways in which informality contributes to repairing the intricacies of water governance in India.

Keywords: visual ethnography; methodology; informality; water governance; India; repair

1. Introduction

In the context of navigating India's complex water governance challenges (Narain, 2000), this chapter presents a methodology that aims to shed light on the underexplored role of informal processes and structures, henceforth referred to as *informality*, in *repairing* the gaps and hindrances in urban water governance in the cities of Bhopal and Bhuj. In this context, repair goes beyond mere technical fixes; it is studied as a transformative approach adept at tackling governance challenges. Despite its associated drawbacks, informality emerges as a critical element in bridging governance gaps, offering nuanced perspectives on the interconnectedness and relationships among actors within this sector (Ahlers et al., 2014; Roy, 2005). Current research methodologies often need to encapsulate these nuanced perspectives (Goodman & Marshall, 2018), indicating the need for an innovative, cross-disciplinary approach.

To fill this research gap, the heart of this chapter lies in a novel methodological proposition: the use of visual ethnography to illuminate the informal practices of water governance. This method navigates moral and methodological challenges through five photographic *routines*. The routines served as photographic praxis to critically engage with the human and non-human actors in Bhopal and Bhuj between September 2021 and January 2022.

I begin with a vignette from Bhopal, focusing on the informal practices of overhead water tank (OHT) supervisor Ram Singh*. This case illustrates visual ethnography's role in uncovering obscured informal practices within complex governance structures. Subsequent sections delve into the concept of informality, exploring its potential as a means for repairing governance structures and processes. Insights gleaned through photographic routines in Bhopal and Bhuj follow this discussion. This chapter concludes with an examination of how visual methods can complement textual analysis and reflections on how my positionality influenced the research trajectory.

2. Why Did Ram Singh Shush Farhan?

In September 2021, during my fieldwork in Bhopal, India, I stepped into the world of Ram Singh, a municipal field supervisor responsible for overseeing the

Visualising Informal Repair **99**

water supply of his assigned zone. His multifaceted duties encompassed monitoring the OHT, maintaining the pipe network and ensuring smooth water delivery to the local citizens.

As part of my study, I conducted interviews with local residents, gathering oral testimonials about their water supply experiences. Repeated narratives of dissatisfaction with the supply emerged due to various factors like inadequate provision, substandard water quality and erratic pressure. Interestingly, I observed their illicit measures to these predicaments, which mostly involved tinkering with the physical water infrastructure themselves. This resourcefulness sparked my interest in Singh's critical role at the OHT, a pivotal node in the water supply network. I was intrigued: how was he dealing with these challenges? What strategies did he employ to ensure a consistent water supply amid scarcity?

As we talked, Singh projected an image of a diligent bureaucrat, committed to the rule book, seemingly untouched by the torrent of obstacles that accompanied water shortages. His responses danced around the challenges, skirting away from acknowledging the issues that his peers openly accepted, e.g. pressure from citizens, biased prioritisation and lack of human and financial competencies. Farhan*, a member of a local political party, present during our conversation, possibly influenced Singh's responses. Yet, Singh's steadfast denial of these challenges left me baffled. Despite my persistent questioning, Singh maintained his silence, amplifying my curiosity about the untold strategies he might have in place.

Unexpectedly, Farhan stepped in, recounting episodes of Singh's benevolence when water was dispensed free of charge to citizens. This revelation, standing in stark contradiction to Singh's narrative, took us both by surprise. Caught off guard, Singh swiftly shushed Farhan, conveying a subtle message that certain information should remain concealed from prying ears. The incident further propelled my curiosity about his underlying strategies, making me linger longer.

Post-interview, I observed Singh, who was perched under the looming water tank, engrossed in his newspaper while a few locals gradually joined him for their evening chat. It struck me how effortlessly Singh blended into the local landscape, sharing laughs and conversations with the passers-by (see Figure 6.1). This realisation became apparent when observing through the camera of my smartphone, focusing on the exchange between Singh and the residents. As an observer, the smartphone's screen served as a visual frame which excluded distractions and allowed me to focus on the exchanges between Singh and the residents. I began to comprehend the significance of these personal relationships in Singh's public service.

I came to the realisation that Singh was trying to suppress any mention of these personal relationships, aiming to project an impartial image of himself. While not necessarily illegal, the subtle revelation of these relationships and Farhan's unintentional disclosure indicated that admitting to the governance challenges would force him to reveal his informal strategies. This could jeopardise his position and potentially lead to his relocation to a different zone, uprooting the network he had painstakingly built over the years.

As I continued to observe and document, it emerged that Singh's team, primarily comprising migrant plumbers, worked in a hostile environment riddled with casteism, threats and intimidation. Singh's personal alliances within the community acted as a protective shield, facilitating a smoother service delivery.

Figure 6.1. Left - The physical infrastructure - overhead water tank; Right - Social infrastructure that enabled access to the resource - in-person relationships. (30/9/2021)

He cleverly leveraged relationships to enable provision (albeit unequally) while ensuring a safety net for his subordinates against local prejudice. Yet, these strategies were deliberately kept under wraps, protecting the integrity of his job and his network. However, these strategies remained hidden, safeguarding Singh's position and his informal ways of water management.

Thus, the incorporation of photographic methods in studying people's cases became an integral part of my ethnographic journey, providing me with a deeper understanding of the interplay between formality, informality and the resilience of urban life. Unearthing the intricacies of urban Indian water management necessitates understanding these clandestine practices. Traditional research methods alone, like semi-structured interviews and desk study, often miss the nuances. Consequently, I propose a combined approach, integrating traditional methods with visual ethnography to unmask the instrumental role of repair in informal water governance.

3. On Performing Different Forms of Repair Through Informal Practices

Actors like Ram Singh often face the challenge of circumnavigating formal procedures to amend service shortfalls. By building networks with key citizens,

Singh reduced potential hostility towards his subordinates, thus ensuring smoother maintenance operations. His manoeuvres within the formal water supply system, coupled with informal water distribution, effectively bridged the inherent gaps in these formal protocols. This was evident when residents grew frustrated with slow services or the use of non-local labour. In response, these personal networks became crucial, fostering understanding, patience and allowing for unhindered work.

Moreover, formal arrangements often involve lengthy bureaucratic processes. However, through nurturing informal networks, individuals like Singh can distribute risks and gather benefits, enhancing service provision through reparative practices. Here, the concept of repair goes beyond technical fixes: it signifies a governing approach to managing transitions. I delve into the concept of 'repair', recognised in the literature as a transformative mode adept at addressing complex governance challenges faced by Indian cities through informal mechanisms. This exploration underscores the need to view the informal as an integral component of urban governance rather than an anomaly.

The literature on repair circumscribes two perspectives. The first conceptualises repair as a reactionary process, striving to maintain the existing state and restore its original properties (Henke, 2017). Singh's use of social capital to address challenges in water supply exemplifies this. The alternate perspective positions repair as a sensibility that guides reparation as a mode of transition (Bhan, 2019). This viewpoint advocates long-term, community-focused approaches to rectify past colonial policies, ensuring equitable service provision. It emphasises collective memory, incremental change and iterative processes (Bhan, 2019; Broto et al., 2021; Perry, 2020). These two facets of repair – reactive and reparative – are not opposed but exist on a spectrum, functioning in hybrid forms based on context.

Reactive repair and reparation require mobilising personal networks, collective memory and local knowledge. Regional languages like Hindi proffer nuanced understandings to expand the meaning of repair with terms such as *Marammat* (returning to the original), *Rafu karna* (bolstering the old with the new), *Dosh rahit* (emphasising faultless repair) and *Sudharna* (seeking betterment for the future). These vocabularies provide a heuristic map for multifaceted repair approaches within given constraints and opportunities through informal means.

Informality, therefore, is pivotal in steering transformative repair processes and structures, especially in managing contested resources. Drawing from the works of Roy (2005), McFarlane (2012) and Ahlers et al. (2014), I align with Roy's (2005) understanding of urban informality as an organising logic – a system of codes governing repair processes. This logic is pertinent in a deregulated state where formal rules exist but are negotiated based on contextual conditions (Roy, 2005). Here, informal governance processes and structures do not operate in isolation or in the absence of the state but are mutually co-constitutive with formality, helping bridge gaps in service delivery (Ahlers et al., 2014; McFarlane, 2012).

The structure of informal governance resembles an ephemeral web that mobilises services as needed (Jaglin, 2014), coalescing when necessary and allocating tasks into manageable units based on availability, capacity and resources, often circumventing formal regulations (Ahlers et al., 2014). With the formation of new coalitions, shared understanding and vocabulary materialise to enable service delivery. These relationships, characterised by their temporary and flexible nature, demonstrate resilience to shocks and adaptability to changing circumstances (Ahlers et al., 2014).

I analyse how informality's organising logic plays a role in addressing governance challenges such as mitigating departmentalisation, extending capacities in resource-deficient situations or nudging behavioural change. Ram Singh's actions demonstrate this adaptation as he negotiates with users to ease access to infrastructure. He confronts challenges, employing emotional intelligence by empathising with his subordinate staff's needs, bridging resource provision gaps and risking his job to meet citizen demands, thus identifying repair pathways within a deregulated context. These diverse repair pathways, laden with obscure narratives and nebulous interpretations, make their understanding a complex task, thus necessitating the development of a non-intrusive methodology to unravel how the informal processes and structures enable repair.

Hence, my research aimed to reveal the intricate ways in which actors perform informality to facilitate repair. I describe the actions as performances due to their embodied meaning and vulnerability to situational contingencies, which prompt individuals to address governance barriers hindering water service provision. This chapter emphasises the centrality of ethnographic methodology in discerning these equivocal and ambivalent practices, enabling an understanding of repair in its various forms in Bhopal and Bhuj.

4. On Capturing and Making Visual Narratives About the Role of Informality in Repair

Based on ethnographic scholarship, I outline a methodological framework to capture the varied and informal manifestations of repair. An ethnographic sensibility provides an epistemological framework for 'experiencing, interpreting, and representing' (Pink, 2013, p. 34) the multifarious performances of informal practices reflexively shaped through social norms and beliefs (Gobo, 2008). I employed textual and photographic methods to explore how repair manifests through informal means. I examine repair through personal networks, local knowledge and grey practices – a realm between legality and illegality, where certain practices are accepted but not necessarily supported by formal codes.

In my investigation of informal water governance in Bhopal and Bhuj, I conducted 64 interviews along with 10 separate observations with users, government authorities, practitioners, non-governmental organisation (NGO) actors and academics. Complementing the interviews, I made *thick* descriptions (Kharel, 2015) to cross-reference participant accounts and unravel the intricate web of informal relations. The ethnographic notes captured the practical execution of formal mandates, highlighting the actual roles of actors and identifying gaps between their actions and prescribed responsibilities. By examining the decision chain of actors at different hierarchical levels, I obtained insights regarding their vulnerabilities and intentions in adopting informal practices. This holistic approach deepened my understanding of the informal management of water resources.

However, investigating repair practices posed three dilemmas:

i. Capturing and accurately representing transient oral accounts are often abstract and challenging to document.
ii. Addressing discrepancies between respondents' oral accounts and observed actions on the ground, resulting from overlooked mundane actions or intentional concealment of facts related to illicit activities.
iii. The moral dilemma of documenting illicit activities, questioning the researcher's responsibility in reporting and the potential implications of being involved in unethical practices.

To navigate these dilemmas, I coupled ethnography with photographic methods. While the former allowed for reflection, clarity and a record of the information, it did have limitations (Adhikari, 2018). Primarily, recording observations introduced a delay, potentially leading to missed real-time details. Photographic methods helped mitigate this issue by providing a visual record that supplemented the textual notes. The immediacy and accuracy afforded by this visual analysis helped bridge the gaps left by textual methods.

In my research, I used a Fujifilm XT3 Digital Camera and OnePlus 9 mobile phone for photography. Predominantly, I utilised my smartphone due to its less intrusive nature. The compact size and perceived casualness of the mobile phone, as opposed to the more conspicuous digital camera, made individuals more comfortable, thereby easing the consent process for photographs. The immediate on-screen viewing facilitated quick assessment and reflection, while the viewfinder or screen frame provided focused perspectives. The photography process often occurred after or alongside verbal interviews, influencing the framing of photographs. Employing an iterative approach, starting with an 'establishing shot' (Thirunarayanan, 2006), I zoomed in and out, juxtaposing fragments with the whole to decode ambiguous oral utterances and address the first dilemma of capturing oral accounts accurately.

To address the second dilemma, which involves resolving discrepancies between narratives and actions, I practised visual ethnography by actively engaging in shared activities with the respondents, such as walking, eating and even waiting in cramped spaces outside offices. I moved with the camera, following the subjects' movements, continuously observing, analysing and photographing while immersing myself in the experience. Using the camera or mobile phone screen, I repeated this cycle of observation and reflection. This sensory approach acknowledges that human experiences are not solely verbal or cognitive but also shaped by sensory perceptions, emotions and bodily sensations (Pink, 2015).

Resolving the third moral dilemma of documenting illicit activities involved adopting two ethnographic approaches: immersive presence (Roncoli et al., 2016) and maintaining distance using the *rear-mirror technique* (Wamsiedel, 2017). Immersion fostered trust and understanding of interviewees' vulnerabilities, capturing implicit cues and adding meaning to photographs. Conversely, the rear-mirror technique helped me maintain a critical distance from illicit scenes and activities. This allowed me to reflect on my biases and influence, ensuring I did not become too immersed in or influenced by the illicit activities being documented.

By maintaining a critical distance, I ensured ethical integrity and respect for participants' confidentiality. Striking a balance between these approaches enabled ethical considerations to guide documentation and analysis while respecting participants' rights and confidentiality.

My background as a photojournalist and documentary photographer significantly influenced my approach. Documentary photography (Hodson, 2021; Kratochvil, 2001) allowed me to delve into the intricacies of subjects over three months. Budgetary constraints necessitated a smaller sample of interviewees focused on a well-connected group to explore repair practices across various levels, which was facilitated by snowball sampling. Conversely, photojournalism (Becker, 1995; Kratochvil, 2001) honed my ability to capture and represent stories within limited timeframes, negotiate morally ambiguous situations and foster agility.

Drawing on these insights, I developed five routines to navigate the dilemmas encountered in my fieldwork. I term them as routines as they were informed by theoretical insights on repair and implemented during fieldwork. These routines serve as a photographic praxis that facilitates reflexive visual analysis. In the subsequent section, I will explain how these photographic routines, applied singularly or combined, helped interpret various forms of repair in Bhopal and Bhuj.

5. Visual Tales of Repair in Bhopal and Bhuj

Examining the informal water governance in Indian cities Bhopal and Bhuj reveals varied impacts on repair processes due to contrasting geographical and socio-political contexts. Bhopal, a state capital in central India, abundant with lakes, leans heavily on the distant Narmada River for water supply. Meanwhile, Bhuj, in an arid region on the north-western national border, rebuilt its water system following a 2001 earthquake, sourcing this from a canal linked to the Narmada River, located 700 km away (Sheth & Iyer, 2021).

Bhopal's water governance is fragmented and dominated by governmental bodies that often overshadow environmental NGOs and civil society's efforts, creating sporadic measures. Despite relying on an external source, the Narmada River, water security concerns appear less emphasised, reflecting a lack of urgency and unified vision for water management. This disconnect is noticeable in a report from the Comptroller and Auditor General of India (2021) and is reinforced by my fieldwork observations.

Conversely, Bhuj, a city hardened by repeated natural disasters, exhibits community resilience and self-organisation (Sheth & Iyer, 2017). Such conditions spur the growth of civil society groups addressing water security issues. However, my study reveals discordant approaches between these civil society organisations and local authorities, side-lining the former's efforts and downplaying the conditions which produced water issues.

Both cities showcased distinctive repair practices in response to their unique circumstances. In Bhopal, local governmental actors grappled with citizens' threatening behaviour (exemplified by Ram Singh) and departmental fragmentation (illustrated by Miheer Soni below). Water users in Bhopal also adopted informal strategies to sustain water provision by tinkering with the infrastructure.

Meanwhile, Bhuj residents demonstrated remarkable resilience, blending their professional duties with personal resolve to address water security issues, embodying the city's strong inclination towards community-led repair initiatives.

a) Scale-shifting photography: Unveiling interpersonal infrastructure as a means to repair

Intrigued by Ram Singh's informal approach to water management, revealed during his interaction with Farhan, I found it challenging to fully comprehend the influence of personal alliances on water access. With the aid of scale-shifting photography, I ventured deeper to try and make sense of the role of these alliances. Following the interview, I stepped away from the spot to capture an establishing shot and found myself instinctively drawn to photographing the larger infrastructure elements. The camera's zoom feature allowed a telescopic focus on subtler elements near and beneath the water tank, eliminating visual distractions within the frame. This oscillation between zooming in and zooming out allowed me to observe the relationship between part and whole, prompting a critical examination of what the infrastructure entailed. The collage of zoomed-in and zoomed-out photographs is seen in Figure 6.2. Initially drawn by the colossal scale of the OHT, the scale shifting led me to realise that the real essence of infrastructure lay in the personal alliances that choreograph the flow of water to the desired recipient.

Figure 6.2. Scale shifting photography at OHT. (30/9/2021)

b) Walking with a camera: Uncovering repair tactics to navigate interdepartmental relations

Miheer Soni*, an Assistant Engineer at Bhopal Municipal Corporation (BMC), deals daily with the intricate balance of maintaining water supply, managing public dissatisfaction and obtaining repair permissions. To comprehend these challenges, I joined Soni on an inspection walk with the State Public Works Department (PWD).

This first-hand experience unveiled the tensions Soni faces and his innovative approaches to alleviating bureaucratic constraints. The assertive demeanour of the higher ranking PWD officers was evident in their tone and gestures. In contrast, Soni displayed calmness as he methodically noted down the requirements, communicating them to his subordinates, illustrating his hierarchical position (see Figure 6.3 right).

However, at the junior level, the hierarchy blurred. I observed camaraderie between Soni's subordinates and the PWD junior reporting team, which offset the stern exchanges among their superiors. Their informal interactions

Figure 6.3. (Left) Soni (in blue checked shirt) waiting for the PWD officers. Meanwhile, his team exchanged greetings with PWD's team. (Right) Soni flanked by his men, displaying support and strength. (28/9/2021)

(see Figure 6.3 left) bridged bureaucratic gaps and expedited operations, contributing to the mending or *marammat* (returning to the original) of siloed operations.

Using a camera to document this walk offered a deeper understanding of Soni's professional environment, revealing nuances missed in our initial interview. While the walk could have been purely observational, the camera provided a focused lens, facilitating real-time analysis without peripheral visual distractions. Through this lens, the intellectual curiosities from our previous conversation – power dynamics, loyalty, subservience, obedience, fear, pride and respect – were visually depicted in their daily context. This inspection walk highlighted Soni's adeptness at navigating within the intricate relational dynamics to ensure operational smoothness.

c) Sensorial knowledge production: Decoding intention and situated expertise

During my interactions with Ramanbhai Patel* and Jyotsnaben Jadeja* in Bhuj, I was absorbed in multi-sensory experiences. Patel, a dedicated citizen, showcased his decade-long quest to get a lake notified, which is a long formal process of declaring a body of water as a lake in an urban area. Despite his unwavering effort, evidenced by stacks of diligently arranged documents, success remained elusive. Similarly, Jadeja, who worked in an action research organisation, conducted informative Sunday walks about the city's water sources and distribution. Her patience was evident as she took time to answer tangential questions, broadening the group's understanding beyond the immediate walk.

While their methods might not yield instant results, they were instrumental in fostering awareness of these issues among citizens. Patel and Jadeja's resilient efforts, showcasing their understanding of the challenges faced, embody the essence of *sudharna* (seeking betterment for the future). Their perseverance was tangible: I felt the weight and aged scent of Patel's paperwork, symbolising the endurance required for such advocacy (see Figure 6.4 left). Likewise, while photographing Jadeja, my own dust-covered state mirrored her disregard for the soiling of her clothes as she addressed inquiries (see Figure 6.4 right). Participating in shared activities with a camera made me aware of the peripheral influences on repair, such as dedication and thorough knowledge, shedding light on their ambitions and challenges.

Visualising Informal Repair 107

Figure 6.4. (Left) Patel presenting piles of paperwork required for lake notification requirements (21/12/2021); (Right) Jadeja engaging in soil-covered Q&A session while kneeling on the ground (19/12/2021)

d) Improvising photographic composition: Strengthening the representation of repair

Visual ethnography, an ongoing dialogue between camera and photographer, allowed my photographs to engage with the conceptual understanding of repair. These photographs embrace both content and composition.

Pareshbhai Patel*, a Bhuj school principal, initiated a systemic change by co-teaching water conservation and pollution to school children. Given the slow pace of educational curricular changes at the state or country level, without further ado, Patel collaborated with advocacy organisations and co-taught lessons as extensions of regular classes. His central position in the Figure 6.5 (left) captures his dynamic energy and optimism, essential for the reparative process of sudharna (seeking betterment).

In another instance in Bhopal, an interviewee highlighted how modern digital platforms like government websites can overwhelm citizens, leading many to use tools like WhatsApp for public participation. Citizens, municipal operators and party workers rely on these groups to share events and complaints, often supported with photographic evidence. This free social media platform effortlessly

108   Neha Mungekar

Figure 6.5.   (Left) The School principal in Bhuj explaining the importance of rainwater harvesting and conservation to his students centred in the photograph (16/12/2021); (Right) A supervisor effortlessly showing WhatsApp-enabled phone to display water kiosk updates in Bhopal's old city (03/12/2021).

coexists with modern digital platforms. The image of a phone showing the WhatsApp platform held by a supervisor (see Figure 6.5 right) illustrates the accessibility and integration of such tools alongside modern digital platforms, embodying *rafu karna* (bolstering the old with the new).

e) Long-form documentation approach: Discovering tools for repair

Observing patterns requires distance and demarcation. Patterns often hide in the mundane details of everyday life, subtly emerging through focused observation. My photographic journey, initially centred on the ordinary, unfolded over months and revealed a coherent pattern.

In Bhopal, citizens expressed concerns over groundwater quality, inadequate water pressure and irregular supply. To address this, they innovatively tinkered the existing infrastructure with everyday objects. The photo series (see Figure 6.6)

Figure 6.6.   First series showcasing ordinary objects to tinker the original physical water supply infrastructure. (3/10/21; 3/10/21; 18/11/21) Second series - Mobile phones becoming a norm to access easily. (6/1/22; 6/1/22; 6/1/22)

spotlights these adaptations, e.g. in the first series: (1) specialised pipes connecting to a water pump for propelling water to upper floors, (2) an unauthorised pressure pump and (3) a pipe for transferring groundwater from private bores into water tankers, subtly hiding their unofficial status. Local authorities were typically aware of these adaptations; some even tacitly approved them as they filled gaps in the water system. In Bhuj, despite available redressal platforms for water issues, grassroots government employees used mobile phones to improve accessibility to water services and respond to emergencies, becoming tools for socio-technical repair.

Upon revisiting the photographs, a recurring theme emerged. Over time, images initially captured for various reasons revealed a consistent theme of inventive adaptations and technology's role in social repair, embodying *Dosh rahit* (faultless repair).

6. Discussion and Conclusion

Through my field experiences and engagement with literature, I have appreciated the importance of informal governance processes and structures facilitating repair across legal, geographical and social contexts. Often undervalued due to their clandestine nature, I employed an ethnographic approach, complemented by digital photography, to capture these expressions of repair. Navigating the dynamics of informal governance arrangements presented me with three dilemmas, wherein the five routines proved invaluable for their resolution.

The first dilemma, ensuring the accuracy of oral accounts, was addressed by employing visual ethnography sensorially. This approach proved a powerful tool for understanding dedication, especially in cases like Jyotsnaben Jadeja's. Oral accounts, while providing hints at her intentions, often left much to interpretation. However, visual cues enabled a comprehensive interpretation of her unspoken markers when decoded using the routines.

The second dilemma was the resolution of discrepancies between oral accounts and actions. For vulnerable individuals like Ram Singh, who was worried about his job, verbal disclosures led him to alter or conceal facts. I cross-referenced with others, such as plumbers and supervisors, to verify Singh's account. This triangulation process highlighted inconsistencies, revealing the complexities of his situation. Additionally, looking through the screen or viewfinder highlighted overlooked elements, like everyday interactions, emphasising the significance of personal relationships within these informal systems.

The third dilemma was the ethical aspect of documenting illicit activities. The notion of 'distance' (Rose, 1997) was crucial in managing ethical challenges during research. Determining the extent of immersion, mainly when covering sensitive topics like illicit water pumps and knowing when to withdraw, was essential. I opted to respect the users' oral accounts, documenting their approaches through the less conspicuous medium – the smartphone. This approach was validated when local authorities acknowledged their awareness of these illicit measures, resolving my moral dilemma.

These routines revealed two types of repair – reactive and reparative. The former is a temporary measure to restore the status quo, while the latter focuses on

110   Neha Mungekar

localised efforts to facilitate reparation. Photographic methods, when incorporated with ethnography, provided a nuanced understanding of these dynamics. Integrating photographs and interview notes enriched the textual analysis, serving as meaningful 'codes' within qualitative coding software like ATLAS.ti.

Being an Indian ethnographer in unfamiliar Indian cities, I encountered 'situated dilemmas' (Ferdinand et al., 2007), influenced by my identity. Consent posed a challenge for some, as formal documentation was required for capturing informal actions in line with my institution's best practices. Affiliation with a Dutch organisation compelled me to have written consent, which a few participants perceived as a liability. To address this, I utilised verbal consent, maintaining ethical engagement while respecting Dutch transparency norms. Balancing these contrasting ethical considerations proved challenging throughout the research process.

Recognising my inherent subjectivity as a researcher was crucial to this study. My Indian nationality offered familiarity with the study sites. This cultural proximity facilitated trust with research subjects, allowing them to share 'open secrets' (Wamsiedel, 2017). Despite sharing an Indian identity, my metropolitan roots in Mumbai differed from the realities in Bhopal and Bhuj. Meanwhile, my Dutch association amplified perceived power differentials. The balance between these experiences guided my approach to power differentials and the concept of distance. The interviews became a platform for mutual exchange and personal reflection, prioritising respondents' motivations and perspectives over purely technological and planning aspects. This approach acknowledged the value-laden, historically contingent nature of oral accounts.

7. Returning to Ram Singh

Ram Singh's shushing gestures highlighted his balancing act between the covert aspects of interpersonal arrangements and formal mandates. Officially, he managed the OHT and water distribution, but pressure from residents led to unequal resource allocation. This deviation built essential personal networks with residents, facilitating operations. His informal management rectified governance processes which were ill-equipped for citizen-based threats.

The camera's lens and employment of the routines served as a gateway, illuminating the latent dynamics inhabiting the space beneath the OHT. Through this visual exploration, it became evident that this seemingly mundane location bore significant weight in dictating the decisions of water distribution.

End Notes

*Indicates pseudonyms used.

Acknowledgements

I thank my supervising committee – Dr Annelli Janssen, Dr Katharina Hölscher and Prof Derk Loorbach – as well as the editors of this book for their invaluable

Visualising Informal Repair **111**

guidance. This research is part of the Water4Change (W4C) programme, supported by the Dutch Research Council (NWO) – (Grant W 07.7019.103) and Indian Government Department of Science and Technology (Grant DST-1429-WRC). I express deep gratitude to all contributors, including the W4C programme's member institutions.

References

Adhikari, D. P. (2018). Ethnographic fieldnote writing: Methodological challenges in the 21st century. *Dhaulagiri Journal of Sociology and Anthropology, 12*, 98–106.

Ahlers, R., Cleaver, F., Rusca, M., & Schwartz, K. (2014). Informal space in the urban waterscape: Disaggregation and co-production of water services. *Water Alternatives, 7*(1), 1–14.

Becker, H. S. (1995). Visual sociology, documentary photography, and photojournalism: It's (almost) all a matter of context. *Visual Sociology, 10*(1–2), 5–14. https://doi.org/10.1080/14725869508583745

Bhan, G. (2019). Notes on a southern urban practice. *Environment and Urbanization, 31*(2), 639–654. https://doi.org/10.1177/0956247818815792

Broto, V. C., Westman, L., & Huang, P. (2021). Reparative innovation for urban climate adaptation. *Journal of the British Academy, 9*(s9), 205–218.

Comptroller and Auditor General of India. (2021). *General and social sectors for the year ended 31 March 2019, Government of Madhya Pradesh. Report 3 of the year 2019.* https://saiindia.gov.in/ag2/madhya-pradesh/en/audit-report/details/115252

Ferdinand, J., Pearson, G., Rowe, M., & Worthington, F. (2007). A different kind of ethics. *Ethnography, 8*(4), 519–543.

Gobo, G. (2008). What is ethnography? In *Doing Ethnography*. SAGE Publications Ltd. https://doi.org/10.4135/9780857028976

Goodman, J., & Marshall, J. P. (2018). Problems of methodology and method in climate and energy research: Socialising climate change? *Energy Research & Social Science, 45*, 1–11.

Henke, C. R. (2017). The sustainable university: Repair as maintenance and transformation. *Continent, 6*(1), 40–45.

Hodson, D. (2021). The politics of documentary photography: Three theoretical perspectives. *Government and Opposition, 56*(1), 20–38. https://doi.org/10.1017/gov.2019.3

Jaglin, S. (2014). Regulating service delivery in southern cities: Rethinking urban heterogeneity. In S. Parnell & S. Oldfield (Eds.), *The Routledge handbook on cities of the global south* (1st ed., pp. 434–447). Routledge. https://doi.org/10.4324/9780203387832

Kharel, D. (2015). Visual ethnography, thick description and cultural representation. *Dhaulagiri Journal of Sociology and Anthropology, 9*, 147–160.

Kratochvil, A. (2001). Photojournalism and documentary photography. *Nieman Reports, 55*(3), 27.

McFarlane, C. (2012). Rethinking informality: Politics, crisis, and the city. *Planning Theory and Practice, 13*(1), 89–108. https://doi.org/10.1080/14649357.2012.649951

Narain, V. (2000). India's water crisis: The challenges of governance. *Water Policy, 2*(6), 433–444. https://doi.org/10.1016/S1366-7017(00)00018-0

Perry, K. (2020). Realising climate reparations: Towards a global climate stabilization fund and resilience fund programme for loss and damage in marginalised and former colonised societies. SSRN 3561121.

Pink, S. (2013). *Doing visual ethnography* (3rd ed.). Sage.

Pink, S. (2015). *Doing sensory ethnography*. Sage.

112 Neha Mungekar

Roncoli, C., Crane, T., & Orlove, B. (2009). Fielding climate change in cultural anthropology. In S. Crate & M. Nuttall (Eds.), *Anthropology and Climate Change: From Encounters to Actions* (pp. 87–115). Left Coast Press.

Rose, G. (1997). Situating knowledges: Positionality, reflexivities and other tactics. *Progress in Human Geography, 21*(3), 305–320.

Roy, A. (2005). Urban informality: Toward an epistemology of planning. *Journal of the American Planning Association, 71*(2), 147–158. https://doi.org/10.1080/01944360508976689

Sheth, D., & Iyer, M. (2017). Opportunities and challenges in upscaling decentralized wastewater treatment plants city wide: Case of Bhuj. *SPANDREL-Journal of SPA: New Dimensions in Research of Environments for Living, 13*, 57–65.

Sheth, D., & Iyer, M. (2021). Local water resource management through stakeholder participation: Case study, arid region, India. *Water Practice and Technology, 16*(2), 333–343.

Thirunarayanan, R. (2006). *Visual communication of mood through an establishing shot.* Texas A&M University.

Wamsiedel, M. (2017). Approaching informality: Rear-mirror methodology and ethnographic inquiry. In A. Polese, C. C. Williams, I. A. Horodnic, & P. Bejakovic (Eds.), *The informal economy in global perspective: Varieties of governance* (pp. 97–115). Springer International Publishing. https://doi.org/10.1007/978-3-319-40931-3_6

Chapter 7

Traceless Transitions: Studying the Role of Drawings and Gestures in Construction Project Meetings

Evelijn Martinius

Vrije Universiteit, the Netherlands

Abstract

This chapter zooms in on how bodily gestures allow negotiations on upcoming works in an underground construction project, to transition into subsequent stages without leaving a trace. The gestures were observed during joint meetings of contractors/project managers in their work at an infrastructure mega project located in an international airport. These gestures conveyed meaning through acts of pointing, circling, shielding and bracketing in front of a digitally screened technical drawing. While these gestures entail no significant engineering skills or training, upon closer analysis, they reveal a refined craftsmanship. The gestures clarify, augment and suggest – but leave no visible, formal trace. The gestures convey meaning ambiguously compared to drawing or sketching – and leave no mark. As such, the meaning revealed through gesture remains tacit craftsman's knowledge. Enveloped within past events, it turns those present in the meeting into gatekeepers: only they have accessed local, tacit knowledge required to interpret the technical drawings correctly and make decisions on upcoming works that can progress infrastructure projects underground on time and within budget. Following the role of gestures therefore gives an account of the informal ways in which engineers negotiate progress in construction work.

Keywords: Gestures; drawings; meetings; negotiation; collaboration; underground

---

Informality in Policymaking: Weaving the Threads of Everyday Policy Work, 113–126
Copyright © 2025 by Evelijn Martinius
Published under exclusive licence by Emerald Publishing Limited
doi:10.1108/978-1-83797-280-720241008

114 *Evelijn Martinius*

Introduction

How many times have we listened to someone, completely captured, listening not just to what they were saying but were attuned with our whole bodies? As their story unfolds and their voice, their gestures and posture pulled us in even closer, as if we are witnessing a story coming into flesh.

We know that the power of gestures originates not from the isolated movement of hands but from a much broader arena that presupposes a sense of common ground among an in-group (Goodwin, 2014). The role gestures can play is closely interwoven with the cultural norms and practices of particular groups. Kendon writes, 'as such, gesturing, like speech, is influenced by cultural values and historical tradition, and its usage is adjusted to the setting, social circumstance, and micro-organization of any given occasion of interaction' (1997, p. 117). The setting of a meeting provides the stage for 'focused encounters' in which speech and gestures are part of the informal yet organisational principles commonly adhered to for communication (Kendon, 1990). Meetings are 'planned events' (Haug, 2013) where people come together with their individual needs to, for example, work out a problem, make decisions together or resolve conflict (Van Vree, 2011).

What might zooming in on the gestures of engineers in meetings tell us about their organisational culture? This chapter argues that four gestures – pointing, circling, shielding or bracketing with hands in relation to screened digital drawings, accompanied by speech – tell us something about the organisational culture in which these engineers operate. In what follows, I explore how gestures allow an informal transition in negotiations between project managers and asset managers from merely brainstorming to decision-making. Project managers are responsible for a timely and within budget delivery of reconstruction work on an underground utility network. The asset managers present must accept the delivered work, after which they will be responsible for maintaining the quality of the network's performance. During a sequence of bi-weekly meetings, they discuss upcoming work on underground utilities and decide how to proceed with unexpected difficulties in the construction work. While bearing different responsibilities, both project managers and asset managers are trained engineers. They are accustomed to working closely with technical drawings that visualise the envisioned 'end stage' of the technical design (see Henderson, 1994). Yet, while traditionally engineers are known to annotate and sketch on these drawings (Henderson, 1994), in this case engineers worked only with gestures. Although they were provided with the software and technical skills to 'make their mark' on these drawings, they did not touch the drawings. And so, I argue, the basis for their decisions cannot be traced by anyone outside of the meeting.

Physical, ephemeral gestures leave no mark. The possibility of touch mobilises touch technologies with the possibility of adding to reality. 'Which meanings are then mobilised for realising the promise of touch?' Puig de la Bella Casa asks (p. 303). Similarly, one could ask: which meanings are left immobile and remain only a gesture? What gestures are not, are touches. Touching is an act to come into contact with, or come to be, someone or something (according to the Oxford Dictionary, accessed 27 July 2023). Touch is prerequisite to the ability to draw:

the pencil has to be picked up in order to touch the paper. Although it does not always require physical connection, to touch someone or be touched also means to be affected by them. In the case of digital touch screens, haptic features invite the possibility of touching the invisible (Puig De La Bellacasa, 2009). It is not only that touch technologies 'make real' what otherwise remains immaterialised, but these technologies also promise their users a potential 'realness'. Like pencil marks on a drawing, digital marks add to reality because they leave a trace.

Gestures, Drawings and Familiar Interaction

It is a Tuesday afternoon. Upon entering the room, the main reference point for the engineers who participate in the meeting is the screen opposite to the table. On the screen the minutes of prior meetings will be displayed, as well as digital technical design drawings of underground utilities. The room is a typical meeting space, square with white walls, a suspended ceiling and fluorescent lights. I attended these bi-weekly meetings for one year as part of a larger ethnographic research project on the boundary negotiations between the project managers and asset managers, in underground infrastructure projects. During this year, the meeting was relocated once. The first location had no touch screen, the second location did have a touch screen TV on which the drawings were displayed. In both locations, the anticipated screening of the digital drawings was central to how meeting participants took their seat in the room. Representatives of the project organisation, asset management department of the airport and representatives of the contractor would pick a seat where they could face the screen. Some would push their chairs back once the drawings were displayed to better see the details. Other than the screen, only one participating project manager would take out his notebook, which he rarely used. Only the chairperson of the meeting and the secretary had a laptop in front of them. The chairperson used this to manage the displaying of minutes and drawings. The secretary used the laptop for keeping notes, for the minutes.

On the agenda for this meeting was the upcoming execution works at the construction site, all indicated using abbreviations for infrastructural elements like pillars, pipes or cables. After the first act of going through the minutes, the next item on the agenda was the discussion of these upcoming works which took up the majority of their hour, or sometimes 1.5-hour, session. These updates on upcoming works spoke to a need that the asset managers, in particular, felt was their last opportunity to have a say over how the reconstruction work was planned and would be carried out.

The aim of these meetings was to align the planning and activities at the construction site among the participants in the room, who each represented different organisations with an interest in the construction area. Participating representatives were responsible for their organisation assets, the underground utilities buried in the area that were to be re-routed or replaced so as to service a new above-ground terminal being built. As a way of resolving the clashing interests between parties, which had become an obstacle to the project progressing, project partners launched a special 'underground' meeting.

116   Evelijn Martinius

Meeting participants were all technically trained, and most of them had worked on the airport's utilities for a long time. They were known as the 'underground people', all experts in their particular underground utilities including electricity, water and gas. While they all shared among each other a technical knowledge on underground utilities, they represented three distinct 'tribes': the asset managers, the project managers and the contractors' managers. The asset managers owned the utilities, and their formal responsibility was to take care of the existing infrastructures, ensure the performance of these assets and arrange timely restoration or maintenance works. Instead of maintenance, project management was responsible for development. 'We are judged by what we deliver', a lead project manager explained. The construction of the project was in the hands of the third group, the contractors, whose management presence at the meetings I observed was mainly concerned with construction works.

In what follows, I zoom in on the gestures that repeatedly were exhibited as participants discussed technical drawings of underground utilities during their wider conversations of upcoming construction work (see Table 7.1).

Table 7.1.   Overview of when technical drawings featured during the meeting.

Part of the meeting	Participants	Chairperson	Screen	Cursor	Gestures
Walk in	Sitting down to face the screen	Takes seat	Off	Not used	None
Opening of the meeting	Going through minutes of previous meeting, discussing any additional agenda points	Seated	On, showing minutes	Not used	None
Discussion on construction work	Discussing upcoming works at the construction site	Standing in front of the drawing	On, showing the drawing	Indicating an area by pointing or drawing lines (that are not saved)	Pointing, circling shielding, bracketing
Closing of the meeting	Round table, rounding off discussion points	Seated	Ignored but showing last discussed drawing	Not used	Not used

Pointing

The chairperson of the meeting, nicknamed John, puts a drawing up on the screen. John works for the contractor. He is still seated and uses the cursor on his laptop to point out a specific blue line. 'This is what we just finished, and this is where we have to go underneath', he comments. 'Good, so that is going well, you are finished on time', the project managers comment as they nod their heads approvingly. One of the asset managers looks more puzzled. 'But that new piece that you are connecting, underneath, does it get connected to these ones over here?', he raises his voice. His comment raises confusion. 'What is he talking about, what are we actually looking at?', the project managers respond.

'There, yes, there is a gas pipeline that is contained in a gigantic PVC wrapping', one of the asset owners comments as he points his finger towards the screen. Then, he sits to the back of his chair, arms folded in front of him. He and the other participants look at the design drawing of utilities that shows part of the location on which construction work will start to renew parts of the utility infrastructure network, by next week. With his comment, the asset manager wants to clarify to the others that the single line on the screened technical design drawing, in reality, is covered by a bundle of PVC material. The single yellow line on paper means in this case a bundle of cables that are buried below. This means that the gas pipe is not as easily accessible as one might expect from just looking at the drawing. However, what seemed like a detailed comment during the meeting exchange I learned earlier was a crucial piece of information. During an earlier conversation I had with one of the project managers, he confided in me that this information type is crucial for meeting project deadlines. Without this information, the contractor would have scheduled less time, run into the PVC wrapping and would not be able to finish the job. With the tight planning schedule they must keep to, such small 'surprises' are actually the reason that projects derail and go over budget. Small comments like these were crucial for the contractor who could now decide how to proceed by scheduling in more time by either using this informal and implicit piece of advice or taking the risk of stopping the work and asking for more budget from his client to deal with the PVC wrapping.

In responding to the comment, the chairperson directs his cursor to the yellow line the asset owner had commented on. He holds the cursor still as it hovers over the yellow line, as if to indicate the focus point. The asset manager does not correct him, so possibly the cursor is now on the right location. Typically, the contractor used his cursor to articulate the specific area or cable of interest for the point on the agenda at the start of the discussion. At this stage, interpreting the drawing was still happening relatively freely and without immediate consequences or informal advice on decisions. In this specific case, the contractor took his cursor to the yellow line as a way to verify the exact location of the PVC wrapping. He made perhaps a mental note of the location but made no mark on the drawing with his cursor. Consequently, the design drawing still showed the misleading information. And therefore, 'officially', the contractor could still claim extra budget because he was not informed of the additional work required for removing the PVC wrapping in order to access the gas pipe he needed to renew. The contractor continues to propose how this new information changes their upcoming work. He remains seated, and his voice is as monotonal as usual. Using the cursor, he is directing the participants' eyes to where the utilities of concern are located. Because of his unimpressed response, and the relatively small additional work that is required to remove the package, he does not add that the project managers can expect a demand for additional budget or time. Still, little interactions like these signalled that despite being in a shared meeting, a shared interest or common goal was not necessarily present. The goal of the contractor was not only to be informed but also to potentially use that information to claim extra budget and more time.

Pointing out specific details on the screened drawing aided the first stage of the discussion; it centred everyone's attention and focus on a specific issue. To support the discussion, digitalised technical drawings were brought onto the screen by the chairperson of the meeting. Usually opened as PDF-files, there was a great deal of zooming in involved so that everyone could read the details plotted on these drawings, also as it was not self-evident to participants where exactly to look. After a drawing was put on the screen, what followed was a moment in which people started to interpret what they could see out loud, to the group, as the contractor tried to direct everyone's attention to a particular piece of infrastructure. Participants mentioned what the piece of infrastructure reminded them of, such as a nearby water sewage, or an electricity distribution point. Or they mentioned stakeholders in that area. Working on the opposite side from a bus stop meant someone had to inform the bus company and the airlines that traffic to their offices might be hindered. Pointing to specific details, using hand gestures or the cursor, helped to direct the scattered, associative interpretations of participants to a specific issue.

Circling

Technical drawings go through several iterations as they are created, reviewed and edited. Similar to the production process, the construction of infrastructures is also first envisioned in a design drawing. These can take the form of three-dimensional (3D) models using specific software for the built environment. Technical drawings iterate through several stages, for example, the terminal was first envisioned in a conceptual design. At this point in the process, technical drawings look more like 3D models, typically visualising the above-ground building or complex in its end stage. The drawing should also provide clients with a sufficient level of detail so that they can estimate the costs, the functionality and the aesthetics of the proposed end stage. During the preliminary design stage, the drawings are reviewed and edited according to stakeholders' input. For example, the client organisation's technological requirements are accounted for. Then, the construction design drawings are made by the contractor. Once the works are finished, the contractor is supposed to provide the project organisation with the 'as-built' drawings, using the coordinates of how the utilities landed in the subsoil. After the project is 'delivered' to the asset managers, the client organisation, the as-built drawings are archived so that the client organisation knows where their assets are buried.

Technical drawings of the utility network were typically put up on the screen whenever there was an unexpected event hindering the planned upcoming construction work on underground utilities. The following shows an example of a typical interaction during a discussion on upcoming works. When there was an issue with unexpected works, John would raise the matter with his clients. In one meeting, he raises concerns about contaminated soil that would potentially delay the start of construction work:

'Where are we?' one of the asset managers asks. 'We're at the corner, opposite to the bus stop'. Pointing at an orange area on a screened, utilities drawing, John indicates where soil is contaminated with PFAS (perfluoroalkylated substances) and has to be removed. 'But did you not remove it just a few weeks back?' a project manager asks. 'We need to go deeper, to get everything out. 'You are working in a delicate corner guys', one of the asset owner's comments. 'And then what is that orange line over there? Are you removing that area as well? There are vulnerable cables lying there'. John's client is worried. John gets up from his chair, and starts to stand in front of the drawings with his back to the rest of the group. He is circling with his fingers over a rather large area that only partially crosses the orange lines. 'This is the working area', he says. He tries to minimise the risk to the asset manager by circling around the orange lines on the drawing. Those represent electricity cables, and their fragility worries the asset owner. Excavations might damage the performance of the network. But his circling finger spurs some concerns with the project managers. 'Well, if you are working that corner, you might as well pick up the works planned in May' a project manager comments, unrelatedly to either the fragile electricity cables or the contaminated soil. 'You will have a technical challenge on your hands in that area in May, so you might as well start the preparations? If you want to be smart with your time ... ' another project manager responds, adding to the concerns of his colleague. The contractor gets impatient. 'Do we need to look at another solution?' he asks, not really getting a response. Asset managers and project managers have started separate discussions by now, debating each other's knowledge on the specific location. Each chimes in from their own expertise. 'I could schedule in a separate meeting for us to go into this' the secretary of the meeting proposes, trying to conclude the discussion. 'Yes, that might be better' the chairperson adds, as he sits down again. This marks the end of their discussion.

This vignette shows how in circling over an area on the drawing, John used the drawing to discuss a change to the planned works but is stopped in his tracks by

120   *Evelijn Martinius*

an asset manager who knows remediation might be a risk to the performance of the telecom and electricity network at that specific location. John initiated this update to inform the others around the table about the surprising finding that the soil in the construction area was contaminated more than had been anticipated in the initial planning phase. However, instead of the contaminated area, the drawing showed an orange line, causing alarm among the asset owners around the table. This generated an idea from the asset manager present. John's announcement on soil remediation was hijacked by worries about vulnerable cables that were buried in the same area. The asset owner ignored John's question about the remediation works given the drawing alerted him to a risk that he then assessed. As the display did not show in any visual way the target area John was talking about, it was easier for the asset owners to just focus on the cables. Given the assumed fragility of these cables, the asset owners were not too eager to support remediation works near 'their' cables. Damaging one of them could happen easily and trigger a major impact on above-ground services.

Circling over an area with a hand and collecting information about a location mirrors how technical drawings are updated with every iteration they go through.

Shielding

> 'It is not clear to me why we are now talking about this line', John says, 'we should look at this area'. He gets up from his chair and now stands in front of the drawing. With his back to the group, he points to the orange line that the asset owner is worried about. 'This particular cable is not of any concern right now'. He turns around to the group. 'You are now starting to discuss future work that just happens to be in the same area'. The asset manager looks at him, eyebrows raised. 'Well at least somebody is thinking ahead – right?' John ignores his comment and turns back around. 'Try not to think about what lies underneath', he says. He folds his hands over each other so as to form a shield that covers up the orange line on the screen. 'We will work around those vulnerable cables; decoupling them is planned for later'. He looks over his shoulder to the asset manager. 'Just remember this is future work .... For now, any work on fragile cables will be suspended, and we just want to remove this area'.

John's shielding with his hands the vulnerable assets worked in two ways: shielding the orange line was a way of removing it from the picture, as well as 'adding' another layer to the map that represented the superficial, contaminated soil that he wanted to remove. With these gestures, and the accompanying words that he will not work on the fragile cables, the asset owners saw no harm in the remediation activities. Augmenting the digital map with his body, John created a hybrid representation that, for this specific moment, facilitated agreement on the remediation activities planned. The participants in the meeting refrained from making assumptions about what lay beneath and did their upmost best to verify information on the drawings. Early on in the project, scans and test trenches of the specific project site were used to calculate the margin of error. These scans and test trenches estimated the 'probability' that the data on the location of utilities on which the designs were based were accurate. Still, each participant was eager to learn from each other, knowing that their tacit knowledge that was built on years of experience told them more about the specific location and network than databases or technical drawings did.

Drawings, sarcastically called 'colouring books' by the participants, were intensely detailed, yet obscured a lot of vital information. The drawings, for example, did not show z-coordinates. In the project, the contractor was tasked with collecting data on the depth of buried utilities. This was business as usual. But the asset managers did not plan to incorporate the z-coordinate in their database. Within their databases, the drawings were instead plotted using the x and y-coordinates. The main argument provided by the asset managers was that the software system was incapable of handling another variable. Moreover, the contractor collected the absolute depth, measured from the sea level. But the airport was located about four meters below the sea level. At the construction site, no contractor would recalculate the absolute measure into a relative measure, the asset managers reasoned. Consequently, the wrong measure would show up on the excavation machine and create the wrong expectations.

'If we manage that information, we are also responsible for its accuracy', one of the other asset managers continued. If a z-coordinate accompanied those drawings, he argued, then this might reflect a level of accuracy that cannot be met in reality. For one, there was the natural 'moving' of cables below ground. They have a range of movement in going below and coming up again but also a range in which they swing from side to side. Providing information on the depth of the utilities was simply redundant and risky. When asked how contractors were supposed to know the depth of buried utilities, a prominent asset manager in the project argued that the z-coordinate was 'a non-issue'. He argued professionals already knew the norms and therefore did not need a z-coordinate. Professionals know from experience and training that gas 'always' has to be buried at least 80 centimetres below, for example. And there were similar norms for all the other disciplines. Thus, the asset managers concluded – measures of depth were not useful.

Additionally, what was not on these digital visualisations of underground infrastructures were the abandoned or 'orphan' cables and the ruins of earlier buildings or constructions. Partially this was to do with the history of the construction site location. The soil in the construction area had not been touched for 30 years, and a lot had since changed. Back in those days, there were not many rules for clearing away anything that was no longer functioning. What could be buried would not be seen, and so 'it did not exist anymore', as one of the asset managers commented sceptically. It is also cheaper to work around old cables and construction than removing everything. And there was plenty of space then, he joked. Nowadays, space is scarce and every inch is valuable, and so part of the work on the construction site now included removing abandoned elements and orphaned cables that took up space intended for new purposes.

122 Evelijn Martinius

In sum, shielding with hands was a way of painting a picture for the others around the table – a way to visualise a local reality *not* displayed on the map. In the vignette shared here, John's announcement on soil remediation was hijacked by worries about vulnerable cables that were buried in the same area. Augmenting the digital map with his hands, John created a hybrid representation that – for that specific moment – facilitated agreement on the remediation activities planned.

Bracketing

'We will first start to work on this area', John said as his hands bracket around parts of the orange line. As the discussion comes to a close, John has gained agreement from the asset managers for his plan to continue removing the contaminated soil. 'Then we will continue here', he comments as his hands move right, following the line. 'And finally, this is the last part that will be renovated', he says, as he moves his hands further right. The gesture his hands make would typically be used once the informal plan of action was decided on. So as the discussion finishes, John translates the plan of action into a timeline. His hands are in an upright position, with some space in between the right and left hands.

When John starts bracketing in front of the technical drawing, this is the first cue to participants that the negotiations were being taken into the planning stage. The time had come to start translating the complexity of the solution they came up with into a workable timeline. As the drawings were static representations, they did not visualise the planning or the construction work as a process. Drawings represent either a future image or an 'as-built' state. The gestures John made add therefore another reality to the technical drawing and to the planning process.

More commonly in contractor–client relations, claiming 'extra work' for unexpected events is a core issue – and so a contractor proposing a timeline is a moment for project managers to pay attention. The project manager wants to control their budget, but the contractor has often tendered for a low price to get the job, meaning that their profits are expected to come from the 'extra work'. This is not only true for small-scale projects but also holds for this megaproject. However, in that informal meeting, money was not (really) an issue. People attending the meeting were not personally managing any budgets. The 'moment' that is created – and it is always the contractor who gets up in front of the drawing – is not simply a performance to legitimise a claim for extra budget. It is also an attempt to find a solution to a problem that cannot be solved in isolation. In bracketing with his hands, John signalled to the others that their time to think along, to 'make sense' again of the surprises and find a collective solution had come to an end. From there on, the contractor again took the lead.

The bracketing with his hands was the last gesture John made before he sat back down in his chair, although it would not be the last time the participants discussed the remediation works that were planned. Knowingly, one of the asset managers continued to look at John with scepticism. 'It's all right with me. We all know that if you start excavating, you always find something you did not expect', he mumbled to himself. It may indeed well be that the same topic would reappear next week, depending on what comes up and derails the plan.

Dust to Dust

My intention in this chapter has been to highlight how gestures, drawings and negotiations temporarily wove together a future vision of the 'whole' underground work that faded as soon as the moment was over. What evidences the temporality of these negotiations about the drawings was how the discussions and annotations remained undocumented. Drawings were not corrected, and remarks about the underground were not documented in minutes. As mentioned previously, there was no real 'end' to the discussion – meaning that no concluding part to the meeting occurred. Participants started to feel the ending of the meeting neared when the clock struck three, and without a formal closing or conclusion, they stood up from their chairs or started talking about football or their weekends. Only once was a remark made by a participant about how to properly close the issues they had actively negotiated during the meeting.

> As the chairperson of the meeting tries to move on to the next point on his agenda, one of the participants in the room stops him. 'Wait a minute' this engineer blatantly interrupts. 'How do we keep track of the actions that we just finalised? Do we keep a record of that somewhere? Or do we just drop them from our list, and we never see them back again?'. He looks around the room at the other participants of the meeting. 'Well, you would have to read the minutes wouldn't you, then you'll see what works are finished?' the minutes secretary retorts. 'Exactly', someone else seconds. 'I make a new report every week. So, you can look into at least 52 reports already'. The questioner cleared his throat as if to announce himself with gravity. 'So, we do not keep a list' he concludes to himself out loud. 'Correct' the minutes secretary chastises. 'We do not keep a list'.

Unlike sketching, or drawing on paper drawings, working with digital drawings as illustrated in this chapter leaves no marks or traces – even though the software and technology allowed for these experts to leave their marks. When opening the file with drawing software, the chairperson of the meeting sometimes started drawing and marking the digital file in order to mark the area of interest or draw the alternative route for a cable that cannot be buried the way it was planned. While this happed occasionally, typically this method was not used. Moreover, when the contractor did draw using his software, he closed the file without saving the changes. What this implies is that the corrections to the official design drawings, or the augmentations to it, were not to be recorded.

Discussion

In his review of anthropological studies on gesture, Kendon suggests that gestures differ between cultures (1997). Thirty years ago, engineers' culture has been characterised as being predominantly visually oriented, and that it gravitates to the

124 Evelijn Martinius

use of drawings and sketches (Henderson, 1994). 'With gestures, speakers use a mode of expression that renders invisible form part of what is meant by the utterance', Kendon argues (1997, p. 112).

Why would engineers gesture and not draw? Goodwin (2003a), for example, shows that archaeologists' ability to 'see' outlines of artefacts in soil rely on symbiotic gestures and that pointing out in the actual soil what is relevant simultaneously references archaeological categories and practices. But in the meetings studied here, engineers' gestures in relation to a technical drawing similarly create a landscape relevant within the setting of construction work on underground utilities (see Table 7.2 for an overview) – although these gestures do not transition into scribbles or sketches. The temporal landscape is only accessible to the meeting participants.

Goodwin argues that gestures build professional vision. In his example, one junior learns to see what the senior archaeologist identifies as meaningful archaeology through following the shapes in the soil that are pointed out to her (Goodwin, 2003b). Consequently, perspicuous actions like pointing can have large political consequences – not just because gestures build what professionals see but also what will be ignored. While an inscription of a pointing action re-organises the domain of scrutiny to invite others' judgement (Goodwin, 2003b), gestures are ephemeral.

It was Taussig (2013) who said he was shocked to discover how his own fondness of drawing with a pencil in a paper sketchbook evoked within him a measure of control over what he saw; something that could serve as testimony to his witness. Like the touch screen that is not touched, the cursor does not draw. Nor do they desire to. There were no marks saved during these meetings, besides the announcements in minutes. Corrections to the drawings, annotations and augmentations evaporated into thin air, leaving it unclear on what grounds who

Table 7.2. Overview of how gestures in relation to a technical drawing concentrated discussions on future work.

Gesture	Drawing	Talk	Implications
Pointing	A line or point	Negotiating dispersed interests	Concentrating all participants towards the same issue
Circling	An area	Negotiating site specific knowledge	Collecting and updating knowledge on the issue in focus
Shielding	An area	Bringing in absent presences	Augmenting the absences in the drawing
Bracketing	Lines on the drawing	Negotiating a work planning	Process oriented proposals related to time and planning work

was to be held accountable. Wanting to draw and wanting to be documented are perhaps different things, although even documentary photographers argue their fondness for their medium comes from its ability to leave a mark and create a testimony. 'It's very important, for me to trace people's histories before I lose them', Nan Goldin wrote about her documentary photographs (Ruddy, 2009, pp. 347–348).

The willingness to be documented, to be noticed and not get lost, perhaps intersects with the willingness to be 'touched', to be affected by another (Puig de La Bellacasa, 2009; Ruddy, 2009). What happens then in a space where professionals turn their back on their pencils and papers? What does it say about the profession of engineers who have been so long associated with their pencils and their large, chalk paper drawings (Henderson, 1994)? What is it to desire a traceless gesture over an observable mark?

Engineers' reliance upon transient, ephemeral and informal gestures in a highly controlled, hyper-transparent and risk averse project environment alerts us to an important undercurrent in their meeting. Possibly, the intimacy in the meeting kindled a tolerance for traceless gestures, keeping the scrutiny of organisational politics outside the meeting. Leaving no trace could protect these engineers against possible backlash on their decisions and secure their knowledge from becoming a shared resource. Evidential knowledge relies on tangible evidence rather than 'bare belief' – and being 'in touch' with its material reality bears an opportunity to participate in re-doing it (Puig de la Bellacasa, 2009). Yet the engineers in this case refrained from re-doing technical drawings. Nor did they

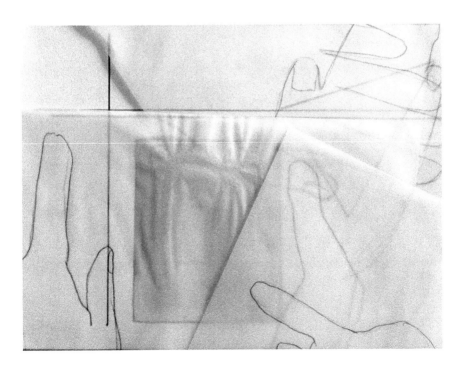

126 *Evelijn Martinius*

seek to build traces to evidence the legitimacy of their decisions. As meetings are considered as the place where interdependency is regulated through talking and decision-making (Freeman, 2008; Van Vree, 2011), it is remarkable that there was hardly any talk or decisions about what goes into the minutes. Record keeping is arguably intrinsic to regulation (Freeman & Maybin, 2011). Tolerating fleeting gestures to steer decisions on future work signals an intimate setting in which insiders grant themselves the liberty to keep accountability in an in-group matter.

References

Freeman, R. (2008). Learning by meeting. *Critical Policy Analysis, 2*(1), 1–24.

Freeman, R., & Maybin, J. (2011). Documents, practices and policy. *Evidence & Policy, 7*(2), 155–170.

Goodwin, C. (2003a). The body in action. In J. Coupland & R. Gwyn (Eds.), *Discourse, the body, and identity* (pp. 19–43). Palgrave Macmillan.

Goodwin, C. (2003b). Pointing as situated practice. In K. Sotaro (Ed.), *Pointing: Where language, culture and cognition meet* (pp. 217–231). Erlbaum.

Goodwin, C. (Ed.). (2014). *The intelligibility of gesture within a framework of co-operative action*. John Benjamins Publishing Company.

Haug, C. (2013). Organizing spaces: Meeting arenas as a social movement infrastructure between organization, network, and institution. *Organization Studies, 34*(5–6), 705–732.

Henderson, K. (1994). The visual culture of engineers. *The Sociological Review, 42*(1), 196–218.

Kendon, A. (1990). *Conducting interaction: Patterns of behaviour in focused encounters*. Cambridge University Press.

Kendon, A. (1997). Gesture. *Annual Review of Anthropology, 26*, 109–128.

Oxford Dictionary. (2023, July 27). *Definition of touch from the Oxford Advanced Learner's Dictionary*. Oxford Learner's Dictionaries.

Puig De La Bellacasa, M. P. (2009). Touching technologies, touching visions. The reclaiming of sensorial experience and the politics of speculative thinking. *Subjectivity, 28*(1), 297–315.

Ruddy, S. (2009). "A radiant eye yearns for me": Figuring documentary in the photography of Nan Goldnig. *Feminist Studies, 25*(2), 347–380.

Taussig, M. (2013). What do drawings want? In N. Curtis (Ed.), *The pictorial turn* (pp. 166–177). Routledge. https://doi.org/10.4324/9781315875873

Van Vree, W. (2011). Meetings: The frontline of civilization. *The Sociological Review, 59*, 241–262.

Chapter 8

Vehicles of In|formality – The Role of the Car as a Mobile Space of Policy and Relational Work

Tamara Mulherin

Northumbria University, UK

Abstract

The materiality of policy worlds – buildings, mobile phones and carparks – has been an under-examined aspect of policy relations. Everyday materialities are routinised in such a way they are enacted as trivial, contributing to an indifference towards the roles they play. In particular, the role of the car and quite what happens aside from driving is largely overlooked. How relations are re-assembled through the small threshold spaces of car interiors, where actors are suspended between two states – neither here nor there – affects everyday work. Latterly, the car has become a complex communicative assemblage for multi-tasking, a coordination centre for telephone, global positioning system (GPS), internet, etc., a place of work, but cars are also places of refuge, comfort zones for affective regulation via the sound system. This chapter explores from a multi-sited, inter-organisational ethnography in rural Scotland how cars are vital in mobilising relations for the implementation of legislation requiring certain National Health Services (NHSs) to integrate with local government social care services. Given rurality, actors' cars were used to travel around the area. I suggest a focus on taken-for-granted materials, like cars, can unsettle policy understandings, engendering thinking beyond 'formal' policy practices, to illuminate acts of implementing 'through things' (de La Bellacasa, 2011). Materialities provide a novel way of interrogating policy practices unfolding in assorted in|formal settings, in this case, conveyed via vehicles. The car is a site whereby often unnoticed doings are produced through relations between bodies,

---

Informality in Policymaking: Weaving the Threads of Everyday Policy Work, 127–144
Copyright © 2025 by Tamara Mulherin
Published under exclusive licence by Emerald Publishing Limited
doi:10.1108/978-1-83797-280-720241009

objects and places. These relations are spatially and temporally enfolded and constitute policy work, particularly in rural areas.

Keywords: Cars; materiality; ethnography; rurality; relationality; policy work

1. What Is It With Cars? Encountering Mobile Interfaces of In|formality

In the early 2000s, long before video conferencing, and smart phones, a common feature of the jobs I worked in as a public servant/manager in rural Australia was the requirement to drive. Whether that was back and forth from the metropolitan policy centre, or across regions for various meetings, driving for hours to meet face to face, even for one hour, was characteristic of these roles. Moreover, sharing rides with other practitioners on long-distance journeys was a regular occurrence. As a practitioner, these mundane experiences attuned me to the activities that go on in these particular mobile spaces beyond being just a mode of transport, especially the relational work associated with mobilising policy, what Peck (2003) describes as 'policies "in motion"' (p. 229), ensuring action at a distance (Carter, 2018).

Figure 8.1. Journey in Kintra. *Source*: Author's own (2016).

Fast forward to 2016, amid ethnographic fieldwork, a time which saw ambitious legislation commence for NHS boards and local government social care services in Scotland, whereby integrated authorities in each local government area were established. The emphasis of the legislation was on reconfiguration of health care and social care services, known as Health and Social Care Integration (HSCI), a flagship policy epitomising public service reform in which normative aspirations of collaboration were central (Mulherin, 2022). And managers – the local policy actors – were expected to implement it. Through the course of fieldwork, I observed how NHS and council managers enacted collaboration as they attempted to operationalise integrated care, interrogating how they worked to both rearrange and hold things together behind the scenes, away from the frontlines of direct care, immersed in spaces of governance and operations.

Ubiquitous objects were central to managers' work, e.g., mobiles and tablets, ensuring their availability when away from their desks. Given Kintra's rurality, all the managers had cars, which they used to drive back and forth from the Council to the Hospital, to other Council and NHS offices and community organisations in the area. Some managers also commuted from across central Scotland and even England. The car was essential for a manager's work, but they were also personal artefacts that belonged to the individual. The extent of driving stood in contrast to apocryphal stories I heard from managers who grew up in Kintra about people not travelling outside their communities, with multiple sites of service delivery reflecting a tenet of the area that I was told was parochialism. While a manager needed to use their car to get to these varied points of delivery, the length of organisational memory and community memory, for a manager, was important to understand.

To situate this chapter, aided by images contained throughout this chapter, my ethnography describes a place I call Kintra,[1] a rural corner of Scotland. A place where the history of the Council can be traced back to the 12th century (Taylor, 2016) and the NHS to 1948 (Lewis, 2001). Kintra was a large rural area with an ageing population of over 100,000 people, with close to 50% living in smaller villages or remote areas. These enumerated particulars, however, are limited in their representations. My early fieldnotes variously described the area as beautiful, a 'rural idyll' with 'sodden fields' and 'rolling hills'; as an 'assault of greenery', 'prone to flooding and snow'; where the 'weighty histories' of towns and villages scattered across the area mattered. Balancing demands from these communities, while delivering services equitably across Kintra, was an enduring dilemma for managers. Kintra was a place where 'national laws and policies were being translated; not just any policy, but particular legislation that was attempting to realise a longstanding ambition of the Scottish Government' (Mulherin, 2022, p. 132). While some staff flippantly referred to it as 'teuchtar-land', 'cut off via topographic barriers', (Mulherin, 2022, p.133). Kintra was connected to other Councils, NHS boards, national agencies and the Scottish Government,

---

[1]Kintra is Scots for country, rurality (www.dsl.ac.uk, accessed 28 November 2020). This name, the names of towns and actors in this chapter are all pseudonyms to protect the anonymity of those involved in the research and the area it took place in.

sustained by technological territories of affiliative objects (Gherardi, 2010, pp. 82-87), including, legislation, policies, plans, emails and people. Geographic distance between Kintra and Scottish government offices in Edinburgh was viewed as advantageous, as they wouldn't attract government attention, from which I inferred NHS Kintra and Kintra Council could do their own thing (Mulherin, 2022, pp. 130–133).

In what follows, I explore the experiences of car travel with managers, and consider through observations how cars affected policy work when treated by practitioners as an inconsequential means for getting around that bore no relation to the delivery of policy; a 'regular occurrence … constituting part of the unreflexive, habitual practice' (Binnie et al. in Holmes & Hall, 2020, p. 9) of doing their jobs. As an ex-manager of rural care services in Australia, the car was vital for sustaining both intra- and inter-organisational relations, not just in being transported here and there but for what went on during journeys and the work involved within. I show how cars mobilised managers on behalf of their organisations, hither and thither, but as personal objects they operated as a threshold, a permeable space between work life and personal life – a generative site of the in|formal. Settings such as cars also allow for informal arrangements in the way they bring actors (and actants) into contact with each other, the consequence of propinquity, i.e., closeness. Given these features, I suggest that a focus on automobility provides a fruitful lens to reveal the connections between different trajectories of policy that develop through blended formal and informal everyday managerial practices within their operational context.

I offer an account of how informality and formality might fold into one another and highlight some of the ways in which this might transform policy intentions. As an unexceptional object unnoticed because of its ordinariness, cars 'are so embedded in the tacit, embodied routines that underpin, but are nevertheless crucial to, everyday life' (Buse et al., 2018, p. 244), contributing to an

Figure 8.2.   Haith Royal Infirmary – wrapped in carparks. *Source*: Author's own (2016).

Vehicles of In\formality   **131**

indifference towards the role they play. A seemingly banal object as a car exposed relations meaningful in their mundanity, which I want to demonstrate had localised effects when it came to policy ambitions, actively constituting relations for policy implementation, with the aim to generate new insights and new questions concerning policy work (Wagenaar, 2018).

I zoom in to share, in excerpts from car journeys with a manager called Samuel, how this affected his role in enacting HSCI implementation, given his 'geographically stretched responsibilities' (Klocker et al., 2015). As the primary care manager, his NHS services were inextricably connected on a day-to-day basis with social care. I show how HSCI policy travelled through entangled modes of in\formality, namely, distributed spatial relations, and simultaneity, where actors are entwined in multiple practices while driving in cars. Managers made the most of journey time while fulfilling the requirement to be present in diverse sites of activity. As Laurier et al. point out,

> while car trips might be thought of as a form of 'suspended animation as it passes from A to B. ... [T]heorists of speed and mobility ... have turned this notion around, animating the suspension, as it were, and placing movement at the heart of how our societies and cultures are continuously organised. (Laurier et al., 2008, p. 2)

In this 'open[ing] up the interior of the car, as it journeys, as a place of import ... and substantial interest for social science investigations' (Laurier et al., 2008, pp. 20–21), I then briefly reflect on the effect of HSCI policy's encounter with the Kintra carescape.

2. The Compounding Everyday Predicaments of HSCI

I shadowed HSCI management team members over five days each in order to aid my understanding of their role, its relationship with HSCI and their approach to collaboration. I spent a lot of time with Samuel, who was the NHS General Manager of Primary Care. He had a wide remit and was well regarded for his diplomatic manner and skills as a trouble-shooter, he prioritised relationship management, appeared to dress in the same navy suit every day and expressed love for his BMW. What follows are extracts of my fieldnotes from between February and April 2016, when he was dealing with operational challenges and the 'politics' of HSCI. His diary was often full, involving meetings across a number of towns. When I began shadowing Samuel, he detailed the dynamics of his job.

> In the car, he talked about being on call for primary care/community and now acute which impacts his weekend. NHS executive directors are trying to combine acute managers and primary care managers to be on a rota. ... Later in the day, as we were leaving the Council, we stood in the carpark while Samuel debriefed with his NHS colleague Frank, (manager of unscheduled admissions),

Figure 8.3. Samuel's Desk. *Source*: Author's own (2016).

about what was a difficult meeting with Council care managers. It was the first meeting I observed where there was explicit disagreement and conflict. We headed back to the hospital and Samuel mentioned that this was the first type of meeting of this kind reviewing and challenging decisions in order to learn for the future and how confronting it was (24 February 2015).

From the outset of my time with Samuel, I was exposed to the dilemmas and discretion entailed in his role. On that day, he was feeling conflicted by the demands for his presence in acute services in the NHS and the imperative to work constructively with social care to address the delayed transfer of care that was straining relations with acute services.

My time with Samuel was unevenly spread over weeks. He began to pick me up from the train station before heading to whatever meeting was first for the day. I was able to listen to him explain his work directly and indirectly via mobile calls where he did not always disclose my presence, necessitating I remain quiet. I quickly learnt his job involved lots of driving given he managed wide-ranging services with staff distributed across Kintra. Consequently, he developed ways to work 'on the go' and fill the 'empty' time in his journeys.

> I meet Samuel as I come out of the station and he's trying to speak to his PA on his Blackberry. He describes a change in his diary, arising from yesterday's informal management meeting. Joanna

Vehicles of In\formality **133**

had done some work on the commissioning document, but it still needed more work, so Chrissie requested he work on it and 'make it look more professional'. On the drive over to Council he gets through to his PA ... and they discussed diary changes. As his mobile was linked through the car, he spoke hands-free. She joked about not liking him today as he can't meet with Stuart or the Deputy Medical Director. He responded about having to go to an afternoon meeting at a GP practice with the new Medical Director, as directed by the NHS CEO. Invoking the CEO brought the conversation to an end as we arrived at Council to meet the Integration Programme Manager. (30 March 2016)

In this extract, Samuel is entwined in various technologies while driving and being responsive to a dynamic context that needs his involvement, where the connectivity of his mobile and Bluetooth technology permitted communication with his personal assistant (PA) for diary management and other work between meetings, including pre-meeting briefings, debriefings after meetings, peer support, discussing plans and agreeing to future action. Over those few days, he became more comfortable with my presence and less concerned about what I heard. This was also reflected in his increased openness about his views on HSCI and seeking my perspectives, which then extended to revealing personal details about the impacts of work on his well-being.

Samuel asked about my reaction to the meeting and the GP's view of their practice and HSCI. He also asked about my PhD and how it will shine a light on their practice. He expressed concern about a lack of an operating model for HSCI and not being authorised to action ideas, such as those advocated by the nurse from the GP practice we'd visited. He put this down to Kintra's history and thinks they perpetuate it by not being clear about what they're managing. ... that what they are doing is an exercise in making it appear like it's something. (30 March 2016)

We get into the car, and he tells me he used to work 55 - 60 hours a week when he also had to manage the acute hospital and ended up having 2 months off to recover. He doesn't do that now. As we head to the train station he talks about work pressures generally. I then said it was good to have had a positive meeting on the HSCI launch day April 1, with Julia being on Radio Scotland and articles in the local papers. I asked why there wasn't more from the organisations today in relation to marking the occasion. He thought there should have been more made of it, muttering something about 'fucking stupid decisions'. (1 April)

As we leave the hospital and get in Samuel's car, he talks about how he's frustrated with his emails and needs to be on top of them as they were 'out of control' – his PA sorts emails ... so he'll need

Figure 8.4. Front and back car parks at Haith Royal Infirmary.
Source: Author's own (2016).

> to spend time in the evening and go through them. He describes email toing and froing at the moment that's getting personal and that he's just said to stop and have a face-to-face meeting. He prefers talking and calling rather than emails. We end up talking about CDs – he's just bought the latest Pet Shop Boys which leads us to talk about our musical tastes and concerts. (4 April)

While Samuel appears to be the kind of 'person-thing … automobilized person' that Thrift (2004, p. 47) describes, given an interdependency with the car supporting him to accomplish his work role, he also used his car for emotional regulation supported by music, but there were tasks that couldn't be done while driving, i.e., reading his emails which were done after hours at home. In his opening up about his work and the progress being made with HSCI, his efforts to support HSCI appeared persistently constrained by NHS arrangements.

> I was in the carpark out the front of the hospital, in between ambulances and cars dropping people off, waiting for a lift from Samuel. He'd already been at Council but came back to get me to return to Council for a meeting about community-led models for local services being promoted by the Scottish Government. As I got into the car, I heard Elvis singing a version of 'Bridge over Troubled Water', and remark, 'You must have a lot on your mind' (assuming he was stressed), to which he nodded but changed the subject and turned his music off. I could see food wrappers flung on the floor of the passenger compartment and in the empty mug holder space in the console. It smelt like a mix of cigarettes and air freshener. There were clothes and documents spread out on the back seats. It looked like he'd been spending a lot of time in his car, although he didn't seem to have his mobile resting in its cradle to take phone calls like he usually does. We chat on the 10-minute drive over to Dochmuir about ideas for setting up a community ward. He'd been questioning these ideas and talked to another manager, who also shared his concerns. I asked about him working on the Commissioning Plan, and he laughed 'No that's this weekend's work'. He then started detailing how he was the Hospital duty manager yesterday and he described the specific directive they are given at the end of every month about meeting

> particular targets, e.g., 95% admissions, so they knew that if they had 4 people go over 4 hours waiting in A&E, it would prevent NHS Kintra achieving their national performance target. I learnt this degree of close monitoring at month's end led to managers influencing clinical decisions, which Samuel wasn't always comfortable with. ... After the meeting finished, while standing in Council's carpark he explained feeling like he's having to deal with so many people and personalities and so many different issues. This conversation continued in the car as he drove me to the train station, where he described being immersed in so much that without the clarity of a model like that of NHS Highland, 'we're in treacle and there are so many different interpretations of what it's about and so people are creating their own realities'. (5 April 2016)

Two main features of his car work stood out, namely simultaneity and sustaining distributed relations. The variety of meetings he attended reflected how broad his role was and the range of services that reported to him, requiring him to be across multiple policy areas, including HSCI. He was explicit about his intentions to talk directly with not just those he managed but colleagues from Council and the community sector. In this sense, he was aware of the policy work entailed in his role, but his relations were dispersed across Kintra, and he determined that his bodily presence mattered to informally sustain these relations. Accordingly, he traded off deskwork with car work, hence the informal workarounds he developed for accomplishing work while driving, simultaneous enactments to allow things to go on. As my time with Samuel came to an end, the cumulative pressures of his work were obvious; he was not just stretched, but he was increasingly stressed. He said they were 'building an aeroplane whilst it's flying, you know, so it's already taken off and it's in the air, but actually it needs to be finished' (6 June 2016). While he expressed commitment to HSCI, he was very frustrated, especially with data production, the resultant waste of energy when new daily data would arrive about the number of beds available and the ill-informed responses based on what he felt was inaccurate data – all emerging from the nexus of practices associated with acuity in the NHS. Despite his lengthy employment with the NHS and grasp of the issues, processes, budgets, personalities and politics, and desire to be across lots of activity, when it came to HSCI, planning activities overwhelmed all other HSCI work, a form of work he had limited involvement in given the expectation of his involvement in operations.

These moments inside and outside the car with Samuel reflected its porosity and salience as a mobile space for shaping practices of policy. However, despite his reparative efforts, Samuel resigned from NHS Kintra within 12 months of the HSCI 'go live' date. His experience exposed that even with the interpretative capacity provided for in the legislation, it relied tacitly on an assumption that policies like HSCI can have an unfiltered and direct effect on sites of implementation, which was counterbalanced by institutional realities in Kintra. This assumption ignored not only care service circumstances in Kintra but also the knotted relations engaged in the process – something my trips in cars revealed (Mulherin, 2022, p. 250).

136 *Tamara Mulherin*

3. In/formal Things

> [...] even as the business people are speeding along motorways, they are likely to be busy doing desk-work: trying to keep up with complaints from clients, requests for help from colleagues and dictating letters to secretaries; trying to keep to optimistic appointment times with clients and colleagues; trying to stay in synch with those who do not have to drive to meetings; trying to do office work with paper documents; and on their mobile phone to recoup time otherwise lost in transit. These varieties of desk work and the dashboard equipment of driving have not been designed to go together, yet the office workers we studied managed to artfully combine them. (Laurier, 2004, p. 264)

While the work going on in cars reveals temporal elements that make journey time productive, to accomplish this relations with things need to be foregrounded. When it came to fieldwork, what I did not grasp initially was the role of materials and how their relations were entangled in intra- and inter-organisational doings. The relatings of objects shifted my attention, slowly transforming my analysis into a part 'ethnography of non-humans' (Gherardi, 2019, p. 211). While HSCI had 'multiple material manifestations' (Woodward, 2019, p. 16), boundary permeability was detectable through rooms as sites of inclusion and exclusion, magnetic entry tags allowing movement around buildings and bodies occupying jointly appointed positions. These objects coalesced in quotidian events, like journeys to meetings, and occasions where I thought clues to how HSCI was being implemented could be discerned. As I endeavour to highlight, these materialities permeated practices of policy in relational ways, and policy permeated materialities in relational ways too; 'not solely determined by human agents but rather through the relationships that unfold between humans, social worlds and more-than-human entities including objects, technologies and environments' (Clark & Lupton, 2023, p. 401). In bringing materiality to the fore, the dualisms that characterise Eurocentric thought (e.g., nature/culture, human/non-human and mind/body) are troubled. Attention is paid instead to the socio-material processes through which meanings and experiences are produced (Clark & Lupton, 2023).

While our entanglements in materials are manifold, I suggest focusing on a mundane object like the car can be used to uncover not only neglected things but also neglected issues in policy work, e.g., the boring (and often frustrating) activity involved in electronic diary management to arrange policy discussions while driving (Star, 1999). Furthermore, when it comes to aiding policy implementation in frontline service delivery, for many care practitioners, travelling is a requirement of the job, and the car is central to how this is achieved. Yet, Ferguson argues, 'the role and meanings of the car [in policy work] remain largely unanalysed ... [and this] makes it appear as if work goes on without movement, that it can be done without professionals ever having to leave their desks' (Ferguson, 2009, p. 276). This approach offers 'a window into capturing prosaic issues usually left by the wayside' (Holmes & Hall, 2020, p. 231); we see how

Vehicles of In\formality **137**

spaces of policy are materialised by others thought of as outside of policy, in contrast to those who shape policy at a distance, the policymakers, politicians and executives who orchestrate the texture of environments where policy implementation takes place with intended and unintended effects.

I contend that attending to materials, in this case cars, combined with geography, allows for a more nuanced understanding of how policies are mobilised from national centres of policymaking to local sites of action in all their connectivity and how they mutate as they move with the iterative actions of multiple actors (Durose, 2011). Additionally, a spatial focus prompts us to consider how policy is configured in particular settings, which practices are facilitated through different spatial contexts and what the implications are of arranging policy implementation and settings as we do. 'Place' implies something more than locality; it also enables 'understanding how different processes and things combine to create the world as it is experienced' (Pink, 2012, p. 23). In this instance, the 'contingent, negotiated and "throwntogetherness"' (Buse et al., 2018, p. 247) of mobile spaces where practices configure policy. Thus, when interrogating materials on the move and spatiality, their mobility is an effect of effort. 'Mobility and ... materiality are themselves relational effects, ... they are an outcome or an accomplishment' (Adey, 2010, p. 18).

The material and social entailments of cars emerge from features like privacy, in which the boundaries are controlled and facilitate ease in terms of informal interactions, mixed with the propinquity afforded by size and seating arrangements. Car's layouts can foster informal interactions in a space where people are physically close, i.e., the blend of the enclosed architecture of the car, the undivided attention that car travellers can give one another and in particular the 'pause-fullness, and slowness, of car conversation' (Ferguson, 2009, p. 281). According to Ferguson (2009, pp. 276–277), the work that goes on in cars is therefore generated through the design of cars, centred around the interaction between the purpose of journeys; the effects of being in movement and the discussion this enables; and how configuration of seating and where people can sit alters power relations between professionals and build trust. By following the mundane materiality of daily work carried out in cars, the informality of automobility and actors' experiences reveal the extent to which policy work is mediated in sociomaterial arrangements in the form of enmeshed technologies, institutions and actors, actively shaping the discontinuous trajectories of policy actors through formal and informal realms of organisational action; understanding these scaffolding conditions for policy mobility can provide a more comprehensive understanding of how in\formality in policy work comes to be enacted. These features make the car a place where policy work needs to be interrogated and analysed (Ferguson, 2009).

To highlight these features, I noted on Day 1 of fieldwork that to shadow the Chief Officer through her day, I needed to accompany her in her car. In our leaving the Council building to the car park to the car, the communicative dynamics between us shifted from orienting statements about the Council, as we were in an open-plan office occupied by the Council's senior management team and administrative staff and where various speech acts could be easily overheard; to a small,

Figure 8.5. Manager's car park at Kintra Council & Public car park at Kintra Council. *Source*: Author's own (2016).

enclosed space where it was just her and I and the conversation shifted to a more open style. By following her through a building, across a car park to her car, became an opportunity for her to describe particular features of the Council and provide more detail about her role, entangled with the car and a GPS. I recognised that being alone in the car provided other possible lines of enquiry to be explored when out of earshot of others and reflective of more forthcoming communication.

> We head off to a presentation the Chief Officer was doing at the College to health and social care students, as part of the consultation on the draft strategic plan for the partnership. We travel in her car to another town, and it is a good opportunity to have some informal conversation. Because of her position her car had a parking space, although someone else had taken it and she'd parked in someone else's spot. She remarked that she'd never had this before and thinks that it is reflective of the hierarchy of the Council. She talked about getting to know the area given how dispersed the towns are. The trip to the College took 20 minutes but she was ably assisted by a GPS. (1 December 2015)

I also came to learn that manager's cars were spaces that could be reached into, via Bluetooth technology, with phone calls received through the car's audio systems and caller id displayed on the dashboard. Ferguson (2009) describes this as where one 'mobility system' – the car – meets another mobility system – computer technology – and permits information gathered on the move to become part of administrative practice and flows around (p. 289). Likewise, the stationary car was a space for managers to take a break, ponder the day's experiences, smoke, eat and make phone calls that they did not want overheard in open-plan offices.

Car interiors were a material, movable space where the informal came to the fore and with that exposed granular regulation of action, on the part of the policy actor associated with implementation. Correspondingly, while I explore how the car is associated with action on the move, its material role in stationary action, e.g., providing an additional space for having lunch, needs to be recognised. Equally, the affordances of the car in facilitating other activities like the after-meeting debrief in the carpark all play a part in enmeshing the informal in the midst of everyday work.

Vehicles of In\formality **139**

4. Porous Mobilities

> [...] what happens in the interior of the car remains largely unex-
> amined ... The inside, however, is perhaps almost too trivial, as a
> space not of state, city and politics but one of family argument,
> refreshments and gossip. (Laurier et al., 2008, p. 3)

There are few human activities more mundane than informal interaction and
few settings in which to study them are more commonplace than cars and carparks. As a site for ethnographic interrogation, cars lack the strangeness to surprise us, as most of us have personal experience with them. Furthermore, Drew
et al. (2022) suggest methodologically that talking in the car has effective advan-
tages over other approaches, '[w]hile people's bodies and minds reside within the
"inner space" of the car, vehicular movement can also unlock their recollections
of the places and things they pass in the "outer space" that extends beyond its
boundaries' (p. 6).

While not necessarily concentrating on vehicles, from Day 1 of fieldwork, the
centrality of cars as the space for what I wrote as 'informal conversations' is indicated in my fieldnotes. I appeared to 'know' or place value on what happened
during car trips as a means to elicit details about HSCI implementation. This
realisation generates questions about the circumstances of policy implementation
as not only associated with places, like Council or hospital buildings, but also
spread across places, away from policy actors' own offices, including ones that
are fleeting or mobile. Analytically, when it came to cars, effects arose from both
the physicality of a space and the patterning of the activity that occurred there.
Something Ferguson (2009) argues is

> central to the management of time, space and relationships in
> people's everyday lives, and to the flows and practices within
> entire societies ... far more goes on in cars than was previously
> understood, as travel time is not simply wasted or 'non' time.
> (pp. 275–276)

As a form of 'practice of everyday life' (De Certeau, 1984), the car enables
the movement of bodies by the millions, and as such is 'so pervasive that it forms
the daily routines often taken for granted' (Drew et al., 2022, p. 6). Thrift (2004)
argues that car travel is a vital means through which humans come to know
the world, which 'reconfigures civil society involving distinct ways of dwelling,
travelling and socialising in and through an automobilised time-space' (p. 46).
He noted 20 years ago that developments in-car technologies, merging software
and ergonomics, were shifting how automobility was being practised, car's habit-
ability and the practices of driving and passengering (p. 51).

Transport was a difficult feature of fieldwork, requiring I travel to and
from Kintra by bus or train, which meant I was a passenger in many car journeys across various towns, an ethnographer positioned 'in motion in the field'
(Birtchnell, Harada and Waitt in Holmes & Hall, 2020, p. 232) centred on
car-related matters.

140   Tamara Mulherin

Figure 8.6.   Access to the Field. *Source*: Author's own (2016).

While car journeys were pragmatic ways for me to both shadow managers as they went about their daily routines, and to get to different locations in a large rural municipality, it soon became obvious that the journeys afforded opportunities to talk with managers about their jobs, involvement in HSCI implementation, assessment of its progress and the impact on their roles. Although not always uninterrupted or alone, having a manager's attention fostered an understanding of their knowledge, experiences and perspectives, and consequently, interesting insights emerged (Drew et al., 2022). Spending time with managers and others in cars made for productive time to build trust.

Cars mobilised relations in what was a form of private space into which work could intrude but on the driver's terms. It was a vehicle, in both senses of the word, to learn about people and places, chat about shared experiences, listen to their versions of events and talk about things not necessarily shared in front of others. It facilitated multidirectional conversation in which researcher/subject relations shifted and discussion emerged organically on diverse topics. Cars were 'a good place for certain sorts of conversations' (Laurier et al., 2008, p. 17).

Five months into fieldwork, my relations with managers evolved and much had happened. While still in and out of cars, I had more to discuss, and managers were at ease disclosing views on numerous matters. The managers with integrated responsibilities had nuanced understanding of organisational differences that they had to navigate figuratively, and literally, by car.

As I got to know each manager over a number of car trips, the trips took on different forms, which highlighted their generative features for ethnographic observation, if trust was established. First, more affective elements emerged as dissonance and emotion were bared in unguarded moments when they divulged concerns about implementation efforts, as well 'matters of life, love and death were discussed, … inter-personal support was given[,] … intense feelings [were] generated – "auto-emotions"' (Ferguson, 2009, p. 276). This was exemplified when accompanying Stuart, the Associate Director of Allied Health, in the Occupational Therapy team leader's car to a meeting with Mental Health Services. He had been working on a restructure of Allied Health Services in response to HSCI and was negotiating with the union, and 'in an agitated manner off-loaded about being challenged about his structure chart and being shafted by a specific individual' (23 February 2016). Often conveyed with affect, the other affordance of cars was stimulating information disclosure on the part of interlocutors for events I was unable to observe. This was apparent one afternoon when I got a lift from the hospital to the train station, where a retelling of an event at the new partnership's board meeting exposed underlying tensions with HSCI.

> As Integration Programme Manager, Chrissie drove me towards the train station, she divulged what happened at the board meeting yesterday and how angry she was. She said 'Claire' (the board Secretary) told the Chairperson to move two items on the agenda to private, items relating to the appointments of Chief Officer and Chief Financial Officer, and that the NHS CEO, who Chrissie then called 'a fucking cunt', did this. … The NHS CEO argued staff appointments shouldn't have staff present. According to Chrissie, Julia, the Chief Officer, had to leave and was very angry … I said, 'I wonder if this was about realising the legislative implications, and Chrissie responded, 'the NHS CEO realises they're losing power'. I thought to myself, I really like car conversations, you learn a lot … but I was shocked by what Chrissie told me. I felt for Julia, what a difficult job. (8 March 2016)

In revisiting my fieldnotes, I realised managers were sharing their views with me in cars from the beginning, with the discussion during these trips often following on from preceding activity that was dominating their attention, such as contentious meetings related to HSCI.

> I went in Julia's car to the hospital for the informal managers' meeting. She talked about the day being difficult, focused on delayed discharge, and said that it was about underlying politics, 'blaming social work for the delayed discharge', but she indicated the situation was more complicated. (5 January 2016).

Subsequently, I began to wonder if there was a third feature; I felt like I was a receptacle for managers to process their feelings about HSCI and express out loud their views when I was in the car, knowing I was a researcher and ethically required to keep things confidential.

5. My Journeys End

> […] mobile policies are not simply travelling across a landscape – they are remaking this landscape, and they are contributing to the interpenetration of distant policymaking sites. (Peck & Theodore, 2010 p. 170)

Witnessing managers' movements as they journeyed throughout Kintra in their cars uncovered the dense relations managers were enmeshed in: relations in the management team, relations with the teams they were responsible for, relations with authorisers and governors and the partner organisations they worked with. These dense relations were conditioned in arrangements with things as well, with the car generating relations in particular ways that affected the implementation of HSCI, as they produced ways to work 'on the go'. In world/s of 'evidence-based everything', what was displayed was the ambivalence and complexity in the workings of automobilised policy as it travelled on trunk roads, town streets and village lanes. Neither hidden nor fully articulated, enfolded patterns of in|formal doings prove essential for understanding the blurred boundaries of threshold spaces, like the car, which are critical for policy mobilisation. As McFarlane explains,

> Informality and formality are as nomadic as people themselves. They have no pre-given geography or political content, progressive or otherwise. They co-constitute and dissolve spaces, becoming politicised or depoliticised at different moments, and they both enable and restrict organisational life. (McFarlane, 2012, p. 89)

Cars were a hybridised workspace, quasi-private artefact; 'a fluid container … a secure base to retreat to, either to be alone to reflect and "contain" themselves' (Ferguson, 2009, p. 291), where managers could listen, chat, generate connections, share experiences, divulge conflict and discuss action. The car is implicated

Figure 8.7. Off on a trip in the snow. *Source*: Author's own (2016).

Vehicles of In\formality **143**

as a locus of affective and embodied relations between policy actors, materialities and spaces of mobility and dwelling, an in|formal, threshold space – the transitory office – where meaningful policy work is conducted that enables the flow of policy work to continue.

Lastly, I propose understanding the affordances of the car and mobilities enriches understandings of policy implementation. While Laurier et al.'s (2008) research explores 'a tentative sociology of passengers and passengering', I want to suggest that analysis of the role and meaning of the car in the mobilising of policy as exemplified in HSCI implementation in rural Scotland adds a further crucial dimension. This entails what goes on within the car as a site of practice and the place of the car and system of automobility in policy arrangements. Apart from differences between the car and other meeting places, there are relations involved in policy work in the car which mark it out as different from work undertaken elsewhere. What goes on in the car is part of the countless iterations of practice that occur at various implementation sites, and it is these entangled relations between them that create the 'fluid' interventions that lead policy to flow in particular directions (Ferguson, 2009, p. 291).

References

Adey, P. (2010). *Mobility*. Routledge.

Buse, C., Martin, D., & Nettleton, S. (2018). Conceptualising 'materialities of care': Making visible mundane material culture in health and social care contexts. *Sociology of Health & Illness, 40*(2), 243–255. https://doi.org/10.1111/1467-9566.12663

Carter, P. (2018). Governing spaces: A multi-sited ethnography of governing welfare reform at close range and at a distance. *Critical Policy Studies, 12*(1), 3–23. https://doi.org/10.1080/19460171.2016.1208109

Clark, M., & Lupton, D. (2023). The materialities and embodiments of mundane software: Exploring how apps come to matter in everyday life. *Online Information Review, 47*(2), 398–413. https://doi.org/10.1108/oir-12-2020-0565

De Certeau, M. (1984). *The practice of everyday life* (S. F. Rendall, Trans.). University of California Press.

de La Bellacasa, M. P. (2011). Matters of care in technoscience: Assembling neglected things. *Social Studies of Science, 41*(1), 85–106.

Drew, G., Skinner, W., & Bardsley, D. K. (2022). The 'drive and talk' as ethnographic method. *Anthropology Today, 38*(3), 5–8. https://doi.org/10.1111/1467-8322.12725

Durose, C. (2011). Revisiting Lipsky: Front-line work in UK local governance. *Political Studies, 59*(4), 978–995. https://doi.org/10.1111/j.1467-9248.2011.00886.x

Ferguson, H. (2009). Driven to care: The car, automobility and social work. *Mobilities, 4*(2), 275–293. https://doi.org/10.1080/17450100902906723

Gherardi, S. (2019). *How to conduct a practice-based study: Problems and methods*. Edward Elgar Publishing.

Holmes, H., & Hall, S. M. (2020). *Mundane methods: Innovative ways to research the everyday*. Manchester University Press.

Klocker, N., Toole, S., Tindale, A., & Kerr, S.-M. (2015). Ethnically diverse transport behaviours: An Australian perspective. *Geographical Research, 53*(4), 393–405. https://doi.org/10.1111/1745-5871.12118

Laurier, E. (2004). Doing office work on the motorway. *Theory, Culture & Society, 21*(4–5), 261–277. https://doi.org/10.1177/0263276404046070

144 *Tamara Mulherin*

Laurier, E., Lorimer, H., Brown, B., Jones, O., Juhlin, O., Noble, A., Perry, M., Pica, D., Sormani, P., Strebel, I., Swan, L., Taylor, A. S., Watts, L., & Weilenmann, A. (2008). Driving and 'passengering': Notes on the ordinary organization of car travel. *Mobilities, 3*(1), 1–23. https://doi.org/10.1080/17450100701797273

Lewis, J. (2001). Older people and the health-social care boundary in the UK – Half a century of hidden policy conflict. *Social Policy & Administration, 35*(4), 343–359. https://doi.org/10.1111/1467-9515.00238

McFarlane, C. (2012). Rethinking informality: Politics, crisis, and the city. *Planning Theory & Practice, 13*(1), 89–108.

Mulherin, T. (2022). *B/order work: Recomposing relations in the seamful carescapes of health and social care integration in Scotland*. PhD, University of Edinburgh, Edinburgh.

Peck, J. (2003). Geography and public policy: Mapping the penal state. *Progress in Human Geography, 27*(2), 222–232. https://doi.org/10.1191/0309132503ph424pr

Peck, J., & Theodore, N. (2010). Mobilizing policy: Models, methods, and mutations. *Geoforum, 41*(2), 169–174.

Pink, S. (2012). Situating everyday life: *practices and places*. SAGE Publications Ltd.

Star, S. L. (1999). The ethnography of Infrastructure. *American Behavioral Scientist, 43*(3), 377–391. https://doi.org/10.1177/00027649921955326

Taylor, A. (2016). *The shape of the state in medieval Scotland* (pp. 1124–1290). Oxford University Press.

Thrift, N. (2004). Driving in the city. *Theory, Culture & Society, 21*(4–5), 41–59.

Woodward, S. 2019. *Material methods: researching and thinking with things*. SAGE Publications Ltd.

Wagenaar, H. (2018). Policy as practice: Explaining persistent patterns in prostitution policy. *The Howard Journal of Crime and Justice, 57*(3), 379–400. https://doi.org/10.1111/hojo.12271

Concluding Thoughts

Chapter 9

Tracing Threads of In/Visibilities: The Knotty Mattering of Policymaking

Lindsey Garner-Knapp[a] and Joanna Mason[b]

[a]*University of Edinburgh, UK*
[b]*Menzies Centre for Health Policy and Economics, University of Sydney, Australia*

Abstract

This chapter focuses on the actors who engage in policymaking to offer alternative understandings of informality and the context in which this occurs. Using ethnographic vignettes from Canada and Australia as illustrations, theoretical and methodological goals are pursued through adopting the anthropological concept of 'traces' to show how informality both mediates and transcends across non-fixed physical, temporal and conceptual boundaries. With an underlying premise that normative understandings of informality are shaped by the policymaking 'black box' metaphor and a lack of access to policymaking spaces and actors, this chapter argues against the association of informality with illegitimate and invisible policy processes. Instead, experience of the policy process gained through professional and ethnographic engagement, or an 'insider' perspective, shifts the researcher's gaze beyond physical barriers or separations to show that 'traces' formed through in|formal encounters create opportunities for relationality through which policy is conceived, deliberated and, in part, created.

Keywords: Informality; policymaking; ethnography; relationality; traces; policy actors

---

Informality in Policymaking: Weaving the Threads of Everyday Policy Work, 147–162
Copyright © 2025 by Lindsey Garner-Knapp and Joanna Mason
Published under exclusive licence by Emerald Publishing Limited
doi:10.1108/978-1-83797-280-720241010

148 *Lindsey Garner-Knapp and Joanna Mason*

The View From Inside

The institutional setting in which policy comes to life poses a natural impediment to public scrutiny of what is involved; thus, the intricate negotiations and debates that government employees engage in to progress policy proposals rarely come to light. By contrast, many chapters in this volume show how ethnographic study allows researchers access to the policy setting and opportunities to observe what goes on from close by and do this over time. These contributions also demonstrate that ethnography benefits from tailored methods, theories and techniques to advance the analytical understanding of a given setting such as 'immersive presence' and 'rear-mirror technique' in visual ethnography (see Mungekar, this volume) and 'vehicular movements' to capture mobile relations (see Mulherin, this volume).

This chapter picks up these threads to consider further what an insider's perspective on the policy setting can reveal, and how being there 'in the moment' destabilises the formal/informal or visible/invisible binary understandings of these processes. As insiders to the policy process, both as embedded researchers and with knowledge gained from professional experience, we found a binary understanding of informality did not resonate. In exploring other conceptualisations, we bring forward the material and temporal aspects of policymaking through attention to the 'ethnographic detail' for how it creates a 'trace' through the knotting together of the past with the present. We pursue this empirically with ethnographic vignettes from our past experiences to illustrate the porous boundaries of informality and formality, dispelling the association of informality with invisibility and illegitimacy in the policy process. By using the anthropological concept of the trace, we can show how ethnographic details encountered in the field accumulate meaning in conjunction with knowledge of what has already occurred and with later reflection on these events. Drawing on Levi-Strauss, Valentina Napolitano states:

> One aspect of an anthropology of traces ... is a capacity for remembering and imagining after an event has ceased and turning the counter-position of apparently uneventful data ... into meaningful traces. (2015, p. 51)

Accordingly, we begin this chapter with the suggestion that one does not know what is needed to make sense of field research until the moment has passed. Only after the fact does this become visible.

Spaces and Traces of Policymaking

In this chapter, we argue that the proliferation of binaries describing where and how policy work is carried out, by whom and to what effect has resulted in line-of-sight qualities being applied to the spatial and material elements of policymaking. The policy literature on informality is littered with binary terminology featuring formal and informal, legitimate and illegitimate and even institutional and discretionary (for example, see Ayres et al., 2017; Bekker et al., 2010; Wimmelmann, 2017). Playing into the policymaking metaphor of the 'black box', these terms conjure up connotations of impenetrability, mystery and shadow which darken an understanding of policymaking and the spatio-temporal boundaries that contain it (Pinch, 1992).

Ethnographic methods are not the core interest of this chapter; instead, these observations introduce a general argument advanced here: ethnomethodologies facilitate opportunities to blur boundaries and challenge binary thinking. In this chapter, we offer alternative understandings of informality that derive from a focus on the actors who engage in policymaking and the spaces in which this occurs. By highlighting the presumption of a physical and visual separation, we harness the concepts of visibility/invisibility and present/absent to argue for a reappraisal of what occurs within and between the *informal* and *formal*, or in|formal (see Mason et al., this volume), arena of policymaking.

Drawing on our experiences of policymaking processes in Australia and Canada, our ambition is to show how visibility and invisibility leave traces which can be knotted together at a later space and time. Our conception of a trace is informed by Napolitano's (2015) work, buoyed by her convincing case for the long-standing influence of this concept on anthropology and her demonstration of how this can be used to further theoretical and methodological goals. Napolitano (2015) writes:

> Traces emerge out of a condensation of stories/histories. I use the word condensation ... to mean a process of compromise and convergence of multiple stories into a knot. That knot has a form and is in space – so that a trace is both a form in space as well as the process through which histories and reminders of different worlds imprint and condense on the given space. When multiple stories from different worlds condense into a trace they become powerful as they stand not only for the singular history. (p. 57)

The extract above shows that Napolitano's concepts of traces and knots draw upon multiple, simultaneous processes. The condensation of multiple stories into knots, we argue, is an active, intuitive process that comes from reflection and deliberation that brings together multiple lived experiences. For us, our discussions and reflections of our time as practitioners offered a process to identify traces from our in|formal policymaking stories which we knot together below.

Ethnographic Reflections: Past–Present Linkages

Further elaboration on our approach to this chapter is helpful preparation for what follows. As former practitioners now in academia, we were motivated by a feeling that the descriptions and explanations we had encountered in the academic scholarship did not accord with our experiences or with our research engagements with government institutions and their staff. Many accounts were positioned in relation to the visible and 'formal' of policymaking – such as the

150   Lindsey Garner-Knapp and Joanna Mason

documents, policies and meetings – with accounts of informal defined precisely by what they lacked: *visibility*. For us, the formal/informal binary did not help explain how the informal matters or reveal how it manifests in everyday policy-making. The conundrum for many scholars is gaining access to what are often perceived as elite spaces (Mikecz, 2012; Ortner, 2010), which we argue reinforces the 'black box-ness' of policymaking processes and its perceived invisibility. Our own access to these spaces occurred precisely because of our work and academic ambitions: as policy employees and ethnographers, we were expected to be *in* these spaces and to contribute to policymaking. Methodologies like ethnography and autoethnography create pathways into these spaces and entry points to make these processes visible.

In writing this chapter, we began with the premise that what can be apprehended and understood about the policy sphere is undeniably knotted together with its past. As co-authors, we are mindful of our disciplinary pasts – foregrounding our own genealogies that have become spun together as residual traces of our ethnographic sensibility (McGranahan, 2018) and policy-as-practitioner attune-ments to government work and what it entails. These lived experiences have infused our interpretive understandings of informality and widened our per-ceived possibilities for how to integrate empirical details and analysis through ethnographic narrative.

Unlike intentional autoethnographic work, the vignettes emerged through reflections and discussions of our past experiences. Our insights come from creat-ing knots between recollections of past histories and our ongoing empirical and professional lived experiences; we are practising ethnography and *writing about people*. In this sense, our method is analogous to Tim Ingold (2014) who writes that anthropological practitioners:

> [...] tread ways of carrying on and of being carried, of living life with others – humans and non-humans all – that is cognizant of the past, attuned to the conditions of the present and speculatively open to the possibilities of the future. (p. 390)

Our approach takes on this tying together of different times and places, things and people while remaining open to new knotty-ness that emerges with the unfolding of time. Ingold (2014) goes on to say:

> The conflation of ethnography with fieldwork is indeed one of the most commonplace in the discipline, and all the more insidious because it is so rarely questioned. That the field is never experienced as such when you are actually there and caught up in the currents of everyday life – that it only stands out when you have left it far behind and begin to write about it – is widely acknowledged. (p. 386)

Ingold's insights on the field rang true for us, for it was only after we left the field or our practitioner environments – and began to discuss those experiences – that we were able to identify ethnographic insights or perhaps *ethnographic threads*. So while we did not conduct ethnographic fieldwork with the intent to garner the stories presented in this chapter, we offer a reflective ethnographic account of our involvements in the policy field.

Ethnographic Policy Vignettes

The first vignette draws from Joanna Mason's (2023) ethnographic study with policymakers in the Australian Public Service. As a narrative, it was constructed from empirical field notes made at the time of research and her concurrent participation in the policy work of the branch in which she was situated – but relied also on post-field reflections. How office space was occupied and utilised is presented through a description of the movements of a single figure, the branch manager. The significance for our understanding of informality accrues through his use of visible and less-visible locations and how this relates to opportunities to interact with his colleagues, showing how occupying a highly visible location within the workspace does not offer better prospects to engage in relational moments with colleagues. Instead, the privacy afforded by unseen spaces fosters work that is procedural, and enacted alone, but which leaves visible threads that appear as communications in staff inboxes.

In the second vignette, Lindsey Garner-Knapp offers reflections on her lived experiences of being a policy advisor for a Canadian local government. She shows that a shared historical moment – invisible to all who were not present in the coffee rooms, offices or hallways – produces unseeable and intangible traces that can be knotted to present policies. It is only through knowing that these encounters have taken place, creating a history, that we are able to 'see' those moments as traces; those histories becoming meaningful at a later point in time. Methodologically, we conceptualise these ethnographic data as traces only after they are brought to matter through knotting together with a future policy decision or act or become interwoven with the relational routines that are central to the practice of consensual policymaking (Napolitano, 2015).

A Multi-functional Workspace

> On my first morning in the office, I eagerly waited for the branch manager to arrive to begin our scheduled meeting which would mark the commencement of my ethnographic research with the department. As he arrived, our greeting was brief and we set off immediately to find a quiet spot to chat. As we walked together through the elongated office, he tutted to himself quietly about a particular meeting room that he liked but had been already occupied. Walking further, we settled on a small, cloistered room, drawing back a heavy, upholstered curtain to take a seat at a small bistro-style table. With limited table space, I balanced my notebook on my knees while I listened to him describe the structure of the department and the policy areas that each of his teams contributed to.

As I settled into office life over the coming weeks and months, it became clear that the branch manager was well regarded by his colleagues. He had a calm and introspective demeanour that was prone to spontaneous bursts of self-depreciating humour which seemed to put others at ease. Despite his senior role and busy schedule that went with this status, he never appeared to be in a hurry. His passage in, out, and through the office could readily be observed by anyone who raised their eyes above their computer screen to gaze into the surrounding office space. His manoeuvres drew my interest as I wondered where he was going and why. As my earliest field confidant and interlocutor, I was curious about his whereabouts for what it could tell me about who he was speaking to and the types of activities that occupied his time. As my research study was focused on observing how policy staff engage with academic research in meeting their policy responsibilities, I was keen to learn about routine and mundane activities around me as staff went about their day.

These movements in and out of the office caught my attention for other reasons too. During earlier negotiations around the practicalities of my fieldwork, the branch manager expressed to me his curiosity of how the physical office environment influenced how staff worked. He had explained that in this open-plan workspace staff had no allocated desks, workstations or offices. Instead, staff were encouraged to work from any location in the building and to adjust their position according to their task at hand. The kitchen area, corridor and adjoining café were all potential workspaces, and in keeping with the 'multi-functional' design of the workspace, an assortment of seating configurations like pods, low and high desks and open benches had been placed throughout the floor for staff to set down with their laptop or engage in conversation. This 'working your way' design aimed to remove physical and operational policy barriers (or silos) that could stifle creativity or impede collaborative work.

Contrary to his stated interests in what behaviours or effects the workspace produces for staff, my observations came to rest on him, in particular his morning arrival in the office and how his routine depended on his agenda for the day. When his time was to be spent mostly in meetings, he would choose a prominent desk in the middle of the office space close to the executive assistants who could alert him to upcoming engagements or pass on critical information. But when his day was less structured, he would move instead to a designated 'quiet' area down the far end of the office. From here he could be seen sitting quietly with his laptop – but only in knowing where to look. The tell-tale sign of this activity

Tracing Threads of In/Visibilities **153**

was when emails began arriving into your inbox with responses to earlier queries, along with general office communications that needed to be sent down the line. When approached by colleagues he would reluctantly rise to his feet and engage briefly in low-volume and perfunctory conversation. While never unfriendly, this would come without the usual half-smiles and informative and interesting asides that would tell you about something you did not ask.

Yet on the days he selected his desk near the executive assistants, he could not be readily located. His choice was not gestured by his bodily presence but by a laptop or backpack on the surface of the desk and a coat slung over the back of the chair. Visible were only these few possessions and an empty chair. Occasionally, he could be seen hovering in the vicinity while in conversation with colleagues, or at their chosen workstation for the day, before moving towards one of the office meeting rooms or towards the lift – only to reappear again at a later point in time. Many of our conversations occurred as the lift doors slid open, and I would find him standing in wait. Oftentimes, we would chat as he passed by my desk, pausing for a minute or two on the way to elsewhere.

Consequently, at his desk no signs could be observed of his habitation or of any past or impending activity at this place. This was not itself remarkable as desks would commonly be left unoccupied – but pens, notebooks, coffee mugs or other personal effects would be present as if a task at hand was still in progress and the occupant would return.

At the end of the workday, the backpack, laptop and jacket would vanish, meaning that the branch manager had departed the building. At his desk nothing was left behind that would serve as a sign of what had, or had not, been that day.

Centred on the branch manager's chosen desk and his movements around the office space, this vignette presents an entanglement of his possessions, and their visibility, with what this inversely signals as bodily absence, and unseen but material, activity. His selection of a desk that could be easily overseen by his staff and colleagues – and hence a signalling of his presence and availability – seems to contrast with his lack of opportunity to utilise this as a space to work, have discussions or attend to policy matters. In relative terms, the lesser-seen desk at the far end of the office was a place to action routine and prescribed correspondence and deliver authorised information to those who required it.

By configuring the backpack and the jacket as a trace that remained at his unused and uninhabited desk allows this scene to become intelligible. As ethnographic details, the items left behind that were visible to others connect his arrival routine and desk selection with his circuitous movements around the office which

154 Lindsey Garner-Knapp and Joanna Mason

allows a knotting together of his trajectories or 'histories' (Napolitano, 2015) through this material and in-the-present assemblage. Only by having observed his movement in and through the office space that surrounded his desk, and in noting how he claimed the desk and left it unattended, do these items become lodged in a history and manifest as a trace to challenge binary understandings of visibility. The far end of the office where the branch manager worked, in contrast, was unseen by others but became a productive space to generate visible communications that populated email inboxes – with the distributed emails and other transactions becoming material traces of this activity.

From the branch manager's visible desk, few signs could be detected for the progression of his policy work and his collaborative efforts – but his usage of the office space as he transitioned to and from planned engagements facilitated opportunistic interactions and conversations with those in his midst. With lesser-seen spaces away from the ear- and eye-shot of others often considered productive for informal relations within policy settings – in unpacking this scene through attending to the traces left behind from the knotting of histories, this association does not appear to hold true. For the branch manager, formal relations as digital correspondence were enacted from a private and unseen space, while unprompted and opportunistic informal interactions occurred in plain sight in the general office space.

This vignette lends itself also to exploring the methodological significance of the trace, the 'ethnographic detail'. Napolitano writes of the 'lingering qualities of materialities "looking back at us", with affective forces of histories' (2015, p. 61). This is in reference to the auratic quality of traces – signalling that this occurs 'when the trace disrupts a given reading and animates the mattering (the becoming important) of things, histories and places' (2015, p. 61). Here, the laptop, backpack and jacket developed auratic qualities of traces as their visibility indicated the branch manager's invisibility, and as ethnographic details upset a simple reading of the situation that the branch manager was present and available. A similar upset occurs when the branch manager stood in wait outside the lift area in anticipation of holding discussions in alternative spaces. Yet in the vignette, this act saw to relational moments that would inform chosen policy actions and pathways. Only later would these interactions materialise into traces that could be seen and recorded, such as in a modified paragraph within a policy proposal or a meeting request to address an emerging policy issue.

By breaking down the stability of these binary associations, and by understanding mundane items as traces arising from a past history, a conclusion can be reached that the multi-functional workspace had indeed achieved its goal – but perhaps not in the way that the design had intended. Claiming a workstation next to a distant colleague for the day was not the means to foster interaction and conversation across policy areas. Instead, it was the visibility of moving through the office, and being seen by colleagues, that allowed for spontaneous or informal relations.

A Coffee Room Chat

Years after working for a local government in Canada, I am still in contact with my former team members and the work they are

Tracing Threads of In/Visibilities   **155**

doing. Social media has made this possible via notifications and live feed updates on platforms like *LinkedIn* and email mailing lists. Hundreds of kilometres away from my former colleagues, I see their workings coming to fruition – policy documents, programmes and the collaborative making of a mural that celebrated and welcomed an under-represented minority group. Despite the chronological and geographical distance, the news of these outcomes fills me with pride, nostalgia and gratitude. These projects, at one time, were the central aim of my work in the policy team. Yet, as time passed, distance grew between myself and that work until this moment when my past was present once again as I read a *LinkedIn* notification celebrating the creation of a mural.

Local governments in Canada are responsible for many of the programmes and policies that impact citizens' lives like urban planning, affordable housing, parks and public art. In this local government, policy and resource allocation decisions were made by the elected mayor and counsellors who were supported by a permanent civil service to implement their decisions.

My role was to support the local government by providing policy research and advice on government policy matters to the senior leadership team. This meant that I regularly interacted with senior leadership and elected officials. All of this work was completed under one roof wherein elected officials and civil servants regularly crossed paths in secure hallways and coffee rooms and also public spaces. My desk was located within metres of the mayor's office and the manager's office, allowing for regular interactions to occur.

As a policy advisor, I utilised a range of tools to inform policy but always with the ethos that 'we advise, they decide'. As an advisor, I understood that I could use the full set of tools to inform the decision-maker including briefings, documents, ad hoc meetings and catch-ups off the side of a desk or in the coffee room. When deciding which tool to use, I often considered timeframes, urgency and bureaucratic processes while also recognising the policymaking process as relational and dynamic.

One day as I sat at my desk surrounded by my team in our shared cubical, I overheard a colleague on the phone guiding a person who was seeking to have a meeting with the mayor and city council. Hearing half a telephone conversation, I learned that a recognised minority group were phoning to inquire about how to develop a stronger relationship with the elected government. My colleague said to the caller that she would look into the best

156   Lindsey Garner-Knapp and Joanna Mason

way to help the group meet this goal. After the call ended, another colleague who had also overheard the conversation suggested that the group fill out an online form as per regular protocol. There was something about this response that did not sit well with me – context matters, and as this group were a recognised minority, a different approach was warranted. Knowing the importance of inclusion and representation of minority groups to the elected government, I swivelled my chair around to contribute to the discussion. Instead of completing an online form, I suggested that it would be better for the elected officials to bypass regular bureaucratic procedures and reach out directly to the group to meet with them, thereby signalling that the local government recognised their importance. My cubical colleagues agreed but were concerned about gaining the appropriate leadership buy-in to the modified programme and the pressure to respond quickly.

From my desk, I could see the doors were open to the mayor's and city manager's offices which indicated that they were both in the building. First, I sought my manager's signoff on the proposed idea before walking over to the city manager's office. Poking my head into my manager's office, I asked: *Can I talk to you about something quick?[1] Sure*, they said. *We got a request for a meeting with the mayor from a minority group representative. Our normal policy is for groups to fill out an online requisition. I sensed that this would be terrible because this group isn't a local sports club but has a recognised minority status*, I advised. *What do you suggest*, they asked. *We get the mayor's office to invite them to a meeting. What do you think?* I responded. After a brief and openly inquisitive discussion, the city manager agreed.

With relief that I had the city manager onside, I went over to the mayor's receptionist to enquire if the mayor was available. At that very moment, the mayor walked up to his office, and I asked if I could speak with him briefly. This request was unusual but welcomed. We had a friendly rapport, and I knew from past interactions that he was interested in inclusive policies and actions. He suggested that we get a coffee and talk on the way. Carrying his mug, we walked along the edge of the cubicles towards the coffee room. In a quiet voice, I said: *We got a request from a minority group that they'd like to meet with you.* Curiously, he asked: *Great. What do we have to do?* Restating the same arguments I shared with the city manager, I suggested that we invite them to a meeting and forego the regular procedures. Continuing with his curiosity and

---

[1]These quotes are from my recollections and are not verbatim.

Tracing Threads of In/Visibilities   **157**

entering the coffee room, he asked: *What do you think we should do?*
I briefly looked around the coffee room hoping that it was empty.
I was aiming to be discrete in providing direct policy advice on a
socially and politically sensitive topic which the mayor may or may
not have been briefed on earlier. Fortunately, the room was empty,
so I suggested that there are many ways that we could be more
inclusive, including meeting with them directly or collaboratively
developing a mural with this group. We discussed several options I
put forward for a few moments, then I returned to my desk.

I shared the proposed outreach approach with several cubical
colleagues throughout the day, discussing also the value of this
particular group and their contribution to our shared culture. I
later learned that my suggestion to conduct the outreach first was
agreed upon. These conversations happened off the corner of people's desks and within the cubical that we shared. That was the end
of my engagement with this outreach strategy and a few weeks
later, I left this role to pursue an opportunity.

This takes me to the current moment and reading the *LinkedIn*
update – 'Municipal Mural for All' is the subject line from the
city's bulletin. Sitting at my desk in Edinburgh, the threads of the
past – my memories – were present. At once, I am taken back to
the hallways, doorways and coffee room in the local government
building. Without connections between these two periods of my
life, I had not followed the progress being made on these outreach
strategies. I was pleased that they implemented my suggestions. I
later learned that the council had implemented all of the suggestions I put forward that day years before in the coffee room. But in
that moment while scrolling through *LinkedIn,* I was remembering
the past in the present, knotting together memories with current
updates, adding a context to what I was reading of a forgotten
observed and shared moment.

My memories of the moments of popping my head into the city manager's
office and sharing a quiet moment in the coffee room with the mayor were the
only traces I had of those previous moments. We neither created a policy document nor a set of minutes following these encounters, but we did create a memory,
a non-visible, intangible trace of these co-created encounters. As my physical and
temporal distance grew from these moments, these intangible, invisible traces
faded from my memory. For me, the policy guidance I gave was shifted to the
periphery of my thoughts – nothing to knot together, just fading reflections on a
time passed.

However, these invisible traces became visible to me through the social network-
ing update and of the making of the mural. Despite my lack of engagement in the
work that took place between the historical moment of sharing my advice and the

later artistic collaboration of the painted mural and media announcement, these temporalities became knotted together, to use Napolitano's term (2015) – an invisible trace became visible as I knotted it with a current event. My role in the becoming of the mural has no visible trace, and it will remain this way. The invisibility of policy guidance, which could be described as an *informal chat* in a coffee room or doorway is the sort of trace that Michel de Certeau describes as: 'the voice that once sounded is lost, the effects and affects that the voice produces can just be heard in the writing of the listener' (Highmore, 2007, p. 97, quoted in Napolitano, 2015, p. 52). The mural is the visualisation, the now visible knot of prior discussions.

The traces here are not tangible things but invisible memories and shared policy ideas of a particular overlapping history (Napolitano, 2015). Unlike a document that moves between different times and spaces creating a textual trace visible in different places, the policy guidance shared briefly in a coffee room creates intangible traces which can only be seen when their concept transforms into a policy matter. In this vignette, the policy process transcends multiple times and places, invisible and visible, but is entangled by multiple shared histories between policy actors who move between these physical spaces and knot together in|visible.

Traces as Theoretical and Methodological Tools

Against this backdrop, we return to our underlying premise that the past informs the present to further explore the 'trace' as a lens formed by overlapping and forward-leaning incantations of the past. For us, Napolitano's argument offered 'new ways of conjuring and operationalizing ethnographic "details"' (2015, p. 47) that could be used to pursue both theoretical and methodological purposes. This has allowed us to pursue twofold and interlinked aims within our discussion of informality and to apply this specifically to the spaces in which it may associate. In attending to the physical and material realm through attuning to what is present/absent, visible/invisible and even seen/unseen – the trace offers a fruitful heuristic for exploring how informality may be apprehended in ethnographic practice and how this enables a unique understanding through a relation with its past. This stance on empirical enquiry and embedded theory places anthropological and ethnographic sensibilities front and centre, along with the lived experiences of the policymaking world – to enable a methodological approach to 'seeing' traces and a conceptual toolkit for constructing interpretations of informality that are disconnected from formality, its binary couplet.

Theoretically, traces allow us to bring together multiple times, spaces and people, weaving between what is visible to the public and what is not or not yet – all the while creating particular traces of histories that are necessary for a particular policy to be developed. These traces are themselves sometimes only visible by knotting together particular shared histories of encounters – both publicly visible and invisible – but are accessible through ethnographic approaches and the situated details that linger as present/visible materialities. We argue that the significance of informal encounters at work may not be their invisibility in the policy process – but how they create traces that mediate between spaces and transcend beyond their original locations.

Methodologically, our concept of 'visibility' can also be used in reference to Napolitano's ethnographic detail – fine-grained and observable specifics – as the building blocks for apprehending the field through participant observation (Spradley, 1980). These elements draw attention to the situated relationality of materialities as a medium for 'seeing' how traces mediate between the past and present by aiding the travel of policy through policy actors, their interactions, and with material artifacts to progress policy work. Through this, we contend that while ethnographic details may be small and easily overlooked, even seemingly inconsequential, these are important for the knotting together of particular pasts which may or may not be visible at the time, into the present. The vignettes in this chapter show how these details become the signs or physical manifestations for/of the threads that connect what may be presently unobservable or absent – having occurred or existed in the past – but leave connective traces that are visible to the attuned researcher and can be harnessed.

Exploring policymaking through the concept of the trace helps us to side-step dichotomised narratives of informality. But in disrupting binaries, the trace deploys a focus on policymaking beyond its present state, or future impacts, through adopting an analytical framework that unites the temporal and material sphere of policymaking while recognising the intricacy of this relationship between past and present. This insight highlights that there is more to be understood about policymaking than is suggested by a linear transition from the past to the future. Yet ethnographic details need not be limited to what is physically present or immediately observable. Morgan Meyer (2012) encourages thinking about an ontology of absence, to see this '… not as an existing "thing" in itself but as something that is made to exist through relations that give absence matter …', and further that 'a more fertile and less dualistic way of thinking [about what is absent or present] is to conceive absence as a trace and as something that needs to be traced' (p. 107). Tracing absence therefore can be achieved when 'absence becomes matter and through which absence comes to matter' (2012, p. 107). Such insights enable the researcher to construct interpretations of informality that can account for the multiple dimensions which are able to be captured through ethnographic research – materiality, temporality and spatiality – and to conceive of these in non-binary terms.

However, not all encounters of the past become meaningful in the present or future, yet some moments become knotted in making a material difference. How this makes a material difference is reflected in Napolitano's message that 'history affects the present not because it is a rediscovery of the past, but because it effectively introduces a discontinuity, a gap, a loss of meaning and a form of violence' (2015, p. 58). It is the invisibility of the past through gaps in time and space that creates the possibilities of knotting in the present – the act of putting together two spatio-temporal encounters to create meaning in the present.

Looking 'With' Materialities

The vignettes and this chapter's analytical claims build towards a subsequent contribution – to explicate the potential for *looking with* the materialities that exist, and have existed, in previous and temporary forms within the policy sphere. This manner of 'looking' derives from the theoretical concept of the trace to enable a deviation from scholarship on public administration and policy that configures common objects such as desks, papers and technologies (Adler-Nissen & Drieschova, 2019; Freeman, 2019; Hull, 2012; Riles, 2006), as sites of analysis – or a way of *looking at* or *upon* these elements. Our proposed focus does not desire to downplay the significance of research into these often visible but unseen everyday materialities of policy, with our goal instead to draw attention to potential other ways to integrate material objects into the analysis of policymaking. We contend that existing scholarship has contributed to an overemphasis on the utilitarian purpose of objects and the resultant impact or effect. This comes at the expense of an analysis of a *means* through which policymaking can be apprehended and understood – hence of methodological importance. For instance, in looking *at* policy documents, instead of rendering the document as an object and subject of analysis, our approach shifts the focus to its adjacent histories – such as during the production of the policy and how it changes through the actions of policy actors in relation with each other. *Prima facie* readings of a policy document may overemphasise stated policy goals and proposed instruments – but through this act passes over the ethnographic detail that allows the researcher to inquire deeper into its history and its making – to 'make visible' its history being made. Unleashed by the right methodology, this perspective allows the researcher to expose the interior of the policymaking black box.

We argue, consequently, that a policy negotiation which materialises in visible marginal traces within a policy document (e.g., email) or policy act (e.g., mural) simultaneously produces relational traces that are affective but not visible. So, while the visible marginal traces get removed from the working copy of the document when the copy is finalised and cleaned, the invisible affective traces remain. These invisible affective traces endure as social relationships, memories, tacit knowledge and trust between the participants of the negotiations and policymaking process. The traces of the relationships are also in the co-written, co-created and co-negotiated policies and policy acts. As these policies are cleaned of authorship in the civil service, only the unseen traces of the relations that are produced through the negotiated texts and policymaking transcend the space and time in which the policy was *made*.

The same is true for serendipitous policy guidance given in hallways, cafes and outside office lifts. These spaces allow for the transfer of ideas between policy staff. The traces they produce include dirty coffee cups, receipts and temporary physical blockages to passers-by. These short-lived traces are often not visible to the public – and at times, intentionally so. Rather, the intention of taking advantage of a serendipitous bumping into a colleague to share advice can be to create a relational and ideological trace – the sharing of an idea – not a physical or tangible trace.

The effects of these invisible traces occur at different times and in different places. In Joanna's vignette, a desk is selected that moulds to the branch manager's agenda of the day. The material trace gets produced when he places his belongings at the desk, marking his presence but then moves away in pursuit of other activities and back again. In Lindsey's vignette, the guidance on possible outreach and inclusion options is enacted through the creation of a mural and regular meetings between the local government and the recognised group.

In these cases, the affective traces bridge the moments between spatio-temporalities. Arguably, as time progresses there are multiple threads connecting to others throughout the policymaking process – some of which create material traces and others affective traces. These different moments become woven together throughout the lived experiences of policymakers – as 'insiders' to the policy setting – yet only some become visible.

Illuminating the Black Box

As policy researchers and former civil servants, our stance in this chapter has been that we have found the policy setting to be more accessible and easier to observe than the conceptualisation of the black box has led us to believe. A focus only on the most visible aspects of policymaking – the published white papers, reports, parliamentary hearings, and press conferences – has had the effect of blinding the public and academic discourse from policymaking processes, particularly from those which are positioned as outside of these visible and formalised spaces. In seeming opposition to these places, we were aware of spaces that are traditionally regarded as existing outside of the 'formal' policy sphere – around the office coffee machine (Visser, this volume), and service vehicles (Mulherin, this volume). These are spaces – or perhaps more aptly described as 'places' due to their accrued meaning and value (Gieryn, 2000) – where policymakers congregate, but for which little is known about how these arenas are utilised, or their fit with their ways of working.

Ethnographic vignettes which we featured in this chapter, constructed from 'insider' policy experiences and later reflections on these and memories, have drawn a focus back onto the actors who engage in policymaking to offer alternative understandings of the construction and maintenance of informality. Through attention to the dichotomies often evoked in grappling with informality and formality, we have argued that while informality normatively occurs under a cloak of 'invisibility', this should not automatically challenge the legitimacy of what occurs in these realms. Through examining the porosity of formal and informal spaces, our chapter has shown how informality both mediates and transcends across non-fixed physical and conceptual boundaries. Ultimately, the significance of informal work arrangements may not be their invisibility or isolation but how traces mediate between time and space and transcend beyond where they originate.

References

Adler-Nissen, R., & Drieschova, A. (2019). Track-change diplomacy: Technology, affordances, and the practice of international negotiations. *International Studies Quarterly, 63*(3), 531–545. https://doi.org/10.1093/isq/sqz030

Ayres, S., Sandford, M., & Coombes, T. (2017). Policy-making 'front' and 'back' stage: Assessing the implications for effectiveness and democracy. *The British Journal of Politics and International Relations, 19*(4), 861–876. https://doi.org/10.1177/1369148117721842

162   Lindsey Garner-Knapp and Joanna Mason

Bekker, M., van Egmond, S., Wehrens, R., Putters, K., & Bal, R. (2010). Linking research and policy in Dutch healthcare: Infrastructure, innovations and impacts. *Evidence & Policy, 6*, 237–253.

Freeman, R. (2019). Meeting, talk and text: Policy and politics in practice. *Policy and Politics, 47*(2), 371–388. https://doi.org/10.1332/030557319X15526370368821

Gieryn, T. F. (2000). A space for place in sociology. *Annual Review of Sociology, 26*, 463–496. http://www.jstor.org/stable/223453

Hull, M. S. (2012). Documents and bureaucracy. *Annual Review of Anthropology, 41*(1), 251–267. https://doi.org/10.1146/annurev.anthro.012809.104953

Ingold, T. (2014). That's enough about ethnography! *HAU: Journal of Ethnographic Theory, 4*(1), 383–395. https://doi.org/10.14318/hau4.1.021

Mason, J. (2023). Illuminating the craft of policy: An anthropological approach to policy ethnography. *Anthropology & Medicine*, Advance online publication. https://doi.org/10.1080/13648470.2023.2242307

McGranahan, C. (2018). Ethnography beyond method: The importance of an ethnographic sensibility. *Sites: A Journal of Social Anthropology and Cultural Studies, 15*(1), 1–10. https://doi.org/10.11157/sites-id373

Meyer, M. (2012). Placing and tracing absence: A material culture of the immaterial. *Journal of Material Culture, 17*(1), 103–110. https://doi.org/10.1177/1359183511433259

Mikecz, R. (2012). Interviewing elites: Addressing methodological issues. *Qualitative Inquiry, 18*(6), 482–493. https://doi.org/10.1177/1077800412442818

Napolitano, V. (2015). Anthropology and traces. *Anthropological Theory, 15*(1), 47–67. https://doi.org/10.1177/1463499614554239

Ortner, S. B. (2010). Access: Reflections on studying up in Hollywood. *Ethnography, 11*(2), 211–233. http://www.jstor.org/stable/24048061

Pinch, T. J. (1992). Opening black boxes: Science, technology and society. *Social Studies of Science, 22*(3), 487–510. https://doi.org/10.1177/0306312792022003003

Riles, A. (2006). *Documents: Artifacts of modern knowledge*. University of Michigan Press.

Spradley, J. P. (1980). *Participant observation*. Holt, Rinehart and Winston.

Wimmelmann, C. L. (2017). Performing compliance: The work of local policy workers during the implementation of national health promotion guidelines. *Evidence & Policy: A Journal of Research, Debate and Practice, 13*(3), 417–432. https://doi.org/10.1332/174426416x14663312126352

Chapter 10

Dénouement: Why the How Comes to Matter

Tamara Mulherin[a] and Lindsey Garner-Knapp[b]

[a]Northumbria University, UK
[b]University of Edinburgh, UK

Abstract

As a backend to this book, we outline the crafting of our collaborative book assembling journey on in|formality in policymaking. Anchored in practitioner experiences, we explore how we encountered the often-discounted dimensions of informal policy processes and the challenges entailed in transversing traditional academic boundaries. We describe the chronological evolution of the project, highlighting the inclusive editorial process and thematic workshops that shaped this book's content. With creativity and thoughtful reflection, we describe how we navigated the complexities of interrogating informality in policymaking without falling into binary distinctions. Ultimately, we show how our efforts underscore the transformative potential of collaborative academia and our ongoing inquiry into in|formality.

Keywords: In|formality; writing; autoethnography; relationality; coproduction; academia otherwise

Introduction

How do you describe it but not name it?

This book would not be complete without chronicling the emergence of its development and central organising concept. That this involved sustained collaboration as a four-strong editorial team and the forging of a shared aspiration is not itself unusual or uncommon. Yet our journey had particular dimensions,

---

Informality in Policymaking: Weaving the Threads of Everyday Policy Work, 163–173
Copyright © 2025 by Tamara Mulherin and Lindsey Garner-Knapp
Published under exclusive licence by Emerald Publishing Limited
doi:10.1108/978-1-83797-280-720241011

164 *Tamara Mulherin and Lindsey Garner-Knapp*

guided by a strong commitment to being co-creative and inclusive, attributes that often struggle to be sustained in standard academic projects.

If we regard the making of an edited book as the careful art of knotting together multiple threads of creative authorship to construct a cohesive volume, then this chapter is an active, reflective 'unknotting' of its making to expose how we co-created it as multiple collaborators. This dénouement is not a resolution or conclusion to our volume but an unravelling of the multiple knots holding it together – leaving the loose ends untied.

This book's origins materialised through 'virtual' pandemic conversations among a group of doctoral students where neither our shared experiences as policy practitioners nor our up-close doctoral research squared with policy theories or descriptive policy prescriptions. We were aware of important literature on the informal in policy work (Bevir & Rhodes, 2003; Colebatch, 2014; Lindblom, 1959; Metze, 2010; Yanow, 1996), as we outline in the Introduction (Mason et al., this volume), but we felt there had been limited empirical studies exploring how and why the informal actually matters in policy.

Practitioner Experiences

Having come to academia with already locally situated understandings of policymaking, we were driven by a curiosity built out of these experiences. However, this was not the only aspect captivating our interest. Our experiences have not been homogeneous, stemming from different orders of governments, settings and countries (Canada, Australia, the Netherlands, England and Scotland). We recognise that all of our experiences have derived from the global north, yet even here we identified many differences from across this policy landscape. Through our interactions and collaborations exploring policy, knowledge, and practice, we concluded that context matters and this position has informed our editorial approach.

We have observed that various scholars writing about policymaking do so from a position of being already situated within an academic discipline and a theoretical commitment. We also have observed, given our backgrounds, that the silos found in government departments are not so different from the silos found between academic disciplines – each creates limits on the kinds of research questions being asked but also how to answer those questions – with similitude to Gillian Tett's (2015) observations. As former practitioners, we brought insights of the lived experiences of policymakers into academia, which opened up different lines of inquiry.

Rules, procedures, paperwork, manuals and protocols were all part of our practitioner experiences in policymaking and public administration settings. These were also ubiquitous in the academic literature on policymaking and public administration when we transitioned into academia. While the documents we produced and the infrastructures that we recreated through our policy work were present in academic discourse, the dominant text-focused methods exclude the people who make those artefacts. It excluded the negotiations at the coffee machine, the resolutions discussed while walking towards the car, the emotions that surface during meetings that never make the minutes and the sketches and scribbles in the margins of drafts that form the input for important policy decisions. Our experiences as policymakers pointed us to the importance of bringing analysis of everyday actions into policymaking research in general, and the role of informality and formality research in particular.

And so, while situated in different disciplines and places in the world, we shared an ethnographic sensibility (McGranahan, 2018) that underpinned our doctoral research. This blend of shared policy praxis, research approach and being mature-age students, all shaped our desire to create something that reflected this, as well as an ambition to undertake a project that embodied doing academia differently.

Chronology of Collaboration

Throughout this book's creation, we committed to a collaborative and open approach both to the way we inquired into informality (now in|formality) and also to our interactions with the chapter author contributors. This approach to the ongoing concept and text development is not dissimilar to the policymaking work we experienced as practitioners. As editors, we welcomed the chapter authors into a process of community building as co-creators of this book and as peers who were equally committed to exploring informality and formality differently. This editorial approach shaped how we engaged with all of the authors throughout this book's formation as it required more intense and frequent collective interactions, meetings and dialogues from the outset. As a result of this commitment, we used multiple forms of engagement, first as an editorial team with brainstorming and co-writing sessions and later with chapter authors starting with preliminary interviews with abstract authors, an introductory welcome, three thematic workshops, ongoing peer editorial team discussions and multiple updates along the way.

Our coming together as an editorial team did not emerge out of a structured group or structured programme but through independent outreach efforts seeking to connect with kindred spirits to do academia differently. We owe our initial discussions to Richard Freeman who put us all in contact. Still, our continued connections are our own and evolved through the development of the ongoing *Policy-Knowledge-Practice Group* (PKP). This virtual international collective emerged during the COVID-19 pandemic as a supportive space for early-career scholars to discuss policy and public administration literature and present work-in-progress to each other. In and through our virtual meetings, we developed relationships, understandings, curiosities and questions, and it was in these spaces where our origin story and this book began.

Our foray into writing a book tentatively emerged through **PKP** members trying something new, the organisation of a conference panel *The informal practices of making policy (work)* at the June 2021 Interpretive Policy Analysis Conference. Led by Sarah Ball and Tamara Mulherin and in collaboration with **PKP**, papers were sought from scholars who were considering informality in policymaking differently. The panel call for abstracts noted that while the work of public policy actors entailed spending their time on varied activities like writing policy, advising politicians and implementing various initiatives, they also spend their time 'hanging out' chatting at the coffee machine, discussing developments in the hallway walking from one meeting to another, having informal discussions before formal meetings or sharing a drink afterwards to make sense of what has happened in formal negotiations (Stubbs, 2015).

As a potential way to garner support for the imagined book, working collaboratively under the stewardship of Sarah and Tamara who supported the ambitions of the book editors as well as the careers of PKP members, the panel offered an opportunity to engage in the academic traditions and curriculum vitae-building exercises necessary for our career development goals and test potential interest in the idea of a book on the topic.

And so, we were interested in re-imagining, re-thinking and re-shaping knowledge about the informal doings of policy actors, exploring the importance of this often-obscured dimension in policy work, whereby aspects like creative discretion, the influence of varied traditions or conventions, dynamic processes (e.g., deliberative approaches, elements of partnership working) and prosaic daily routines inflect the ongoing interplay between formal/informal dimensions in policy work.

Building on the success and interest garnered at the IPA conference, the editors pushed forward with further discussions resulting in the production of a call for abstracts for a book. Proposing that informality is part and parcel of the everyday process of – relational and entangled – policymaking, an enabling force, we sought expressions of interest to develop chapters which present thick descriptions and analysis of (then) in/formal policymaking and the work that actually resonates with policymakers, resembling what they do from day to day. Even at this early stage, we sought to do something novel and break from academic conventions of rigid chapter structures, seeking alternative approaches to the writing, format and presentation of chapters including ethnographic, narrative, poetic, visual or graphical representations. This ambition to challenge the dominant essay format proved difficult in practice, yet our call was well received by ethnomethodologists from around the globe – and predominantly from women scholars. Our commitment to creative interpretations went beyond the chapter texts and informed the artwork used throughout this book, produced by our collaborator, the artist-weaver Emma Weale, which we discuss below in greater detail.

As interest in our emerging book grew, chapter abstracts filtered into our inboxes, and we felt a shared relief that we were not alone in our inquiry into informality – our community of interest was growing. With a commitment to doing academia differently, we met virtually with each abstract contributor to better understand their understanding of in/formality and their intentions with their chapter. This relational approach helped us identify a cohesive set of chapters for this book while allowing more traditional interpretations of informality to find alternative publication outlets.

As we reviewed the abstracts, a number of themes were derived. Once we had the chapter abstracts, as editors we discussed a) what holds these abstracts together and b) what themes could continue to do the work of understanding

Dénouement **167**

informality as in|formality as we describe in the Introduction – or what these bridge in relation to the informal–formal divide. In our meetings prior to the first workshop, we identified five themes. The goal then of our first workshop was to bring the authors into the bookmaking process by having them inform and advance our understanding of the themes and how the themes related to informality. Our invitation to the first online workshop sought to bring all chapter authors to discuss the themes which we generated as associated with informality in policymaking including, boundaries, networks and relational infrastructure, traces, response-ability (Haraway, 2016) and knowledge mastery. After productive discussions in the workshop, we asked authors to consider which of the possible themes their work would further develop in their chapter. From this, as editors, we narrowed the themes to three, and following the authors' responses, we assigned the authors themes to further develop in their chapters. These themes also worked as the foundations for sorting the chapters between the editors. Each editor was given two chapters from two different themes so that there was some overlap and consistency in how the themes were developed in the chapters. Additionally, we approached editing as a collaborative endeavour working in pairs to give additional support to the authors and to each other as editors.

A second set of workshops clustered on the themes, and we brought together the chapter authors within their thematic cluster to listen and learn from each other, specifically recording how each author was developing the theme throughout their chapter and to support each other's progress. Chapter contributors provided longer drafts of their chapters to share and discuss what the theme meant to the author and how they were working with it. In these thematic groups, the other authors provided feedback to each other – a co-creative collaboration to build up our conceptualisation of informality. This was part of our process of doing academia differently; we brought the authors together as a collective and provided a platform for further interrogation of the theme and the concept of informality not as a fixed category but as one that was emerging through our interactions.

A third workshop was timed to enable all authors to bring their chapters to fruition by sharing an almost finalised version of their chapter with the group. Every workshop aimed to provide a space for each author to discuss the ideas underlying their developing chapter and to give and receive peer feedback. Bringing the chapter authors together regularly meant that we developed a community of co-inquirers into the topic of informality in policymaking alongside the production of this book.

Each workshop incorporated a creative visual exercise to encourage new ways of thinking about informality. Shared images related to fieldwork and words associated with informality in policymaking brought together as word clouds were two of the creative tools we used to spark conversations during these collaborative sessions. These creative endeavours wove their way through this book as part of the learning experiences we participated in during our inquiries into informality in policymaking. A number of these images appear in the preceding chapters and more are presented below.

Taking seriously Herbert Blumer (1954) that scholars ought to interrogate assumed concepts, each of these workshops aimed to do just that through deliberation, reflection and inquiry. Undoubtedly, our discussions during the workshops informed our conceptualisation of informality (and formality) in policymaking. Figures 10.1 and 10.2 show changes in the words associated with informality in policy(making) from the beginning and end of the first half-day workshop. And rather than moving towards a consensus on what 'informality' is, the term became more bifurcated, contextual and a-normative. These are the roots of our neologism in|formality.

Figure 10.1. First Word Cloud from the first workshop, January 2022.

Figure 10.2. Second Word Cloud from the first workshop.

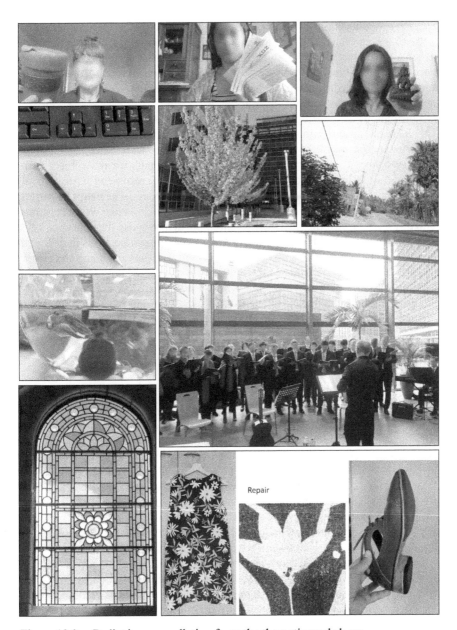

Figure 10.3. Padlet images, collation from the thematic workshops.

Figure 10.3 is from the second set of workshops where chapter authors contributed to a shared Padlet[1] collage, combining visual metaphors from our individual

---

[1] What is Padlet? Padlet-for-online-teaching-and-learning.pdf (imperial.ac.uk) (accessed 25 March 2024).

research on policymaking. Once again, these images highlight the uniqueness of each context in which in|formality emerged for the authors of this book, from invisible repair work making something a-new, to the impermanence of pencil markings, to community-making efforts via shared coffees and to the pastoral care of a cubical fish. These material objects matter in the making of policy, yet they are not homogeneous or uniform.

Throughout the development of this edited manuscript, we were challenged with how to inquire into 'informality' without falling into an extant binary relationship. We asked: how do you interrogate the concept when the complementary concept – the formal – is so deeply entangled with the subject matter? These questions and challenges in representation resonated with each of the chapter authors in trying to describe their encounters. The chapters in this volume take different approaches to dealing with this challenge. Whereas some critically engage with the way their research participants use the concepts, others show the work that the concepts do and the meaning it acquires in different contexts, while others refrain from using the terms, rather analysing the everyday practices, materials and spaces that have not received detailed scrutiny in existing accounts of policymaking. We have co-inquired into the production of informality and formality, their meanings and affordances through ongoing open discussions about it from various contexts from around the globe. Even as the creation of this book has come to an end, we are all aware that our inquiry into informality continues.

Threads of In|formality Through Art

The cover of this book is a physical metaphor for our interpretation of the role of in|formality in the policymaking process. Emma Weale, an artist-weaver from Edinburgh, Scotland, crafted the tapestry and photographed the process that encases this book. The fibres that start the tapestry are the warp threads which are equally spaced and run vertically. The weft threads are then woven, often of different colours, forward and backward through the warp threads. The weave of weft threads builds on previous rows, slowly building a completed tapestry. Throughout the process, the weft threads move from the front of the tapestry, which generates the intended image and then to the back of the tapestry, which faces a wall when later displayed. Yet, these are the same weft threads moving between the front, the back and in-between. The totality of the tapestry – the front, back, sides and form – emerges as the craftsperson (Emma in this case), carefully transforms threads into a fabric. This haptic process resonated with our interpretation of the informal and formal in the policymaking process. People, documents, meetings, thoughts, memories and values move through places, spaces and traces over time, and while there may be insights into the process via public records, the craft of policymaking is akin to the weft threads moving forward and backward among the warp threads. Here, informality and formality are enmeshed together and often part of the same thread – in|formality enmeshed and interwoven together.

Authorship and Sharing Credit

Authorship, recognition and citation are meaningful practices within the academy, and these practices have not gone unnoticed in the literature (Liboiron et al., 2017; Macfarlane, 2017) or during the creation of this book. Authorship order can be a sensitive topic in academia as it can be linked to career advancements including 'prestige, promotion and pay', making the ordering of co-authorship a potential battleground (Macfarlane, 2017, p. 1195).

From the beginning, we sought to identify a fair system that reflected the collaborative nature of our approach – this was no easy feat. There were multiple author-ordering strategies that we could choose from, yet each came with its own bias. From the Vancouver Protocol to unconventional methods like random competitions, to circumvention strategies like laboratory group names (Liboiron et al., 2017), authors from across disciplines have tried to identify the optimal strategy to establish equity in the author order. Each method of determining who counts as an author or what order they are positioned in is informed by a particular set of principles – often related to the contribution or value of the contribution. We were challenged to identify a strategy that recognised the equal but different contributions of each of the editors and, equally, the contributions of our author collaborators.

The *Vancouver Protocol* has been widely accepted by various disciplines and has informed publishers' policies including Oxford Press and Cambridge University Press (UCP, 2024). Here, three conditions must be met to afford authorship credit:

> Authorship credit should be based only on substantial contributions to (a) either conception and design or else analysis and interpretation of data and to (b) drafting the article or revising it critically for important intellectual content and on (c) final approval of the version to be published. (ICMJE, 2014, p. 149)

Emerald Publishing subscribes to the updated *Vancouver Protocol* also outlined by ICMJE which include the three criteria above and (d) 'agreed to be accountable for all aspects of the work in ensuring that questions related to the accuracy or integrity of any part of the work are appropriately investigated and resolved' (n.p.).[2] While the *Vancouver Protocol* sets out a baseline for inclusion of who should (and should not) be designated authorship, we found this protocol to be lacking in identifying the ordering of authors within this collaborative project.

Offering a feminist approach, Max Liboiron and colleagues (2017) have developed an approach to authorship ordering, prioritising 'process and equity rather than system and equality' (p. 3). This feminist-informed approach takes seriously

---

[2]https://www.emeraldgrouppublishing.com/publish-with-us/ethics-integrity/research-publishing-ethics#authorship

172 *Tamara Mulherin and Lindsey Garner-Knapp*

the importance of author ordering and prioritises equity, consensus, valuing care work and social location when establishing the order (Liboiron et al., 2017). Adding these values to the *Vancouver Protocol* helped us address some of the challenges we faced in reordering our authorship as we compiled the manuscript.

In an attempt to avoid authorship disputes later on, the four editors agreed to an arbitrary approach and resorted to alphabetical order but with a commitment to foregrounding the collective of the book-making (Mason, notes, 20 July 2021). However, as time passed and each of our positions changed, the original decision to follow the alphabet was re-evaluated and collectively questioned whether it truly signalled the co-creative and collaborative efforts of the group. The challenge of addressing this at the end of a collaboration is to avoid approaching it as a retrospective score-keeping exercise where nobody wins. Instead, our ambition was to identify a strategy where we could all be better off – not identical but improved in our authorship acknowledgements. We maintained the editorial authorship by the last name – recognising the 'formal' tradition in academia – and the Introduction authorship by first name – recognising the 'informal' and familiar relationships between us. With these authorship-ordering choices, we recognise that in the making of this book, we each contributed differently while utilising the variety of skills and aptitudes we each brought into the collective.

Reflections

Doing academia differently is possible – this book is confirmation of that. As mature, early-career academic women with children and familial responsibilities and limited prior experience in the academy, but extensive experience outside of it, particularly in policy settings, our efforts counter the scripts for doing academia and challenge accepted conventions along the way to collaboratively, creatively, committedly, craft this book to share our experiences. Together with our chapter authors and collaborators, we have learned a great deal – some aspects were easier than anticipated and others not so much.

When it came to the positive aspects of co-producing this book, we felt it was quite easy, like mopping the floor – you just keep moving. Bookmaking is built on transferable skills developed outside of the academy (e.g., organising events, writing, minutes, publishing reports). We had incredible support from senior academics editing, reading, and promoting our efforts. There were some surprises, whereby we had to let a chapter go. While these moments disrupted the flow, we learnt by doing, picking a supportive publisher, knowing timeframes, and being open to addressing difficult moments.

And as we come to the end of this book and our collaboration, while a dénouement might be understood as pulling the strands together to resolve matters, its meaning in French is untying or unravelling,[3] so while some loose ends need to

---

[3] Oxford English Dictionary, dénouement – quick search results. Oxford English Dictionary (oed.com), accessed 25 March 2024.

be re-woven, there remain some hanging, inviting us to 'follow the threads where they lead in order to track them and find their tangles and patterns' (Haraway, 2016) in the in|formal and in the effects of the relations generated.

References

Bevir, M., & Rhodes, R. A. W. (2003). *Interpreting British Governance / Mark Bevir and R. A. W. Rhodes*. Routledge.

Blumer, H. (1954). What is wrong with social theory? *American Sociological Review, 19*, 3–10.

Colebatch, H. K. (2014). Making sense of governance. *Policy & society, 33*(4), 307–316. https://doi.org/10.1016/j.polsoc.2014.10.001

Editors, *International Committee of Medical Journal*. (1994). Uniform requirements for manuscripts submitted to biomedical journals. *Canadian Medical Association Journal, 150*, 147–154.

Haraway, D. J. (2016). *Staying with the trouble: Making kin in the Chthulucene*. Duke University Press.

International Committee of Medical Journal Editors. (1994). Uniform requirements for manuscripts submitted to biomedical journals. *Canadian Medical Association Journal, 150*(2), 147–155.

Liboiron, M., Ammendolia, J., Winsor, K., Zahara, A., Bradshaw, H., Melvin, J., Mather, C., Dawe, N., Wells, E., & Liboiron, F. (2017). Equity in author order: A feminist laboratory's approach. *Catalyst: Feminism, Theory, Technoscience, 3*, 1–17.

Lindblom, C. E. (2020). The science of "muddling through", 19 Pub. Admin. Rev. 79 (1959). *Communication Law and Policy, 25*(4), 451–455. https://doi.org/10.1080/10811680.2020.1805947

Macfarlane, B. (2017). The ethics of multiple authorship: Power, performativity and the gift economy. *Studies in Higher Education (Dorchester-on-Thames), 42*(7), 1194–1210. https://doi.org/10.1080/03075079.2015.1085009.

McGranahan, C. (2018). Ethnography beyond method: The importance of an ethnographic sensibility. *Sites: A Journal of Social Anthropology and Cultural Studies, 15*, 1–10.

Metze, T. (2010). New life for old buildings: Mediating between different meanings. In H. K. Colebatch, R. Hoppe & M. Noordegraaf (Eds.), *Working for policy* (pp. 75–90). Amsterdam University Press.

Stubbs, P. (2015). Performing reform in south east Europe: Consultancy, translation and flexible agency. In J. Clarke, D. Bainton, N. Lendvai, & P. Stubbs (Eds.), *Making policy move: Towards a politics of translation and assemblage* (1st edn., pp. 65–93). Bristol University Press. https://doi.org/10.2307/j.ctt1t89fpb6.

Tett, G. (2015). *The silo effect: Why putting everything in its place isn't such a bright idea*. Hachette UK.

University of Cambridge Press (UCP). (2024). *Research integrity: Guidelines on authorship*. University of Cambridge Press. Retrieved March 18, 2024, from https://www.research-integrity.admin.cam.ac.uk/research-integrity/guidance/guidelines-authorship

Yanow, D. (1996). *How does a policy mean? Interpreting policy and organizational actions*. Georgetown University Press.

Afterword

Afterword: Reflecting on In|formality

Peregrine Schwartz-Shea[a] and Dvora Yanow[b]

[a]*Department of Political Science (Emerita), University of Utah, Utah, USA*
[b]*Guest Professor, Knowledge, Technology, and Innovation Sub-Department, Department of Social Sciences, Wageningen University, Netherlands*

> *Keywords*: Ethnographic evidence; everyday policymaking and implementation; expectations for Weberian bureaucracy; interpretive methodological thinking; situated meaning

In|formality, the term of art created by this book's editors, could be said to name a paradox. Humans make policies through formal, written rules and procedures which offer the promise of certainty, but that promise is constantly challenged as the rules and procedures must always be enacted anew, in time and *in situ*, by particular social actors. These actors may 'choose' to act (or act habitually) 'by the book' or to innovate at the margins, responding 'informally' to the many aspects of a situation that formal rules can never cover, all the more so in a rapidly evolving social world. The term marries two ordinary language words – formality and informality – in a way that focuses on their interrelationships. In coining it, the editors draw attention to those linkages and what we think we know about them: the vertical bar ('|') halts our normal reading habits and invites us to reconsider the meanings of the two components. Alternative punctuation marks – a slash (as in 'in/formal') or a parenthetical [(in)formal] – would not halt our reading as readily, given their commonality. The visual disruption of the less common orthography is what makes the editors' intervention so arresting. Their introduction and the nine substantive chapters they have curated dig deeply into what in|formality can mean in an array of public sector settings, professions and cultures. In a situated, contextualised manner, chapter authors theorise social actors' continual (re)making of their worlds as they encounter settings that evolve.

In this reflection on those chapters, we assess this theorising, drawing on the contexts of our respective scholarly domains. In the initial section, we revisit the two concepts that are central to this volume from the perspective of language use. We then attend to definitional quandaries and how the editors have handled them. Next, we turn to an issue of power implicit in these considerations which

---

Informality in Policymaking: Weaving the Threads of Everyday Policy Work, 177–192
Copyright © 2025 by Peregrine Schwartz-Shea and Dvora Yanow
Published under exclusive licence by Emerald Publishing Limited
doi:10.1108/978-1-83797-280-720241012

178 Peregrine Schwartz-Shea and Dvora Yanow

we find lurking across the chapters. Subsequently, we take up the complexities of informality as revealed in chapter treatments. In the final section, we engage the implications of the book's analyses for how we theorise and for methods and methodologies.

The Language of Formality and Informality

The editors' introduction to the book implicitly calls for attention to the language of in|formality. Especially when structured that way with the vertical line, in the context of their critique, the negating prefix, in-, 'marks' the word. As linguists, anthropologists and others invoke the idea, marking distinguishes its object from the customary, presumedly 'normal' case of the unmarked term (see, e.g., Jakobson, 1969, p. 321; Waugh, 1982, pp. 299–301; Zerubavel, 2018). Marking a term designates it as not usual, not expected, a deviation from the norm. In that sense, the unmarked 'formal' stands as the normal case, with 'in|formal' pointing to unexpected exceptions that violate the norm. Moreover, in many societies, the 'non-normal' character of a marked term lends it an inferior or otherwise negatively valued difference from the more 'value-neutral', unmarked term.

But what if the 'informal organization' that we encounter in these chapters *were* the norm, with explicit rules and formally written procedural manuals being the exception? That is the direction of thought to which the introduction alludes. How did it come about, we might ask, that 'formal' became synonymous with explicitly articulated protocols and rule-following? A back-of-the-envelope consideration of analyses undertaken in public administration, public policy and organisational studies points to the 'formal' organisation as the heritage of Weberian bureaucracy theory (Weber, 1946). As the study of organisations progressed into the 20th century, growing attention to 'the human side of enterprise' (McGregor, 1957) and the developing 'human relations' school of thought gave rise to the idea of 'the informal organization': those aspects of organisational life which include the human actors who people bureaucratic structures, their acts, and their interactions, alongside structural design issues. In other words, the very framing of Weber's rules for bureaucracy – requiring offices, hierarchy, authority and the other characteristics he codified, notably separated from human actors – shaped theorists' and managers' expectations for organisational design. Those came to be understood as an organisation's 'formal' aspects. Any 'deviation' from those expectations would be deemed unexpected and abnormal, a concept that by the end of the 19th century had developed both in the non-judgemental sense of 'statistical deviation from the norm' and, importantly for this discussion, in the negatively judgemental sociological sense of 'deviance' described by Durkheim in accounting for suicides (Hacking, 1990).[1]

---

[1]Weber's ideas are still relevant today, as Bouckaert (2023, p. 23) argues, claiming that Western European bureaucratic structures remain neo-Weberian: '... what was going on, it seems, was the modernization of the Weberian tradition, not its outright

Afterword **179**

Tensions between 'formal' and 'informal' are not new. We have encountered expectations for appropriate 'organizational behavior' before, also framed by Weberian understandings. In policy studies into the 1970s, these characterised ideas about implementation, which should unfold, according to the then-accepted view, from written policies adopted by way of formal legislative processes and transmitted to the administrative side of the (presumed) politics–administration dichotomy. Implementation that did not follow suit – that did not implement the formal policy as it was written – was deemed 'abnormal', in some fashion (Yanow, 1987, 1990; see also Fox, 1978, 1990, Pressman & Wildavsky, 1984 [1973]). This is also one way of reading Michael Lipsky's examination, from the late 1960s and 1970s, of street-level bureaucrats. His iconoclastic 1978 chapter 'Standing the study of implementation on its head' is basically an argument countering a Weberian framing of policymaking processes (see also Rowe, 2025). Likewise, the organisational culture literature of the 1970s (e.g., Turner, 1971) and beyond could be read as a reaction against the expectations set by a Weberian framing of the 'normal' organisation, shaping expectations that all organisational acts should be conducted explicitly, with a singular meaning for all actors and no place for tacit knowledge. The chapters in this book also turn 'formality' on its head, suggesting, in effect, that the face-to-face interactions and primary ties that are present in organisational life, like those of family and small towns or villages, are more the norm than what Weber's 'Protestant Ethic' posited in replacing them with expectations for regulated, objectively impersonal ties. This book contributes additional settings and theoretical framings in which to explore these tensions.

Definitional Quandaries

In bringing together a set of authors whose work is rooted in actual practices to collaborate on what could otherwise be a rather abstract topic, the editors make two explicit moves. First, although they review relevant academic treatments of informality and formality in the book's introduction, they resist articulating a priori definitions, choosing, instead, to ground the concept in chapter authors' empirical research and the practice-based definitions emerging from those encounters. This decision aligns with a second move, an explicitly interpretive methodological emphasis which sees context specificities, rather than generalisations abstracted from them, as essential to scientific understanding and explanation (see, e.g., Polkinghorne, 1983, Prasad, 2005, Rabinow & Sullivan, 1979), such that what 'informality is … is given meaning in everyday action …

---

rejection: a process of addition, not demolition'. This is so, he says, despite public administration reforms over the last decades resulting from dissatisfactions with the effectiveness of public policy and administration, leading to new administrative forms: contracting out public services, performance measurement and performance management of public servants, and the co-production of services by more than government agencies alone – the so-called governance turn.

180   Peregrine Schwartz-Shea and Dvora Yanow

acquir[ing] meaning through enactment and in situ' (Mason et al., Introduction, p. 12). The particularity of these empirical understandings can, in turn, be compared with academic literatures to assess the 'truth value' of their theory-based, a priori definitions.

In the chapters, formality appears to be the simpler phenomenon to recognise in the policymaking contexts engaged, as it is associated with 'the official' and its visible trappings of 'published white papers, reports, parliamentary hearings, and press conferences' (Garner-Knapp & Mason, Chapter 9, p. 161). The importance of those trappings – and their subsequent entailments – for the regulation of decision-making and accountability to others is strikingly evident in Evelijn Martinius' 'Traceless Transitions: Studying the Role of Drawings and Gestures in Construction Project Meetings' (Chapter 7). The engineers she observes pointedly refrain from recording their revised understandings and decisions, resting the legitimacy of their acts on their professional standing and expertise rather than on written records. They appear to understand that if outsiders were able to inspect the recorded decisions, they might disagree with the engineers' judgements (p. 123). Dictionary definitions[2] of 'formal' point in similar directions, to what is 'officially sanctioned or recognized', with such cognates as documentation, authorisation, legality and legitimacy (*Oxford Learning Dictionary*, Definition 2). Synonyms include dignified, approved, validated, endorsed, accepted and proper, all of them positive in their connotations. These connoted meanings fit comfortably with the discussions of the concept in academic literatures, specifically the 'distinct[ive] Anglo-American and European Public Administration traditions described as the Wilsonian, Westminster and Westphalian traditions based on application of idealised, consistent and impersonal rules for the design and implementation of policies in response to politically defined objectives' (Mason et al., Introduction, p. 7, citations deleted).

On 'informal', the *Oxford Learning Dictionary* features cognate terms that are also commonly regarded as positive attributes: relaxed, open, friendly, comfortable, everyday. *Merriam-Webster* defines informality as 'an absence of formality'; Vocabulary.com, as not following 'any particular rules'. Other dictionaries add elements that gainsay Wilsonian, Westminster and Westphalian traditions: 'Not organized; not structured or planned' (*Wikipedia*); 'irregular' (*Collins Dictionary*). In recent times, dictionary compilers have drawn more on field collections of naturally occurring language as their definitional base, thereby increasingly capturing words' actual (i.e., descriptive) usages, rather than the prescriptive recommendations of expert dictionary editorial board members in past practices (Alan J. Cienki, personal communication, 2015). The definitions of formal and informal and their synonyms may, then, reflect common usage, emphasising the positive, normative dimensions of both terms. The extent of the influence of these proclivities on scholarly theorising is unclear. What is apparent, however,

---

[2]These draw on the *Britannica*, *Cambridge Dictionary*, *Collins Dictionary*, *Oxford Learning Dictionary*, *Merriam-Webster*, Vocabulary.com and *Wikipedia*, all accessed on 24 October 2023.

is that, according to the editors, in relevant academic literatures 'informality' is 'associated with the private sphere or equated with...unstructured, spontaneous, unpredictable and face-to-face interactions', with emotions such as trust and with attributes such as speed and flexibility (Mason et al., Introduction, p. 8). They observe that the common juxtaposition of the two terms in these literatures fosters a binary opposition that links 'formal' with legitimacy and 'informal' with illegitimacy. These problematic associations are one of the editors' primary concerns. Furthermore, in our reading of the chapters, we find that the echoes of these associations also influence political aspects of who decides what is formal or informal.

Power and Politics in In|formality

Reading across the chapters of this volume brings into focus a complication that can muddy scholars' understanding of informality. Assessing the character of informality in policy-related settings and, specifically, whether it is viewed as legitimate or illegitimate depends on which social actors have selected or designed the particular institutional arrangements under study. In the classic Weberian setting, as noted above, 'informality' is understood negatively, an illegitimate departure from the formal policy that politicians and policymakers have decided upon. Embedded in this understanding is the determination that government officials alone are the legitimate decision-makers, their authority deriving from their positions ('offices', in Weber's language) in government. The judgement about which actors are entitled to be making substantive policy decisions has been solidified in the still-rehearsed politics–administration dichotomy: only elected officials should be deciding policy arrangements; administrators should be involved only with implementing those legislator-determined policies following the letter of 'the law'. Decision-making authority – the legitimacy for acting – rests with the former, not the latter. Unstated in these formulations is the relationship between authority and power. Even as the plausibility of the existence of discretion-free administrative action has been resoundingly critiqued, the narrative force of that politics–administration dichotomy remains salient and influential, reflecting some citizens' and activists' inferences that administrators – and, in the United States at the moment, 'the administrative state' as a whole – have acquired *political* power that they should not have.

What is notable in some of these book chapters is that it is *policymakers* who are themselves choosing informality: they do not judge it as illegitimate per se but, instead, as a way to enhance policy effectiveness. The character of informality may itself be different in these two kinds of settings – certainly in terms of its legitimacy, but likely on other dimensions, as well. Book chapter discussions suggest some lines along which these differences might be systematically mapped *and* the extent to which differences in the meanings and acceptability of informality depend on the perspectives of powerful policymakers. These differences can be seen longitudinally both within a single agency (as Claire Bynner shows in Chapter 1) and by comparing cases across chapters.

Bynner's '"Knowing the System": Public Administration and Informality During COVID-19' maps such differences over time, demonstrating the contingency of policymakers' evaluations of informality's legitimacy. Prior to the pandemic, expectations of rule-following formality in the distribution of grants to service providers were the norm; during the pandemic, by contrast, policymakers allowed and even encouraged informality in the delivery of grants to service providers, understood in terms of an 'ethic of care' to prevent suffering during lockdown. Bynner's setting reflects some of the institutional changes that have moved governing away from Weberian forms, e.g., awarding contracts to a dozen or so local community groups that replaced government employees in providing public services. Despite this significant change, Weberian notions of accountability are still in evidence among administrators who allocate government funds. Even when informality was encouraged, the chief administrator who was Bynner's interlocuter adapted processes of accountability to the local council, which mimicked traditional Weberian forms (p. 31). Tellingly, that chief administrator also anticipated a post-pandemic return to the prior, 'business-like' bureaucratic culture of rule-following due to the resilience of those forms of practice (Bynner, p. 34).

Two other chapters explore the administrative consequences of policymakers' choices of cross-organisational policy designs. Comparing them also reveals contingent evaluations of the legitimacy of informality. In 'Vehicles of Informality – The Role of the Car as a Mobile Space of Policy and Relational Work' (Chapter 8), Tamara Mulherin focuses on how service delivery administrators must adapt their practices when formal policy changes require 'certain National Health Services (NHSs) to integrate with local government social care services' (p. 127). E. Lianne Visser's 'Catching Up with Catching Up: Collaborative Policy Work, In|Formality and Connective Talk' (Chapter 5) explores the phenomenon of informal, interpersonal 'catching up' within the context of cross-organisational, collaborative meetings between local policymakers and the leaders of the non-profit service provider. In both chapters, it is powerful policy actors – legislators – who have deliberately chosen administrative arrangements that, from their perspectives, warrant informal collaborations. In contrast, in Bynner's more traditional Weberian setting, 'informality' was not part of the policy design, but it became legitimate under crisis conditions. Differences in policy settings may affect the character and persistence of informal practices, with Bynner's administrator fearing a return to more formal processes that ignore an ethic of care, whereas Mulherin's and Lianne Visser's administrators understand that informal processes are necessary to meet legislators' policy goals.

These may also be compared with another chapter, which shows how 'informal governance' based on cross-organisational arrangements might affect the understandings and practices of informality, depending on which actors hold the most power in particular relationships. In 'Mastering Informality in Diplomacy' (Chapter 3), Kristin Anabel Eggeling and Larissa Versloot focus on sovereign governments as organisations. In what is perhaps the oldest example of cross-organisational informality, diplomats recognise the boundaries between informality and formality as essential, even as they understand those boundaries to be porous and malleable for purposes of reaching formal governmental agreements.

These actors share some features with Lianne Visser's administrative policymakers, who coordinate with leaders of non-profit, government-funded, social service organisations concerning the common need to develop and maintain relationships of trust. But the non-profit leaders depend on the administrative policy actors in ways that diplomats representing their governments do not depend on their own administrative counterparts. Diplomats do serve at the will of their governmental superiors, but their charge is not contractual and their interactions are with their diplomatic counterparts. In contrast, social service non-profits have contractual obligations to serve their clientele in specific ways. Non-profit leaders know that funding can be withdrawn – a within-organisational fact of life – even as they 'catch up', informally, with policy actors who can influence contract renewal. For this reason, the non-profit leaders would seem to have less autonomy to re-fashion their informal practices than diplomats: the former might overstep their lines of authority and be called out as acting illegitimately by those who hold the public purse strings, emphasising once again, alongside setting-specific meanings, how powerful actors decide the legitimacy of the 'informal'.

To the extent that particular events and trends – pandemics, wars, increasing immigration, accelerating climate change – are 'bringing the state back in'[3] yet again, governmental decisions about the legitimacy of informality may constitute a useful arena for observing how power affects interrelationships between the two concepts. State actors may use both informal and formal cross-institutional arrangements to negotiate agreements, bringing the question of the implementation of states' negotiated policies to the fore. Will informality in implementation be understood as legitimate or illegitimate? The two chapters set in India illustrate some of these complexities of legitimacy as frontline staff bend policy rules to fill performance gaps, enabling the delivery of water and of electricity, respectively, to marginalised populations. Such rule-bending may shore up the legitimacy of the state government even as they mean staff risking their own jobs, depending on how their managers respond to their acts. The risk is clearer in Neha Mungekar's water case in 'Visualising Informal Repair: Exploring Photographic "Routines" in Ethnographic Methodology' (Chapter 6, p. 106). By contrast, in Meera Sudhakar's electricity case in 'The Informal Work of Policy Maintenance: Making Space for Local Knowledge in Indian Rural Electricity Governance' (Chapter 2), an accommodation appears to have been reached where the malleability of quantitative estimates of 'free' electricity usage is recognised by staff and managers alike, providing legitimacy to staff's discretionary decisions (p. 42).

Overall, reading across these chapters with attention to questions of political power surfaces a key area for future research on informality. How does the identity of who decides whether informal arrangements are legitimate affect informal practices? Existing literature on this point is not clear. Sociologist Barbara A. Misztal's

---

[3]See Evans et al.'s 1985 *Bringing the State Back In*. The argument at that time was that scholars had not paid sufficient attention to the state, instead focusing on the importance of society and societal structures.

184 Peregrine Schwartz-Shea and Dvora Yanow

argument, discussed in the editors' introduction, is that 'informality is just as necessary for creating order as formality and that a balance needs to be found between the two' (Mason et al., Introduction, p. 8). However, Misztal does not engage the matter of who has the privilege – the power – of deciding that balance. The editors join the late political scientist James C. Scott's *Seeing Like a State* to the conversation. In contrast to Misztal, Scott offered an explicit appraisal of the political relationship between the two concepts. In the full passage from the original, he writes: 'Formal order ... is *always* and to some considerable degree parasitic on informal processes, *which the formal scheme does not recognize, without which it could not exist, and which it alone cannot create or maintain*' (2008 [1998], p. 310, emphases added). More research of the kind presented in this volume could bring further, explicit attention to such questions of power in formal/informal relations.

The Informality in In|formality

As noted above, one of the editors' key goals is to disrupt dichotomised usage in academic literatures that equate 'the formal' with legitimate and 'the informal' with illegitimate (Mason et al., Introduction, p. 12). They argue that such usage has blocked in-depth scholarly investigation because the equivalence delegitimises local knowledge. The book chapters do not replicate these binary divisions, instead adding detail and nuance to existing academic treatments of the meanings and practices of informality. Some of this has been highlighted in the preceding discussion.

First, the six chapters already mentioned provide thickly described ethnographic evidence that informal processes used by street-level actors may be indispensable to achieving formal policy goals. In both Mungekar's and Sudhakar's chapters (Chapters 2 and 6), informal, discretionary strategies assisted Indian state governments in delivering vital infrastructure goods to marginalised and rural communities, consistent with formal policy goals. In Mulherin's Chapter 8, an automobile flips between its constitution as a formal space and an informal one, sometimes serving as an office for official conversations by telephone, at other times as a more casual setting for sharing information among travellers. This flexibility fostered a more effective use of travel time to the distant areas where policy programmes were delivered to clients face to face, something the new policy formally required. Likewise, informal activity made it possible for diplomats in Eggeling and Versloot's Chapter 3 to forge difficult, formal cross-governmental agreements, much as the seemingly irrelevant catching-up conversations in Lianne Visser's Chapter 5 built and maintained the cross-organisational relationships essential for consistent, formal policy delivery. And in Bynner's Chapter 1, it was the informal decisions taken by a higher level administrator to cut out certain stakeholders that helped get monetary resources delivered quickly during a pandemic, as the local council desired.

Second, what constitutes 'the informal' cannot be generalised; it depends on local circumstances. A comparatively private space enabled engineers to make decisions off-the-record (Martinius' Chapter 7); events or crises, such as the COVID-19 pandemic, loosened or abbreviated standard operating procedures

(Bynner's Chapter 1); a staff member's independent judgement call – about a light bulb (permissible) versus a new appliance (not permissible) – provided electricity to a poorer rural inhabitant in Indian electrification (Sudhakar's Chapter 2). Moreover, how the informal is constituted can change over time *within* settings as actors challenge existing boundaries (the diplomats in Eggeling and Versloot's Chapter 3) or as a policymaking space itself alternates between formal and informal activities (the automobile space in Mulherin's Chapter 8).

Two chapters not yet discussed reinforce both of these points while bringing new theoretical ideas into play. In 'Tracing Threads of In/Visibilities: The Knotty Mattering of Policymaking' (Chapter 9), Lindsey Garner-Knapp and Joanna Mason use two quite different vignettes from their respective practitioner experiences to revisit the character of informality. They argue that informal encounters leave 'traces' – impressions left by human action after those actors are no longer around – which 'mediate between spaces and transcend ... their original locations' (p. 158). In one vignette, the traces of an informal, off-the-record, relatively invisible conversation between a staff member and a policymaker bore formal fruit years later in a most visible policy change. In the second, a manager habitually made his presence known to staff through traces of informal action – leaving his computer on top of a particular desk in the centre of the available office space and draping his coat over the desk chair, only to promptly abandon the desk to walk around the floor. At other times, he made himself even less visible, 'hiding' in a less central location when he wished not to be disturbed. The authors contend that understanding policymaking and a particular policy's origins and implementation may require attending to such traces of action and interaction, a concept that underscores the challenges of identifying and researching the informal. Making the study of traces more central would open up a new focus for research on informality, alerting researchers to phenomena that other analytic lenses may render marginal or non-existent.

Second, in Chapter 4, 'Bureaucratic Hustling and Knowledge Shuffling – Informality within Swiss Public Administration', Lisa Marie Borelli theorises aspects of informal activity which revalue it as a way of achieving goals. Her setting presents a key feature of the modern, administrative (Weberian) state: governments promulgating laws to promote their residents' general welfare. For instance, individuals must have licences to drive cars legally, and building contractors must meet earthquake safety codes. In turn, frontline workers seek to ensure that people comply with such requirements. The municipal office Borelli analyses deals with registration of residents relative to activities such as marrying, requiring proofs of residence or moving to new locations (p. 71). Office staff assist clients in filling out the requisite forms, and, in turn, that paperwork makes residents legible to the Swiss state.

Rules and forms are both complex, and the flow of people coming to the office can fluctuate unpredictably. When those encounters are delayed or deemed overly long or unfair, at a minimum the 'general welfare' that governments seek to promulgate may seem even more remote from residents' everyday lives. To assist the municipal office in meeting its formal policy goals more efficiently and effectively, staff have developed two informal practices to handle periods with a high volume of clients: 'hustling', the collective routines developed to manage the workload; and 'shuffling', the activity of consulting one another to verify rules, for example, or obtain quick advice on a complex file. These practices are intended to ease such formal encounters with the administrative state, in settings which, as Soss (2005) has argued, are the locations where residents commonly experience the phenomenon of being governed. They are forms of bureaucratic 'coping', an idea introduced by Lipsky (1980), and one of Borelli's contributions is to show that such coping can be a collective response to workload stress, not only an individual strategy. Moreover, such informal work practices 'can indeed be codified (internally) and institutionalised, yet not written down' (p. 69). They are known, collectively, in worksites, are subject to innovation and may eventually be formalised. In Borelli's view, 'formality creates a framework that stabilises social processes which are then regulated by informality, e.g., through producing flexibility and reducing complexity' (p. 69, citations omitted).

Cracking apart the formal = legitimate/informal = illegitimate binary reveals additional aspects of informality not evident in the academic literature reviewed by the editors or in dictionary definitions. For example, Visser (Chapter 5) and Borrelli (Chapter 4) both re-situate scholarly understandings of informality. Visser's analysis of catching up returns to Goffmanian symbolic interactionist roots, emphasising how social actors must understand each meeting anew, requiring scripts based on prior interactions to be revised. Borrelli helps readers comprehend how 'routines' can remain informal or, alternatively, achieve more formal, institutionalised status if they successfully ease agency interactions with clients. Both authors challenge commonly assumed conceptual associations: a script or a routine might *seem* to be formal, but, in these two chapters, informal traits abound, as scripts are inhabited anew and routines developed through everyday acts, talk and even discussions about whether they should be formalised.

Two other themes emerge from comparing chapters. One is the ways in which elements of the material world can enable or block informality as they shape its relationships with formality. Mungekar's photos on water delivery practices (Chapter 6), for example, document how ordinary objects are used to modify the original water supply modes; Chapters 2, 3 and 8 provide still other examples. A second theme is the significance of the 'face-to-face'. Often treated in the literature as 'informal' (and lesser), it is re-valued by the actors observed in both Chapters 3 and 8. As Eggeling and Versloot observe, European Union (EU) treaties legally require 'bodies' to meet together in face-to-face interactions to enact agreements (Chapter 3, p. 63).

Methodological and Methods Implications

In their introduction to the book, the editors underline what they see as the requisite situatedness of studying in|formality, and each chapter demonstrates what such contextualising can contribute to understanding the interplay of formal policymaking and administrative structures and informal organisational and social realities. Although the editors do not dwell on the methodological and methods implications of that emphasis, in our reading these are evident and worthy of

Afterword **187**

explicit reflection.[4] Attention to context and situated meaning-making translates quite clearly into interpretive *methodological* thinking, with its emphasis on meaning-making that is context specific. Implicitly arguing against the sole utility of research 'findings' based on distance, of statistical (and other forms of) control and of the necessity of quantification, the authors bring readers into their settings' contexts.

'Accessing' situated meaning itself translates into particular forms of research *method*: those that introduce researchers to the everyday worlds of social actors (policymakers, administrative heads, frontline implementors and so on). Chief among these are conversational or 'ordinary language' interviewing (Fujii, 2018; Schaffer, 2014 [2006]) and participant observation or ethnography (e.g., Pachirat, 2018; Schatz, 2009), at times supplemented by textual or other material evidence of interactions and processes observed, often repeatedly, over time. Each chapter demonstrates the many ways in which methodology, methods and theorising are mutually implicating. This book shows what can be gained from theorising informed by research grounded in the everyday worlds of policymakers and their practices: the chapters reveal what the hard work of grounding theorising in empirical evidence can achieve.

To illustrate this point, consider, first, the implications of its opposite: theorising that retains physical and/or emotional distance between researchers and their 'subjects', not getting close to the social actors under study because such proximity would produce, in this view, bias or partiality. The epistemological value of distance is a key methodological presupposition of such a positivist-informed, often variables-based approach to research (Yanow, 2014 [2006]). Historically, the methods implied by that methodological idea have been those which produce the quantitative evidence making statistical analyses possible. Research practices that do not rely on such numerical evidence and statistical analyses, as Shames and Wise (2017, p. 815) relate, produce 'findings' that some deem not trustworthy because they are not 'scientific'. Such views devalue the non-quantitative evidence produced by proximity.

Against such an approach, the chapters in this volume demonstrate how a practice-centred study of in|formality benefits from interpretivist methodologies and methods, especially field-based, ethnographic ones, as researchers observe and experience 'up close' the events and interactions that are fundamental to everyday in|formal practices. This closeness enables them to tap into the tacit knowledge that underlies collectively held values, beliefs and sentiments, alongside the explicit reasoning which these inform.[5] Chapter authors observe, interact with and learn from setting-specific social actors in specific field settings, about

---

[4]We distinguish between methodologies – sets of ontological and epistemological presuppositions – and the methods that are based on these and enact them (Schwartz-Shea & Yanow, 2012, p. 4).

[5]This was Charles Taylor's point in his landmark 1971 article, 'Interpretation and the sciences of man.' He argued that these tacitly known values and beliefs are intersubjectively produced and, therefore, overlooked by variables-based research approaches (what he called the 'categorical grid of behavioral political science'; Taylor, 1987 [1971], p. 56).

188 Peregrine Schwartz-Shea and Dvora Yanow

whose practices, formal and informal, they endeavour to theorise. The specificity of those settings, actors and practices matters because, as the chapters show, what constitutes 'the informal' depends on 'local' circumstances.

Chapter authors all draw on field evidence generated using various methods. Bynner, for instance, focuses on a single interview of a key interlocutor; Eggeling and Versloot draw on ethnographic observation, as do Visser, Borrelli and Sudhakar; Mulherin shadows the managers she observes; Mungekar elaborates on visual methods involving photographs; and Martinius explores drawings. This emphasis on field evidence is not happenstantial: the book's four editors and at least some of the chapter authors came to their academic positions from the worlds of policy practice, possibly encountering discrepancies between the academic literatures they read and their own practitioner experiences. Garner-Knapp and Mason's chapter, for instance, originated in reflections on their work as civil servants (Chapter 9, p. 161); Bynner notes how her own prior experiences were similar to those of her interlocutor (Chapter 1, p. 27). That these scholars bring their prior personal experiences to bear on their research studies is not considered problematically biasing in interpretive methodology but, instead, as advantageous, as those experiences potentially inform their analyses (e.g., grasping what a practitioner might have observed and herself done in other settings), enabling them to probe what people are doing and how they are responding to their own settings. Making such experiences explicit – what the methodological literature calls 'reflecting on the researcher's positionality' – fosters potential comparative analysis in addition to empathic insights and understanding (see, e.g. Shehata, 2014 [2006], Soedirgo & Glas, 2020).

With respect to ethnography, specifically, its unparalleled advantage lies in enabling comparison between the values 'espoused' by social actors, whether in writing or in interviews, and those that are 'enacted' *in situ*. These differences lie at the heart of the tensions between formal and informal and are evident in a number of the chapters, especially in Mungekar's, where her interlocuter, Singh, steadfastly denied using the informal strategies he was actually seen applying to water management (Chapter 6, p. 99). In some academic literatures, particularly those concerning administrative discretion, any gap between espoused legislative goals and implemented policy carries the whiff of illegitimacy – of secret, undocumented decisions taken behind closed doors, for instance. Part of what this volume highlights is how interpretive ethnography and other methods can open up differences between 'espoused' and 'enacted' values in the study of in|formality. If it is the case that rules can never cover all contingencies, interpretivist ethnographic methods are ideal, even necessary, for studying, finding patterns in and theorising such moments of improvised action.[6]

---

[6]Too often, the strengths of ethnography are overlooked and their limitations emphasised – mirroring, perhaps, the ways in which the strengths of quantitative approaches are assumed and their limitations downplayed or ignored. Instead, as the chapters in this volume attest, ethnography can be a powerful method to address particular sorts of research questions.

We mention three of the many examples this book provides. Eggeling and Versloot's method for studying dynamic diplomatic practices (Chapter 3) permits and encourages iterative observations that can reveal emergent patterns over time, bringing to light the key analytic point that diplomats *re-make* boundaries (e.g., definitions of country interests) to be able to forge agreements. Martinius' ethnographic evidence (Chapter 7) shows that engineers, an occupational group typically devoted to explicit measurement of phenomena, can recognise a limit to the human ability to model every element of a complex project in ways that make everything explicit. They understand the limits of the formal, digitised, end-product pictures they are viewing, resisting the addition of detail: adding a z-coordinate to those drawings, one engineer argued, 'might reflect a *level of accuracy that cannot be met in reality*' (p. 121, emphasis added). Third, Visser analyses the role that sociability plays in policymaking (Chapter 5), in which much of what is happening (e.g., actor positioning) is essential, albeit tacitly known and recognised. Actors need to figure out the present situation so they will know how to conduct themselves in future meetings; if they do not understand their place in 'the meeting', some may be working at cross purposes. Whereas this sort of talk is not part of most accounts of policymaking, Visser argues that it is significant for the relational practices that are central to collaborative work. It was her sustained observation and associated fieldnotes that allowed her to 'see' a seemingly mundane, boring practice, to ask why it repeatedly occurred and to make a case for its importance for policy work. These and insights in other chapters provide telling evidence that could not have been obtained through more distance-preserving methods, such as survey questionnaires, focus groups or brief observational visits.

In sum, the book's chapters reveal dimensions of informality and its intertwining with formality which escape dominant ways of understanding policy and policymaking: the chapters contest easy judgements of legitimacy and illegitimacy, they demonstrate how informal/formal entanglements shift by and within settings and they show how understandings of in|formality can be shaped by material objects. The chapters engage different kinds of actors (diplomats, EU officials, municipality workers), different kinds of settings (cars, offices, meeting tables) and different kinds of acts ('catching up', drawing, 'hustling'/'shuffling'). Demonstrating the mutual implication of methodology, methods and theorising makes this book as a whole a potentially exciting theoretical reframing of the 'informal', a theory-building that starts from – indeed, is rooted in – empirical examples drawn from chapter authors' lived experiences. Their significance for future theory-building lies in the range of literatures suggested by different chapters, which could extend their arguments still further:

- in *gesture studies*: interactions with cognitive metaphor studies as developed in the last 25 years (see, e.g., Cienki & Müller, 2008);
- in *practice studies*: phenomenological approaches (e.g., Schatzki, 2001; Yanow, 2015; Yanow & Tsoukas, 2009), including
  - o in international relations (e.g., Büger & Gadinger, 2014; Epstein, 2008);
  - o studies of specific practitioners, such as John Forester's planners (2012);

190 Peregrine Schwartz-Shea and Dvora Yanow

- in studies of *the material objects* used in acts and intersections, including in work and other practices; for instance:
  - o architects' design practices mediated by various 'tools', such as the pencil (Ewenstein & Whyte, 2009), the mediating role played by maps in scientists' interactions (Latour, 1999);
  - o Henry Petroski's analysis of *The Pencil* (1990) at the intersection of engineering, economics and culture, or Julia Paley's study of the situated meanings of material objects such as televisions and kitchen appliances to residents of a Chilean barrio encountering the census-taker (2001, p. 154);
  - o spatial analyses (e.g., of city halls, Goodsell, 1988, or hospital hallways, Iedema et al., 2010).
- in *research methods*: turn-taking and other aspects of conversation analysis as developed in ethnomethodology; visual methods, including still and moving photography and visual ethnography (see, e.g., Taussig, 2011). Several of these chapters also add to the long history of ethnographic studies of bureaucracies (e.g., Blau, 1963 [1953]; Crozier, 1964; Kaufman, 1960; Selznick, 1949; and more recently Dubois, 2010).

Such are the promises of cross-disciplinary work, of which this is a prime example, in which scholars from various academic backgrounds (among them anthropology; see Shore & Wright, 1997, Shore et al., 2011) take up policy analysis, joining their voices to those from many other fields and challenging readers to consider the paradox of in|formality in policymaking.

References

Blau, P. (1963 [1953]). *The dynamics of bureaucracy*. University of Chicago Press.
Bouckaert, G. (2023). The neo-Weberian state. *Max Weber Studies, 23*(1), 13–59.
Büger, C., & Gadinger, F. (2014). *International practice theory*. Palgrave Pivot.
Cienki, A. J., & Müller, C. (2008). *Metaphor and gesture*. John Benjamins.
Crozier, M. (1964). *The bureaucratic phenomenon*. University of Chicago Press.
Dubois, V. (2010). *The bureaucrat and the poor: Encounters in French welfare offices*. Routledge.
Epstein, C. (2008). *The power of words in international relations: Birth of an anti-whaling discourse*. MIT Press.
Evans, P., Rueschemeyer, D., & Skocpol, T. (Eds.). (1985). *Bringing the state back in*. Cambridge University Press.
Ewenstein, B., & Whyte, J. (2009). Knowledge practices in design: The role of visual representations as 'epistemic objects'. *Organization Studies, 30*(1), 7–30.
Forester, J. (2012). Learning to improve practice: Lessons from practice stories and practitioners' own discourse analyses (or why only the loons show up). *Planning Theory and Practice, 13*(1), 11–26.
Fox, C. J. (1978). Biases in public policy implementation evaluation. *Policy Studies Review, 7*(1), 128–141.
Fox, C. J. (1990). Implementation research: Why and how to transcend positivist methodologies. In D. J. Palumbo & D. J. Calista (Eds.), *Implementation and the policy process* (pp. 199–212). Greenwood Press.

Fujii, L. A. (2018). *Interviewing in social science research: A relational approach*. Routledge.

Goodsell, C. T. (1988). *The social meaning of civic space*. University Press of Kansas.

Hacking, I. (1990). *The taming of chance*. Cambridge University Press.

Iedema, R., Long, D., & Carroll, K. (2010). Corridor communication, spatial design and patient safety. In A. van Marrewijk & D. Yanow (Eds.), *Organizational spaces* (pp. 41–57). Edward Elgar.

Jakobson, R. (1969). Appendix III. Autobiographical notes on N.S. Trubetzkoy. In N. S. Trubetzkoy (Ed.), *Principles of phonology* (Transl. Christiane A. M. Baltaxe, pp. 309–323). University of California Press.

Kaufman, H. (1960). *The forest ranger*. Johns Hopkins University Press.

Latour, B. (1999). Circulating references. *Pandora's hope: Essays on the reality of science studies* (pp. 24–79). Harvard University Press.

Lipsky, M. (1978). Standing the study of public policy implementation on its head. In W. D. Burnham & M. W. Weinberg (Eds.), *American politics and public policy* (pp. 391–402). MIT Press.

Lipsky, M. (1980). *Street-level bureaucracy*. Russell Sage Foundation.

McGregor, D. (1957). The human side of enterprise. *Management Review*, *46*(11), 22–28.

Pachirat, T. (2018). *Among wolves: Ethnography and the immersive study of power*. Routledge.

Paley, J. (2001). Making democracy count. *Cultural Anthropology*, *16*(2), 135–164.

Petroski, H. (1990). *The pencil: A history of design and circumstance*. Knopf.

Polkinghorne, D. E. (1983). *Methodology for the human sciences*. SUNY Press.

Prasad, P. (2005). *Crafting qualitative research: Working in the postpositivist traditions*. M.E. Sharpe.

Pressman, J. L., & Wildavsky, A. (1984 [1973]). *Implementation* (3rd ed.). University of California Press.

Rabinow, P., & Sullivan, W. M. (Eds.). (1979). *Interpretive social science*. University of California Press.

Rowe, M. (2025). *Researching street-level bureaucracy: Bringing out the interpretive dimensions*. Routledge.

Schaffer, F. C. (2014 [2006]). Ordinary language interviewing. In D. Yanow & P. Schwartz-Shea (Eds.), *Interpretation and method* (2nd ed., pp. 183–193). M.E. Sharpe.

Schatz, E. (Ed.). (2009). *Political ethnography*. University of Chicago Press.

Schatzki, T. R. (2001). Introduction: *Practice theory*. In T. R. Schatzki, K. Knorr Cetina, & E. Savigny (Eds.), *The practice turn in contemporary theory* (pp. 10–23). Routledge.

Schwartz-Shea, P., & Yanow, D. (2012). *Interpretive research design: Concepts and processes*. Routledge.

Scott, J. C. (2008 [1998]). *Seeing like a state*. Yale University Press.

Selznick, P. (1949). *TVA and the grass roots*. University of California Press.

Shames, S. L., & Wise, T. (2017). Gender, diversity, and methods in political science. *PS: Political Science and Politics*, *50*(3), 811–23.

Shehata, S. (2014 [2006]). Ethnography, identity, and the production of knowledge. In D. Yanow & P. Schwartz-Shea (Eds.), *Interpretation and method* (2nd ed., pp. 209–227). M.E. Sharpe.

Shore, C., & Wright, S. (Eds.). (1997). *Anthropology of policy*. Routledge.

Shore, C., Wright, S., & D. Però (Eds.). (2011). *Policy worlds: Anthropology and the analysis of contemporary power* (2nd ed.). Berghahn.

Soedirgo, J., & Glas, A. (2020). Toward active reflexivity. *PS: Political Science & Politics*, *53*(3), 527–531.

Soss, J. (2005). Making clients and citizens: Welfare policy as a source of status, belief, and action. In A. L. Schneider & H. M. Ingram (Eds.), *Deserving and entitled: Social constructions and public policy* (pp. 291–328). State University of New York Press.

Taussig, M. (2011). *I swear I saw this: Drawings in fieldwork notebooks, namely my own.* University of Chicago Press.

Taylor, C. (1987 [1971]). Interpretation and the sciences of man. In P. Rabinow & W. M. Sullivan (Eds.), *Interpretive social science: A second look* (pp. 33–81). University of California Press.

Turner, B. (1971). *Exploring the industrial subculture.* Macmillan.

Waugh, L. R. (1982). Marked and unmarked. *Semiotica, 38*(3–4), 299–318.

Weber, M. (1946). Bureaucracy. In H. H. Gerth & C. Wright Mills (Transl. and Eds.), *From Max Weber* (pp. 196–244). Oxford University Press.

Yanow, D. (1987). Toward a policy culture approach to implementation analysis. *Policy Studies Review, 7*(1), 103–115.

Yanow, D. (1990). Tackling the implementation problem: Epistemological issues in policy implementation research. In D. J. Palumbo & D. J. Calista (Eds.), *Implementation and the policy process* (pp. 213–227). Greenwood Press.

Yanow, D. (2014 [2006]). Neither rigorous nor objective? Interrogating criteria for knowledge claims in interpretive science. In D. Yanow & P. Schwartz-Shea (Eds.), *Interpretation and method* (2nd ed., pp. 97–119). M.E. Sharpe.

Yanow, D. (2015). After mastery: Insights from practice theorizing. In R. Garud, B. Simpson, A. Langley, & H. Tsoukas (Eds.), *The emergence of novelty in organizations* (pp. 272–317). Oxford University Press.

Yanow, D., & Tsoukas, H. (2009). What is reflection-in-action? A phenomenological account. *Journal of Management Studies, 46*(8), 1339–1364.

Zerubavel, E. (2018). *Taken for granted.* Princeton University Press.

Index

Academia 4, 149, 164
Accountability 7, 9, 30, 40, 41, 42, 43, 47, 57, 70, 126, 180, 182
Administrative practice, 68, 138
Affect, 68, 141, 182
Anthropology, 148
Asylum practices, 69
Australia, 128, 130, 149, 164
    Public Service, 151
Authorship, 171–172
Autoethnography, 150

Bartels, Koen P. R., 9, 23, 83, 92
Binaries, 10, 148, 159
Binary, xvii, 4–5, 10–11, 14, 26, 70, 77, 148–150, 154, 158, 170, 181, 184, 186
Blumer, Herbert, 5–6, 14, 167
Boanada-Fuchs, Anthony, 5–6
Boanada Fuchs, Vanessa, 5–6
Boundaries, 5–6, 13, 15–16, 43, 48, 56–62, 64, 92, 137, 139, 142, 148–149, 167, 182, 185, 189
Boundary work, 56, 59, 61, 62
Bureaucracy, 4, 7–8, 11, 14, 34–36, 40–43, 68, 70, 77, 178
Bureaucratic, 15, 25–26, 29, 31 34–35, 40–41, 43, 48, 68–69, 72, 77, 101, 105–106, 155–156, 178, 182, 185–186
    actors, 7–9
    offices, 72
    processes, 25–26, 34, 101, 155
    system/s, 31, 69
    work, 69, 77
Bureaucrats, 68–71, 73, 75, 88, 179
Business-like approach, 33–35, 182

Canada, 149, 154–155, 164
Care, 34, 172, 182
Cars, 128–131, 134–142
    in|formal things, 136–138
    journeys (*see also* trips), 130–132, 136–137, 139
Case workers, 74
Catching up, 15, 83, 86–92, 182, 184, 186, 189
Citizens, 36, 41, 43, 71–72, 99–100, 104, 106–108, 155, 181
Collaboration/s, 24, 33, 71, 75–76, 83, 86–87, 90, 92, 129, 131, 158, 163–165, 167, 172, 182
Collaborative governance, 83
Community
    grants, 29, 32
    groups, 24, 26, 32–34, 36, 182
Community of practice, 61
Conventions, 8
Conversation/s, 6, 15, 40–41, 54–55, 57, 59, 82–84, 87–88, 90, 99, 106, 116–117, 133, 135, 137–141, 152–157, 164, 167, 184–185, 187, 190 (*see also* Talk)
    car, 137, 141
    informal, 41, 87, 138–139
    institutional, 83, 88, 90
    ordinary, 88
Coping strategies, 70
Council, 28, 33, 129–133, 135, 137–139, 155, 157, 182, 184 (*see also* Local Government and Municipality)
COVID-19 pandemic, 14, 24, 30, 33, 35, 37, 55, 58, 60, 63, 75, 165, 182, 184 (*see also* Pandemic)
Crisis, 24, 26, 30, 34, 36, 182

194 *Index*

Decision-making, 5, 24, 29–31,
58, 68–69, 82, 114, 126,
180–181
Deliberation/s, 48, 54, 87, 149, 168
Development process, 48
Dichotomy, 9, 179, 181 (*see also*
Binaries)
politics-administration, 179, 181
Dilemmas, 8, 101–104, 109–110, 132
Diplomacy, 15, 55–60, 62–64, 182
Diplomatic, 56–64
informality, 57–58
negotiation, 55
practice, 57–58, 60, 187
protocol, 57
rules, 61
skill, 15, 56
work, 15, 55, 63
Diplomats, 15, 55–64, 182–185, 189
Discretion, 6, 68–71, 77, 131, 166,
181, 188
Discursive practices, 88
(*see also* Institutional
conversation)
Documents, 10, 12, 40, 58, 71, 73, 75,
87, 106, 134, 136, 150, 155,
160, 164, 170
Documentary photography (*see also*
Photojournalism), 104
Documentation, 31, 68–69, 75–76,
104, 110, 180
Drawings, 16, 114–116, 118–125, 180,
188–189

Entanglements, 8, 10, 13, 14, 23, 134,
151, 189
Ethnographic
approaches, 4–5
detail, 148, 153–154, 159–160
evidence, 184, 189
methods, 40, 83, 149, 188
narratives, 150, 166
policy vignettes, 151
reflections, 149
research, 15, 82, 115, 151, 159

Ethnography, 15–16, 98, 100, 103,
107, 109–110, 129, 136,
146, 148, 150, 187–188,
190, 192
Ethnomethodology, 14, 190
European Union (EU), 15, 54–59,
61, 186
Everyday, 4, 9, 27–28, 36, 56, 60,
69–71, 73, 87–88,
108–109, 130–131, 138,
150, 160, 166, 180,
185–187
action/s, 12, 15, 165, 179
life, 70–71, 108, 130, 139, 150
practice/s, 12, 26, 70, 170

Feldman, Martha, 12, 15, 68, 70, 77
Feminist
approach, 171
political theory, 36
theorising, 11
Fieldwork, 26, 55, 71, 87, 98, 104,
129, 136–137, 139–140,
150–152, 167
Floorwalker/s, 72–75
Formal
accountability, 40–42, 47 (*see also*
Accountability)
arrangements, 101
organisation, 27, 178
policy, 48, 91, 126, 161, 179,
181–182, 184–186
process/es, 25, 30, 34, 36, 58, 96,
106, 182
work, 60–61
–informal boundary, 48
Formality, 4–5, 7–12, 14 –15, 17, 48,
55–60, 63–64, 68–70, 74,
100–101, 130, 142, 158,
161, 165, 168, 170,
178–180, 182, 184, 186, 189
(*see also* Informality)
language of, 178
Freeman, Richard, 9, 13, 90–92, 126,
160, 165

Index   **195**

Frontline
  actors, 69 (*see also* Street-level
    bureaucrats)
  staff, 68–69, 71, 74, 77, 183
  workers, 15, 68, 70–71, 76, 185

Gestures, 15–16, 55, 105, 110, 114–116,
    118, 120, 122–126, 180
  bracketing, 114, 116, 122, 124
  circling, 114, 116, 118–120, 124
  pointing, 114, 116–119, 124
  shielding, 114, 116, 120, 122, 124
Gherardi, Sylvia, 4, 83, 88–90, 130, 136
Global South, 41, 48
Goffman, Erving, 7–8, 55, 83, 90
Governance
  electricity, 14, 40, 41, 183
  practice/s, 27, 41, 87
  system/s, 14, 26, 30, 32, 36–37
  turn, 8, 179
Government/s, 6–9, 24, 29, 33, 41–42,
    46, 60, 102, 104, 107, 109,
    129–130, 134, 148–150,
    164, 179, 181–185
  actors, 9, 102
  Local, 14, 24, 26–28, 129, 149,
    151, 154–157, 161, 182
    (*see* Local Government)
  offices, 129
  officials, 28, 181
Grosz, Elizabeth, 9, 11–12

Identity construction, 89
Immersive presence, 103, 148
Implementation, 179–180, 183, 185
In/formal
  things, 136
  work, 60, 64
India/n, 14–15, 40–43, 98, 100–101,
    104, 110, 183–185
  Towns and Cities
  Bhopal, 98, 100, 102, 104–105,
    107–108, 110
  Bhuj, 98, 102, 104–110
  Karnataka, 40, 42

Informal
  activity, 26, 36, 61, 184–185
  chat, 158
  community groups, 26
  consumption, 45–46
  conversations, 41, 87, 139
  diplomacy, 56
  gestures (*see* Gestures)
  governance, 9, 101, 109, 182
  housing, 48
  interaction/s, 36, 57, 105, 137,
    139, 154
  policy practices, 87
  practice/s, 8–9, 14–15, 41, 46, 55,
    57, 61, 68–72, 74, 76–77,
    91, 98, 100, 102, 165,
    182–183, 185
  knowledge production, 72
  process/es, 7, 10, 15, 30, 68, 98,
    102, 182, 184
  talk (*see also* Conversations and
    Interactions)
  work/ing, 14, 33, 36, 55, 58–61,
    64, 135, 161, 183, 186
Informality, 4–17, 25–27, 41, 46–48,
    55–60, 63–64, 68–71, 74,
    76–77, 91–92, 98, 101–102,
    130, 137, 142, 148–151,
    158–159, 161, 165–168,
    170, 177–186, 189
  definitional quandaries, 177–179
  (un)codified and routinised ad hoc
  practice, 69
  boundaries of, 56, 60, 148
  concept of, 6, 11, 13, 56–57, 98,
    167
  diplomatic, 59
  in relation, 9
  language of, 178
  matters, 4–5
  methods to study, 15
  in repair, 102
  thinking with, 6
Ingold, Tim, 11, 150
Integration, 129

196   Index

Institutional
    Conversation/s, 83, 88, 90
Interaction (*see also* Informal
    interaction)
Interpretive approaches, 11–13
    methodological, 179, 187

Knotting together, 148, 151, 154,
    157–159, 164
Knowing, 11, 14, 27, 33–34, 44,
    59, 64, 92, 109, 121, 141,
    151–152, 156, 172, 182
Knowledge/s, 5–6, 13–15, 27–29, 32,
    35–36, 41, 43, 45–46, 48,
    68–69, 71–77, 88–92, 101–
    102, 106, 116, 119, 121,
    124–125, 140, 148, 160,
    164–167, 179, 183–185, 187
    forms of, 41
    Informal, 32, 35, 43
    informality as response to
        imperfect, 48
    local, 14, 101–102, 183–184
    mastery, 5, 13, 167
    practical, 32, 36, 41, 89
    production, 72, 106
    tacit, 27, 121, 160, 179, 187
    technical, 35, 116
Koutkova, Karla, 5–6, 10–11

Lipsky, Michael, 8, 68–69, 179, 186
Lived experiences, 4, 6, 149–151, 158,
    161, 164, 189
Local authorit/ies, 26–27, 30, 33, 104,
    109
Local governance, 10, 27–28
Local government, 14, 24, 26–28, 104,
    129, 151, 154–157, 161,
    182, (*see also* Authority,
    Council and Municipality)
Local
    knowledge, 14, 101–102, 183–184
    need/s, 32–33
    pandemic responses, 26
Lockdown, 24, 26, 29–30, 32, 62, 182
Luncheons, 62

Manager/s, 12, 15, 27, 29, 30, 55,
    58, 82–91, 128–135, 138,
    140–142, 151–157, 160,
    178, 183, 185, 188
    Asset, 114–121
    Project, 114–119, 122
Materialit/ies, 60, 62–63, 136–137,
    143, 154, 158–160
Materials, 4–5, 11–13, 15, 29, 71,
    136–137, 170
McFarlane, Colin, 10, 12, 91, 101, 142
Meeting/s, 4, 9–10, 16, 29–31, 34,
    54, 58–64, 82–84, 86–87,
    89–92, 114–119, 122–126,
    128, 131–136, 138, 140–141,
    143, 150–152, 154–157,
    161, 165–167, 170, 180,
    182,185–186, 189
    agenda/s, 31, 54, 57, 59, 61, 64, 84,
        88, 90, 115–117, 123, 141, 152
    chair/person, 31, 54, 84, 88, 90,
        115–119, 123, 141
    collaborative, 83, 88, 182
    formal, 10, 55, 59–62, 64, 166
    informal, 10, 55, 59, 122
    minutes, 84, 87, 115–116, 123–124,
        126, 157, 165, 172
    participants, 84, 86, 88–90,
        115–118, 120–124
    partnership, 28–29, 36
    pre-, 59, 91, 133
    physical, 29–31, 58, 63
    room/s, 15, 62–63, 81–84, 86, 91,
        151, 153
    virtual, 28, 55, 165
Method/s, 15, 40, 83, 98, 100,
    102–103, 106, 110,
    148–150, 178, 186–190
Methodolog/ies, 9, 14–15, 55, 98,
    102, 139, 149–151, 154,
    158–160, 166, 178–179,
    183, 186–190
    implications, 186–187
Misztal, Barbara, 7–8, 26, 55, 57–59,
    64, 68, 91–92, 183
Mobilit/ies, 131, 137–139, 143

Mundane, 12, 70, 75, 83, 87, 103, 108, 110, 128, 136–137, 139, 152, 154, 189
Mundanity, 131
Municipality, 68, 71, 84–88, 140, 189 (*see also* Local Authority, Local Government)

Narrative, 40, 83, 87, 89–91, 99, 102–103, 150–151, 159, 166, 181
National Health Service (NHS), 24, 28, 129–135, 141, 182
Negotiation/s, 10, 41, 44, 54–55, 58–59, 61–62, 87, 114–115, 122–123, 148, 152, 160, 164
Netherlands, 15, 82, 84, 87, 164
Network/s, 5, 7, 13, 15, 26, 33, 40–42, 62, 69, 92, 99, 100–102, 110, 114, 117, 119–121, 167
creation, 83
Non-government organisation (NGO), 9, 28, 102, 104 (*see also* Community Groups, Community Organisations, Third Sector, and Voluntary Organisations)

Organisation/s, 4, 6–8, 11, 24, 27, 29, 33–34, 41, 46, 56, 70, 77, 82, 87, 89, 102, 104, 106–107, 110, 115, 118–119, 129–130, 133, 142, 165, 178–179, 182–183
Voluntary, 24, 33–34
Community, 24, 33, 129
Organisational, 7, 9, 14, 41–42, 44, 68, 72, 74, 77, 87–89, 114, 125, 129–130, 136–137, 140, 142, 178–179, 182–184, 186
culture, 114, 179
identity, 89
life, 142, 178–179
practices, 68
routines, 68, 77
structures, 7, 72

Pandemic, 14, 24–30, 32–37, 55, 58, 60, 62, 164–165, 182–184 (*see also* COVID-19 pandemic)
Performance/s 6, 9, 35, 40, 42–43, 46–47, 56, 58, 87–88, 91, 102, 114, 116, 119–120, 122, 135, 179, 183
Photographic methods, 100, 102–103, 110 (*see also* Method/s)
Photojournalism, 104
Polese, Abel, 6
Policies, 7–8, 25, 45, 68–71, 77, 101, 128–130, 135, 137, 141, 150–151, 155–156, 160, 171, 177, 179–181, 183
Policy
actors, 4, 9, 11, 13, 129, 137, 139, 143, 158–160, 166, 182–183
discourse, 40, 47
practice/s, 87, 91, 188
implementation, 68, 131, 136–137, 139, 143, 179–180, 183, 185
maintenance, 14, 39, 183
plans, 87
work, 4–5, 8, 13, 15–16, 69, 82, 87–88, 130–131, 135–137, 143, 148, 151, 154, 159, 164, 166, 182
Policy-Knowledge-Practice International Working Group (PKP), 165–166
Policymakers, 13, 15, 70, 82–84, 86–87, 90–91, 137, 151, 161, 164–166, 181–183, 187
Policymaking, 4–7, 9, 13–14, 16–17, 68–69, 83, 89, 91–92, 137, 141, 148–151, 155, 158–161, 164–168, 170, 179, 180, 185–186, 189–190
black box, 149–150, 160–161
context/s, 4, 6, 9, 48, 180
everyday, 4, 150, 177

198 *Index*

process/es, 13, 149–150, 155, 160–161, 170, 179
sites of, 9, 28, 135, 137, 141
spaces, 5, 8, 13, 16, 58–59, 61, 69, 128, 137, 142, 148–152, 154–155, 158, 160–161, 170, 185
Political power, 181, 183
Post-Soviet informality, 10
Power relations, 26, 41, 137
Practice-theoretical studies, 14
Practices, 8–9, 11–12, 14–15, 26, 34–36, 41, 43–48, 55, 58–59, 61, 68–74, 76–77, 87–88, 91, 96, 98, 100–104, 110, 114, 124, 130–131, 135–137, 139, 165, 170–171, 179–180, 182–190
administrative, 6, 27, 68, 138
connective, 15, 83, 91–92
governance 27, 41, 87 (*see* Informal)
relational, 92, 189
repair, 103–104
work, 15, 70, 186
Practitioners, 4, 6, 8–9, 11–12, 55, 57, 77, 102, 128, 130, 136, 149–150, 164–165, 185, 188–189 (*see also* actors, Policymakers)
Public administration, 4, 6–8, 14–15, 27–28, 34–35, 68–71, 74, 160, 164–165, 178–180, 182, 185
Anglo-American and European, 7, 180
Public administrator/s, 7, 14
Public policy, 4, 9, 165, 178–179 (*see also* Policy)
Puig de la Bellacasa, Maria, 114–115, 125

Re-making, 30, 35
Reactive repair, 98, 101, 109
Rear-mirror technique, 103, 148

Relational, 5, 11–12, 16, 34–36, 82–83, 92, 128, 136–137, 149, 154–155, 159–160 166–167, 182, 189
dynamics, 106
moments, 151, 154
ontology, 36
skills, 35
traces, 160
work, 16, 128, 182
Relationality, 12, 159
Relationship/s, 4–6, 9–11, 15, 26–27, 30, 33–34, 36, 55, 57, 83–84, 86, 89–92, 98–100, 102, 131, 136, 139, 154, 159–160, 165, 166, 170–172, 181–184, 186
personal, 91, 99, 109
social, 7, 28, 34, 69, 74, 90, 160
Repair, 15, 40, 43, 98, 100–109, 170, 183
Routines, 8, 12, 15, 27, 60, 68–70, 72–74, 76–77, 98, 104, 109–110, 130, 139–140, 151–153, 166, 184, 186 (*see also* Organisational)
hustling, 15, 69–70, 73–75, 77, 185–186, 189
shuffling, 15, 69–71, 75–77, 185–186, 189
Rules, 5, 7–8, 27, 29–30, 32–36, 40, 44, 56–59, 63, 68–69, 74–75, 77, 83, 91, 121, 164, 177–178, 180, 183, 185–186, 188
formal, 9, 56, 58, 60, 62, 64, 76, 101, 177
Rural, 13–16, 40–46, 48, 128–130, 140, 143, 183–185

Schwartz-Shea, Peregrine, 13, 16, 187
Scotland, 15–16, 27, 129, 133, 141, 164, 170
Scott, James C., 10, 184
Sensemaking, 83, 88, 90–91
Sensitizing, 5–6, 11, 14
Situated meaning, 187, 190

Index 199

Skill/s, 4, 13, 15, 35, 55–56, 63–64,
115, 131, 172–173
Social, 10–11, 13–14, 24, 36, 44,
47–48, 55–58, 61, 64, 69,
71, 77, 88, 98, 100, 102,
109, 114, 131, 137, 157, 172
actor/s, 58, 177, 181, 186–188
bonds, 55
capital, 101
social care, 129, 131–132, 138, 182
identity, 89
life, 12, 58, 70
media, 55, 61, 107, 155
policy, 76
relations/hips, 7, 16, 28, 34, 69, 74,
88, 90, 160
service, 183
theory, 7
world/s, 57, 136, 177
work, 141
Sociology, 7, 55, 143
Space/s, 5, 7, 11–16, 27, 30, 58–59,
61, 64, 69, 74, 91, 103,
110, 115, 121–122, 125,
128–130, 134–135, 137–140,
142–143, 148–155, 158–161,
165, 167, 170, 182–185
informal, 61, 161
physical, 13, 158
work, 82, 152
Speech (see also Conversation, Talk),
90, 114, 137
Streamlining, 30–31
Street-level bureaucracy, 8, 77
Street-level bureaucrats (see also
Frontline), 68–70, 75, 88, 179
Structure–agency dichotomy, 9
Switzerland, 71

Talk, 15, 27, 54, 57, 60, 84–85, 87–90,
99, 117, 120, 123–124, 126,
131, 133–135, 138–141,
156, 182, 186, 189 (see also
Conversation, Speech)
Tapestry, 4–5, 170

Technical
drawings, 16, 114–116, 118–122,
124–125, 180, 188–189
knowledge, 35, 116
Third sector, (see also Non-
Government Organisation,
Community Groups,
Community Organisation)
Touch, 33–34, 58–59, 62, 64, 114–115,
119, 121, 124–125
Traces, 16, 123, 126, 148–151, 154,
157–161, 167, 170, 185
Trust, 8, 26, 55, 83, 87, 103, 110, 137,
140, 160, 181, 183

United Kingdom, 14, 25, 27

Vancouver Protocol, 171–172
van Hulst, Merlijn, 5, 8–9, 83
Visibilit/ies, 16, 149–150, 153–154,
158–159, 185
Visual, 98–99, 102–106, 109–110,
120, 149, 166–167, 169,
177
ethnography, 15, 96, 98, 101, 103,
107, 109, 148, 190
methods, 15, 98, 188, 190
narratives, 102
Vulnerable communities, 24, 31, 36

Wagenaar, Henk, 4, 9, 27–28, 91,
131
Water, 4, 15, 27, 98–102, 104–110,
116, 118, 134, 183, 186
governance, 98, 100, 102, 104
management, 100, 104–105, 188
Weale, Emma, 166, 170
Weber, Max, 7, 68, 178
World Health Organisation (WHO),
24
Writing, 4, 6, 27, 61, 64, 87, 150, 158,
164–166, 172, 188

Yanow, Dvora, 4, 13, 16, 164, 179,
187, 189

www.ingramcontent.com/pod-product-compliance
Lightning Source LLC
Jackson TN
JSHW011307171224
75586JS00004B/42